NOT TRAUMA ALONE

The Series In Trauma And Loss
Consulting Editors
Charles R. Figley and Therese A. Rando

NOT TRAUMA
ALONE

Therapy for Child Abuse Survivors in Family and Social Context

Steven N. Gold, Ph.D.
Nova Southeastern University

BRUNNER-ROUTLEDGE
ALERE FLAMMAM
Taylor & Francis Group

USA	Publishing Office:	BRUNNER/ROUTLEDGE
		A member of the Taylor & Francis Group
		325 Chestnut Street
		Philadelphia, PA 19106
		Tel: (215) 625-8900
		Fax: (215) 625-2940
	Distribution Center:	BRUNNER/ROUTLEDGE
		A member of the Taylor & Francis Group
		7625 Empire Drive
		Florence, KY 41042
		Tel: 1-800-634-7064
		Fax: 1-800-248-4724
UK		BRUNNER/ROUTLEDGE
		A member of the Taylor & Francis Group
		27 Church Road
		Hove
		E. Sussex, BN3 2FA
		Tel.: +44 (0) 1273 207411
		Fax: +44 (0) 1273 205612

NOT TRAUMA ALONE: Therapy for Child Abuse Survivors in Family and Social Context

1 2 3 4 5 6 7 8 9 0

Printed by Edwards Brothers, Lillington, NC, 2000.
Cover design by Ellen Seguin.

A CIP catalog record for this book is available from the British Library.
∞ The paper in this publication meets the requirements of the ANSI Standard Z39.48-1984 (Permanence of Paper).

Library of Congress Cataloging-in-Publication Data

Gold, Steven N.
   Not trauma alone : therapy for child abuse survivors in family and social context / Steven N. Gold.
     p. cm.
   Includes bibliographical references and index.
   ISBN 1-58391-027-1 (alk. paper)
   1. Adult child abuse victims—Rehabilitation.   I. Title.

RC569.5.C55 G65 2000
616.85′8223906—dc21   00-023643

ISBN 1-58391-027-1 (case)
ISSN 1090-9575

With Love and Appreciation
to
Peggy,
my life partner,
whose profession
is mental health counseling,
but who has made
growing and sustaining our family
her calling,
and
to
Andrea,
Lylah,
and
Adam,
the three most wonderful, precious children in the world.

CONTENTS

PART III
ACQUIRING TOOLS FOR DAILY LIVING:
THE STRUCTURE OF THE THERAPEUTIC PROCESS

SERIES FOREWORD

Nearly thirty years ago, I sat down with my first Vietnam combat veteran interviewee and asked him what it was like to look back on his war experiences and *not* become disoriented, disillusioned, afraid, or mad. My sense was in those early days that I was finding something few others had found. I reasoned that no one had bothered to ask war veterans about life after the war. I was wrong, of course.

War veterans had been interviewed by journalists as long as there have been journalists talking to war veterans. Hearing and learning from those interviews is another matter. We tend to be a rather selective species in terms of acting on what others perceive as the truth. Therefore, until Vietnam, no war veterans had ever protested a war while the war was still being waged. Indeed, there have been only a few other instances of such an act worldwide, throughout history. As a result, a government established, for the first time in history, a mental health treatment program for war veterans.

Today the Vet Center (Readjustment Counseling) program is a part of the Department of Veterans Affairs (DVA), and one of its most celebrated and successful programs in the organization's history. The major problem, however, is that no matter how hard they try, the DVA is unable to treat Post-traumatic Stress Disorder (PTSD) in all veterans who seek treatment. As a result, more than 50,000 war veterans receive a pension because of this permanent disability. However, the success rate for treating PTSD is far better in other populations. One such group is childhood survivors of child abuse.

There was a time in this country when child abuse was not discussed. This book is about post-modern psychotherapy for people abused as children—a systems sensitive, transgenerational, goal-oriented, respectful approach to helping people of all ages confront, manage, and draw strength from overcoming a legacy of maltreatment. From the first moment I understood Professor Gold's thesis, I knew that this gentle and wise approach had great promise for a wide group of traumatized people. This includes survivors of child abuse, but is not limited to them.

In this timely book, Gold also ventures into new territory that requires new ways of viewing and helping the traumatized. Gold's book evolved from his work with traumatized people two decades ago. Gold's initial experience with survivors, in the late 1970s and early 1980s, was with his individual clients. As noted earlier, the modern view and acknowledgement of child abuse and family abuse generally did not exist only two decades ago. Rather than seeking help as a "survivor," as Gold notes, they entered treatment for any of a large variety of reasons that we now know are consequences of trauma.

Of special importance, however, was his work in his Sexual Abuse Survivors Program early in the 1990s. Later, he established and now directs the Trauma Resolution Integration Program (TRIP) of Nova Southeastern University Community Mental Health Center. At the heart of TRIP is what Gold calls "the indispensability of interpersonal relationships to developing the capacity for living well" in spite of surviving horribly traumatic events. The book is a confluence of clinical, empirical, and training experiences related to adult survivors of child abuse. Gold's approach in his clinic at Nova Southeastern University draws upon three missions: provision of psychological services in a specialized area; training graduate students in service provision in that specialty; and ongoing research based on data collected from clients receiving services. He found that the "abuse trauma" model failed to encompass much of what I have come to see as being some of the most essential and debilitating aspects of their life experiences. It can act to impede recognition of other realms of data and alternate avenues toward therapeutic progress.

The book is divided into three parts. Part I delineates the family/social context model for understanding and treating adult survivors of prolonged child abuse and reviews sources of support for this approach within the research and professional practice literatures. Gold describes his family/ social context conceptual model in chapter 4. Clients are encouraged to discuss their history of recurrent childhood abuse, but are assisted to go beyond that aspect of their life. According to Gold, overt incidents of abuse merely comprised a single component of a much more pervasive childhood atmosphere of coercive control, contempt, rejection, emotional unresponsiveness, and a lack of training in fundamental abilities necessary for effective daily living that for most of us are so second nature we do not even realize they are learned.

The Gold Model asserts that the chaotic and ineffective interpersonal environment is a risk factor among survivors of prolonged child abuse, no matter the age. Therapy involves insuring that the vital interpersonal competence and social effectiveness often learned in childhood is assessed and, if needed, taught to the client. In addition, the client is enabled to fully face and cope with her or his family-of-origin environment.

The remaining two parts of the book are a wonderful guide for applying the model in a variety of clinical practices. The goal of the treatment model is to enable clients to acquire tools to manage emotional discomfort, stay present and focused, and engage in critical thinking, and to equip them to apply these capacities to relinquish maladaptive behavior patterns previously relied on as means of reducing distress. While processing traumatic material is not the primary focus of contextual treatment for abuse survivors, it is retained as one aspect of a broader approach to intervention. Toward the end of their therapy, clients begin to explore and develop capacities for effectively engaging in fundamental aspects of adult living, such as establishing and maintaining intimate relationships, a gratifying pattern of sexual functioning, mutually rewarding affiliations with friends and family, stable work adaptation, and responsible money management.

Thus, this book offers an alternative to abuse-focused therapy that forces exposure of the past, having the client endlessly process the traumatic material. Rather, the Gold Model focuses on the acquisition of adaptive living skills. In my opinion this approach is appropriate with most adult survivors. There is an acknowledgement of the abuse, but the focus quickly moves on to the "so what?" question: Now that you are here, how can we help you become a survivor, not a victim? This is an important and historic paradigm shift from a deficit to a requisite model of psychotherapy with the traumatized.

Gold believes, wisely, that his is the first in a series of efforts to clearly articulate the best ways of helping the traumatized survive and thrive. Unlike other clinical innovators, he is a builder, not a defender refusing to allow his protocol to shift with evidence and experience. This progression is inevitable as this new paradigm is adopted not only by clinicians treating adult survivors of child abuse, but also by traumatologists struggling to help any number of people throughout the world.

He and I both welcome your ideas generated from this book. Both of us are journal editors and welcome articles on these topics. This Series, certainly, would welcome book proposals that contribute constructively to viewing and helping the traumatized.

Charles R. Figley, Ph.D.
Series Editor and Director,
Traumatology Institute, Tallahassee, Florida

FOREWORD

The contemporary study of child abuse and neglect has been underway for nearly three decades. During this time period, much has been learned about abuse and its range of initial and long-term aftereffects, resulting in the development of a number of theoretical and conceptual models. Perhaps the most significant of these research and clinical findings to our conceptual understanding has been the recognition that child abuse constitutes a form of traumatic stress that holds an inordinately high potential to impact and to traumatize both the child victim in its immediate aftermath and the adult survivor across the life span. A number of research studies on the initial and long-term aftereffects of abuse found that they frequently met criteria for the diagnosis of Posttraumatic Stress Disorder (PTSD), in its acute, chronic and/or delayed forms, and that PTSD was often an overarching diagnosis encompassing a number of commonly associated aftereffects. More recently, as additional research data have accumulated, a number of clinical researchers have noted that the PTSD model is not a perfect fit for the aftereffects of abuse and suggested another conceptualization which they labeled Complex PTSD or Disorders of Extreme Stress, Not Otherwise Specified (DESNOS). The Complex PTSD model stresses the developmental implications of abuse, especially in terms of the alteration of fundamental aspects of personal and interpersonal development.

These conceptual models, in turn, have led to the emergence of treatment models, both for children dealing with the effects of contemporaneous abuse and for adults whose abuse occurred in the past. The "first generation" model, based on the PTSD formulation, emphasized identifying and working through the abuse-trauma and its aftermath, while the "second generation" model, based on the Complex PTSD formulation, put more emphasis on a sequenced course of treatment beginning with personal safety, stabilization, and skill-building undertaken before any directed work with the abuse-trauma. In response to the critiques of the recovered memory controversy, the latter model also incorporated guidelines and recommendations for working with abuse memories (whether they were never forgotten and continuously accessible to the patient or forgotten or repressed for a period of time and then remembered in delayed fashion).

With the publication of *Not Trauma Alone: Therapy for Child Abuse Survivors in Family and Social Context*, psychologist Steven Gold builds upon this conceptual and treatment progression and adds yet another dimension that is trauma-responsive but not exclusively trauma-focused. As the title implies, he stresses that adult survivors are affected not only by the abuse-trauma, but also by the family and social contexts that surround such abuse. He emphasizes that these contexts may be much more subtle and less evident to the observer (i.e., emotional neglect and maltreatment involving the lack of a secure base due to interpersonal chaos and involving rejection, abandonment, unresponsiveness, belittlement, contempt, coercive control, lack of training in life skills, and lack of training in essential self-regulation skills) than more frank abuse (i.e., physical and sexual abuse) but that their potential for damage is enormous and should not be minimized. Furthermore, these forms of neglect and maltreatment usually form the matrix within which more overt forms of abuse occur and flourish. Moreover, they are major risk factors that increase a child's vulnerability to further abuse and revictimization and constitute a direct source of many of the difficulties survivors experience in adulthood. Thus, the multitude and complexity of problems manifested by adults abused as children and brought to treatment are cumulative and developmental within this family context, rather than only the result of distinct and identifiable incidents of abuse.

The treatment model that is presented in this book both builds upon this conceptual expansion and considerably extends the Complex PTSD treatment model. Labeled the family contextual treatment model, it provides a cohesive theoretical and treatment framework for working with adult survivors of prolonged child abuse and the myriad problems and difficulties they bring to treatment. The model stresses treatment priorities rather than a strict sequence of treatment, priorities determined according to the singular circumstance and needs of the individual. A clear progression of treatment priorities is outlined, however. Treatment is predicated upon the direct teaching of problem-solving and coping skills along with cognitive interventions to develop critical judgement and reasoning, in addition to more traditional emphases. A principal goal of the treatment plan is teaching clients how to reduce, modulate, tolerate, and manage distressing emotions without resorting to self-harm or other problematic strategies for affect management. The development of affect modulation skills, along with other essential skills, fills in gaps from the past, often providing some immediate relief and improvement in present day life and functioning. These skills also provide tools that are needed to directly approach and re-work the abuse-trauma, a strategy employed as necessary, according to the individual's ongoing and/or residual symptoms. In this model, personal recovery is not predicated on the recovery of memory; rather, present-day life and functioning are underscored as primary, with trauma resolution secondary, undertaken as indicated and in the interest of symptom resolution and personal integration.

Not Trauma Alone is an important book and a brave clinical contribution due to its shift away from a strict abuse-trauma orientation to one that is more trauma-responsive and more encompassing. It is evidence-based and pragmatic. Its author has mined a number of sources of data in developing the conceptual and treatment model so eloquently presented here: his considerable clinical experience in treating adult abuse survivors, much of it derived in a specialty outpatient clinic devoted to this population which he founded in the early '90s at Nova University; his experience training and supervising doctoral level graduate students in the treatment of this population; and, the aggregate research data obtained from the hundreds of adult survivors treated in the clinic over the years. Steven Gold is a skilled clinical researcher with a special affinity, understanding, and empathy for the plight of adult survivors of pervasive and prolonged abuse. His book reflects these attributes; his carefully thought-through and articulated family contextual model broadens our treatment armamentarium considerably.

Christine A. Courtois, Ph.D.
Psychologist, Independent Practice and
Clinical and Training Director and Co-Founder,
The CENTER: Posttraumatic Disorders Program
The Psychiatric Institute of Washington
Washington, DC
Author of Recollections of Sexual Abuse: Treatment Principles and
Guidelines *(1999),* Adult Survivors of Child Sexual Abuse:
A Treatment Model *(1993), and* Healing the Incest Wound:
Adult Survivors in Therapy *(1988).*

PREFACE

☐ Background

This book is the product of a confluence of clinical, empirical, and training experiences related to adult survivors of child abuse. My initial experience with survivors, in the late 1970s and early 1980s, was with individual clients who were in therapy with me. Those were the years immediately prior to the emergence of the disturbing awareness among professionals and by society at large, that child abuse was infinitely more widespread than had previously been realized—and even more damaging than had been imagined. At that time, the word "survivor" had not yet entered general usage in reference to people whose childhoods were marked by severe and repetitive experiences of abuse. The clients I saw in those days, therefore, did not seek therapy because they were "survivors." They entered treatment for any of a large variety of reasons: because they had difficulty controlling their alcohol and drug consumption; because their attempts at establishing intimate relationships were marked by volatility and misery; because despite, in many cases, impressive intellectual capacities and lofty career aspirations, they could not manage sustained work productivity. Their complaints, symptoms, and lifestyles overlapped and varied in numerous ways, yet they shared the haunting frustration that, hard as they might try, peace of mind and effective living constantly seemed to elude them. Today many of these clients would be known as "survivors." They shared, beyond other commonalities, a history of continuing maltreatment in childhood and adolescence. The guiding concepts of "trauma," "abuse," and "survivorship" were invaluable to me and to countless other practitioners in opening up new ways of understanding and responding to the difficulties with which these clients were grappling.

In 1990, I established an outpatient treatment program for adult survivors of childhood sexual abuse, the Sexual Abuse Survivors Program (SASP). The program was housed within a community mental health center administered by the graduate psychology division of Nova Southeastern University (NSU). It was based on a specialty clinic model that had been developed by Mary Ann Dutton when she founded a domestic violence treatment program at the NSU Community Mental Health Center. Frank DePiano, then Dean of the graduate psychology training programs, actively encouraged other faculty to adopt the same structure by creating additional specialty clinics at the Center. The model integrated three missions: provision of psychological services in a specialized area; training of graduate students in service provision in that specialty; and ongoing research based on data collected from clients receiving services. It has now been almost a decade since SASP was originally established. Several hundred clients with child abuse histories have received treatment at SASP, extensive research data have been collected on almost 400 of them, and over 50 psychology doctoral students have received supervised clinical training in working with survivors.

My supervisory, teaching, and research experiences at SASP, combined with my own experiences as a practitioner working with adult survivors of child abuse and other forms of trauma, exposed me to a rich conglomeration of clinical observations and empirical data. Those multi-faceted experiences have led me to conclude that the concepts "trauma," "abuse," and "survivorship," although indispensable components in understanding these clients, are not sufficiently comprehensive to optimally address their treatment needs. The "abuse trauma" model fails to encompass much of what I have come to see as being some of the most essential and debilitating aspects of their life experiences. As with any perspective, the "abuse trauma" model, while illuminating certain areas, simultaneously can act to impede recognition of other realms of data and of alternate avenues toward therapeutic progress.

One of the experiences that has most strongly convinced me of the limitations of these concepts has been the therapy I have conducted in my private practice with survivors of child abuse and other forms of trauma. Working with a range of trauma types has afforded me the opportunity to observe important ways in which ongoing maltreatment in childhood is connected with considerably different difficulties and calls for a radically divergent course of treatment than those associated with either single-event or recurring trauma in adulthood. I felt it was important that the practicum trainees and interns I supervise have access to a similar variety of clinical experiences. As a consequence, SASP has been renamed the Trauma Resolution Integration Program (TRIP), and now serves not only adult survivors of child sexual abuse, but also survivors of child physical abuse and survivors of single-event trauma occurring in adulthood.

The truth is that even today, with the greatly expanded awareness of child abuse and its effects, the overwhelming majority of clients we see at TRIP with long-term histories of child abuse do not contact the community mental health center because they consider themselves "survivors." Rather, they seek out psychological services for the very same reasons as the clients I saw 20 years ago, before the "discovery" of "abuse trauma" did: because comfortable, productive living seems continually outside their grasp. A history of recurring childhood abuse is one crucial, clinically relevant characteristic they share, but it is not by any means the only one. Overt incidents of abuse merely comprise a single component of a much more pervasive childhood atmosphere of coercive control, contempt, rejection, emotional unresponsiveness, and a lack of training in those fundamental abilities necessary for effective daily living that for most of us are so second nature we do not even realize they are learned. The type of atmosphere that frequently accompanies overt acts of child abuse, the enduring detrimental impact this atmosphere has on life adjustment, and the remediation of that impact, constitute the subject matter of this book.

☐ Overview

The book is divided into three sections. Part I delineates the empirical evidence, clinical observations, rationale, and socio-political analysis that contributed to the development of a family/social context model for understanding and treating adult survivors of prolonged child abuse. Chapter 1 frames the historical and social forces that formed the context from which trauma-based models of child abuse and its impact emerged. It also raises questions about some of the complications and that can arise from centering the treatment of abuse survivors on the processing of traumatic material.

Chapter 2 reviews empirical findings supporting an alternative conceptualization of the nature and etiology of the psychological difficulties experienced by abuse survivors. This literature includes the observation that the constructs of trauma and posttraumatic stress disorder do not adequately account for the wide range of symptoms and problems commonly found among abuse survivors. The bulk of this chapter is devoted to an overview of a fairly extensive, but not widely recognized, body of empirical literature regarding the family environments of child abuse survivors. This research suggests that many of the problems manifested by survivors may have their origins in this family context, rather than solely in the discrete incidents of abuse.

An extensive verbatim transcript of a therapy session with a male survivor of ongoing childhood sexual abuse is presented in Chapter 3. This transcript was chosen because it provides a particularly vivid and detailed first person account of the type of family of origin environment identified by the research reviewed in Chapter 2. It also will be helpful to practitioners in illustrating the value of a nondirective approach to exploratory interviewing in working with clients with an extensive history of abusive treatment and of interpersonal relationships marked by emotional unavailability, abandonment, and betrayal. In addition, this session transcript nicely illustrates the three major elements of contextual therapy: development of a collaborative alliance; construction of a contextualized conceptualization; and the acquisition of daily living skills.

Transcripts of client interviews also appear in Chapters 11 and 15. In these cases and in all instances where case material is presented, names were changed to protect anonymity. Explicit permission was obtained from clients to use their transcript segments. These clients were also provided with a manuscript copy of the chapter in which their interview transcript appeared to allow them to review this material in context and to provide them with the opportunity to express any objections they may have had to the way the material was presented.

Chapter 4 is devoted to describing the family/social context conceptual framework on which the skills-centered approach to treatment for adult survivors of child abuse is based. This conceptualization builds on the historical, empirical, and clinical data presented in the three previous chapters. The family/social context model proposes that the chaotic and ineffective interpersonal environment in which survivors of prolonged child abuse often grow up represents a risk factor that makes children particularly vulnerable to ongoing abuse and is a direct source of many of the difficulties they manifest in adulthood. The failure of a deficient family environment to transmit the skills needed to adequately manage the complexities of adult functioning is seen as being at least as important as the traumatic impact of overt abuse in explaining and resolving these individuals' problems and symptoms.

Chapter 5 discusses some of the conceptual intricacies introduced by the recognition that child maltreatment can take a variety of forms, each with a differential impact. Research findings on the divergent and overlapping effects of various forms of abuse are summarized. The further compounding of these different types of maltreatment via their interaction with being reared in an ineffective family environment is also addressed.

Taking into account the conflict-ridden and deficient nature of many abuse survivors' family-of-origin environments appreciably broadens one's perspective on their adjustment problems. This view, however, still falls short of providing a comprehensive understanding of the origins and nature of survivors' difficulties. Chapter 6 considers the impact of the interpersonal context of the larger society, beyond the family, on the adjustment of abuse survivors.

Part II explores the clinical implications of the family/social context theory laid down in Part I. Chapter 7 consists of an extensive examination of the challenges encountered in developing a collaborative therapeutic relationship with someone from a chaotic and unsupportive family background. Due to their repeated experiences of abandonment and betrayal, survivors of prolonged child abuse often harbor both intense interpersonal dependency needs and an acute wariness about getting close to others. The various manifestations of these conflicting interpersonal forces, as well as suggestions for how to manage them, are discussed.

Survivors of prolonged child abuse often present with a wide range of difficulties, as well as intricate and confusing histories. It is imperative that therapists develop a cohesive conceptual framework in order to organize this material. Chapter 8 addresses the ongoing process of creating and modifying the conceptualization of a case in order to guide treatment in a coherent fashion.

As a consequence of the multiple problems that most survivors of prolonged child abuse experience, effective treatment requires the achievement of a number of objectives. Optimal progress depends on addressing therapeutic goals systematically. Both the general structure comprising the contextual model of treatment for survivors of prolonged child abuse and the rationale underlying it are delineated in Chapter 9.

It is in Part III that the specific goals and concrete interventions comprising the contextual treatment model are explicated. A cornerstone of the contextual philosophy is that the ultimate aim of treatment is not merely to resolve problems, but to teach clients methods for adaptation and problem resolution that will lead to continued gains long after formal therapy ends. This approach follows logically from the concept that many of prolonged abuse survivors' difficulties stem from never having learned basic adaptive living skills.

Chapter 10 covers the cardinal goal of the treatment plan—teaching clients how to reduce, modulate, and manage distress. In the presence of overwhelming emotional discomfort, it is unrealistic to expect that clients will have the ability to concentrate on mastering other practical living skills. In addition, the higher the clients' general level of distress, the more vulnerable they are to experiencing a range of symptoms such as panic attacks and flashbacks, and the more likely they are to engage in self-harming addictive and compulsive patterns of behavior.

A sizable proportion of prolonged child abuse survivors routinely experience dissociative symptoms that interfere with their ability to stay focused in the present. As with distress, there is a limit to how much clients can learn when their ability to concentrate is tenuous. Chapter 11, therefore, discusses how to teach clients to modulate and disrupt dissociative reactions.

One pervasive area in which many survivors of prolonged child abuse were deprived of learning is the exercise of critical judgement and reasoning. Effective cognitive intervention for these clients, therefore, entails not just facilitating modification of the content of their thinking, but, more importantly, teaching them strategies for conceptual processing itself. Methods for accomplishing both of these aims are covered in Chapter 12.

To the degree that clients have acquired tools to manage emotional discomfort, stay present and focused, and engage in critical thinking, they are equipped to apply these capacities to relinquish the maladaptive behavior patterns that they previously relied on as means of reducing distress. A detailed strategy for accomplishing this is outlined in Chapter 13. This approach has the advantage of being easily adaptable for disrupting a wide range of problematic behavior patterns.

While processing traumatic material is not the primary focus of contextual treatment for abuse survivors, it is retained as one aspect of a broader approach to intervention. Methods for addressing and resolving the impact of trauma that are particularly well-suited to survivors of prolonged abuse are reviewed in Chapter 14. Particular attention is paid to issues of timing and of modulating the way in which abuse experiences are addressed at various points in treatment.

Once the component skills comprising the contextual therapy model have been acquired, and abusive experiences have been assimilated in a way that prevents them from disrupting current functioning, a series of further changes is set in motion. Clients begin to explore and develop capacities for effectively engaging in fundamental aspects of adult living, such as establishing and maintaining intimate relationships, a gratifying pattern of sexual functioning, mutually rewarding affiliations with friends and family, stable work adaptation, and responsible money management. This culminating phase of contextual treatment is described in Chapter 15.

The epilogue comprising Part IV returns to the question of social context. The model presented here is grounded in the contention that it is ultimately at the broad level of social context that we must look to understand child abuse, deficient family systems, their perpetuation, and their debilitating impact on the individual. From the perspective of interpersonal context, therapy for abuse survivors that lacks an adequate comprehension and appreciation of the role of society in perpetuating and compounding these conditions is likely to be at best limited in its effectiveness, and at worst misguided and detrimental.

☐ Aim

Not long ago, it seemed that our treatment philosophy at TRIP diverged substantially from that of most other professionals specializing in working with abuse survivors. Our approach of making the acquisition of adaptive living skills, rather than the detailed processing of traumatic material, the cornerstone of our therapeutic model elicited criticism or even outright derision at times. Increasingly in recent months, I have been heartened to hear my colleagues assert in presentations at professional meetings that trauma-focused treatment is not productive with most survivors of prolonged child abuse. It is my hope that the model proffered here will provide practitioners working with survivors with both a productive alternative perspective for understanding the problems experienced by survivors, and an effective set of methods for helping them overcome these difficulties. I envision the model, in the form in which it is presented here, not as the final word on a finished product, but as the presentation of an emerging perspective on and approach to therapy for child abuse survivors that will undergo considerable evolution and refinement in the years to come.

Steven N. Gold
Fort Lauderdale, Florida
December 1999

ACKNOWLEDGMENTS

Much of this book is about people who feel profoundly alone—who in fact have, to a great degree, been left to make their way through life fending for themselves. Any substantive goal in life is achieved not in isolation, but with the support and assistance of those who we are fortunate enough to count among our friends, family, and colleagues. Throughout the process of writing this volume, I have been intensely aware that it represents an intersection of the personal and professional influence of countless people, over many, many years.

First and foremost, I wish to express my gratitude to Charles Figley, who initiated this project by inviting me to write the book. Charles has not only made enduring, vital contributions to the establishment and development of the field of traumatology in his own right, but more than anyone I can think of, has been active in encouraging, supporting, and promoting the work of others. He is one of those rare individuals whose stature as an internationally recognized professional is matched by the scope of his warmth, compassion, and humanity.

Among those with the most immediate impact on the content of this work, are the doctoral students who comprised the clinical and research staff of the Trauma Resolution Integration Program (TRIP) of Nova Southeastern University Community Mental Health Center, originally known as the Sexual Abuse Survivors Program. Kelly Chrestman, the doctoral student who assisted me in establishing TRIP during its first years existence, from 1990 through 1992, strongly affected the structure and direction of both the clinical and research efforts of the program. By 1992, TRIP had grown to the point that the administration of clinical and research functions formerly handled by Kelly needed to be overseen separately. From then until 1994, Dawn Hughes assumed the position of Research Coordinator, developing and refining the data collection, data entry, and data base management components of the research program. She was succeeded until 1997 by Jan Swingle, who was instrumental in helping to direct some of the first research studies conducted at TRIP, from conception through publication. Until recently, Barbara Lucenko assumed the responsibilities of Research Coordinator. Barbara played a key role in navigating the program through a period when both the membership of the research team and the number of professional presentations and publications generated by it have increased rapidly. Due to the expansion of the research team, it became necessary to create a separate Data Entry Coordinator position, filled first by Erica Hill and subsequently by Melissa Cott. In the summer of 1999, Melissa took over as Research Coordinator, and the Data Entry Coordinator position she vacated has been filled by Shirin Bazaz. I will always be indebted to all of these women for the skill, time, and remarkable dedication they have exhibited in developing and maintaining the creative and productive research program that currently thrives at TRIP. I also want to express my appreciation to the doctoral students who, along with the Research and Data Entry Coordinators named above, have collaborated with me as co-authors on professional publications—Jon Elhai, Arian Elfant, Christopher Heffner, Stephen Russo, Laura Hohnecker, and Cheri Hansen—and to my faculty colleague Alfred Sellers, who provided methodological and statistical consultation and served as co-author on several of these projects.

In addition to those doctoral students who assumed administrative responsibilities on the research team, I want to thank those doctoral students who assisted me in the organization and administration of service programs at TRIP as Clinical Coordinators. I consider myself especially lucky to have been associated with Laura Hohnecker, the first individual to serve in this capacity. Laura began her doctoral studies after almost 10 years of extensive clinical experience working with survivors of severe child abuse and treating dissociative disorders. I know that I learned at least as much from her as she did from me. It is especially gratifying to me that she and her successors, Sheri Knight, Robyn Hightower, Christopher Heffner, Stephen Russo, Ann Booth, and, currently, Jessica McIninch, have all, through their devotion and clinical skill, helped to a build a level of quality into the service program at TRIP of which we can all be proud. Along with several TRIP team members already mentioned, Ted Masino graciously shared clinical case material used for illustrative purposes in this volume.

Three other doctoral students were more directly involved in the production of this book. When I first began preparing the manuscript, Steve Gonzalez helped to obtain library resources for me. As the project progressed, Rob Seifer assumed this duty as well as assisting in transcribing material from video- and audio-taped sessions. During the composition of the third and largest section of the book, Heather Kimmel not only took charge of obtaining library resources and drafting correspondence related to the project, but volunteered to take on the extensive chores of proofreading the initial draft of the entire work and compiling the index. I am grateful to all three of them not only for the competency with which they executed these tasks, but also for their unfailing patience and cheerfulness in doing so.

Beyond the doctoral trainees who collaborated with me in the development of the clinical and research programs at TRIP, many aspects of the treatment model presented here have been influenced by my mentors and colleagues. Among the faculty in my doctoral training program, I am keenly aware of the enduring impact of Al Rabin, my major professor, and of Bert Karon and Henry Clay Smith, on my way of thinking about and approaching clinical issues. Similarly, Camella Serum, my clinical supervisor on internship, and Don Beere, my clinical supervisor in the years immediately after I completed my doctoral degree, have strongly shaped my perspective as a practitioner. More recently, my outlook on working with child abuse survivors has been honed by the invaluable input of my associate in independent practice, Denise Strauch, through her peer supervision. I am also indebted to those colleagues whose expertise in and passion about the pressing need to acknowledge and arrest interpersonal violence in our society has been deeply inspiring and sustaining to me—Laura Brown, Christine Courtois, Mary Ann Dutton, Jan Faust, Bob Geffner, Margo Rivera, Joy Silberg, Susan Wachob, and Lenore Walker.

The irony that working on this book, which emphasizes the importance of parenting and family life, infringed on the time I spent with my wife Peggy and our children, Andrea, Lylah, and Adam, was not lost on me. The fact that they have reacted by expressing excitement about the progress and completion of the manuscript, rather than complaining about the inconveniences the project created for them, has been for me a moving testament to their love and support. I can only hope to repay them by doing my best to make up for lost time in the coming years.

While writing about the indispensability of interpersonal relationships for developing the capacity for living well, so many family members, colleagues, and friends came to mind who have had a profound impact on my own well being that I cannot possibly mention all of them. I do, however, want to acknowledge in particular: my parents, Shirlee and Len Gold; my maternal grandparents, Frances and Louis Bernstein; my paternal grandparents, Rachel and George Gold; and my dear friends Wendy Morris, Ned Rousmaniere, Ken Bertram, Robin Zucker, and Winnie Griffieth. It is from and with them that I have learned many of life's most important lessons.

Above all, I want to thank my own therapy clients with a history of prolonged child abuse as well as those clients who participated in the treatment and research programs at TRIP. It has been an honor and a privilege to know these people. For many of them, one of their greatest concerns has been to spare others the pain that they have suffered. For example, those whom I approached with the request to include excerpts of transcripts from their therapy and follow-up interviews in this volume were not only agreeable, but eager to share their experiences in the hope that others might benefit. It is through their willingness to trust me and the clinical and research staff at TRIP enough to educate us about what they have endured and how it has affected them that we have obtained the knowledge to develop the conceptual and treatment model presented here. I can only hope that in the process, they have been enriched as much as I have.

ABUSE IN CONTEXT: THE CONCEPTUAL FRAMEWORK

From a historical perspective, widespread recognition among mental health professionals of the prevalence of child abuse and its long term adverse impact on psychological functioning is a relatively recent development. Contemporary awareness of abuse and its effects has, from its inception, been intimately related to the concepts of trauma and posttraumatic stress disorder. This section traces the emergence of these constructs, considers some of their limitations, and proposes, based on empirical and clinical evidence, an alternative conceptualization of the sources and nature of the difficulties in adult adjustment that are commonly experienced by survivors of childhood abuse. It presents the argument that survivors of prolonged child maltreatment often grow up in family environments that fail to teach them many of the fundamental daily-living skills required for effective adult functioning, and that this, as much as the discrete incidents of abuse to which they have been subjected, is the source of many of their difficulties.

CHAPTER

Abuse: The Trauma Model

Abuse. Trauma. Not very long ago, these were not words that were encountered with any regularity. In a remarkably short span of years, they have become part of everyday speech. In the process, these two words have come to be so closely associated with each other that they are sometimes used interchangeably. What happened during that relatively brief period of time to transform our thinking about issues that, until then, had remained invisible to so many of us?

Around 1980, several social and academic trends converged to catalyze a recognition of the prevalence of child abuse and of its potentially devastating effects on adult functioning. Over the subsequent twenty years, growing awareness of maltreatment of children has had a profound influence not only on theory, research, and practice in psychology, but on society as a whole. Before the 1970s the topic of child abuse was almost entirely absent from psychological literature (Kempe & Kempe, 1978; van der Kolk, Weisaeth, & van der Hart, 1996). In contrast, there are now several professional journals devoted entirely to child maltreatment. Countless articles on the topic appear in journals devoted to a more general readership, and numerous books have been published on the subject. In the popular media, coverage of some aspect of child abuse is regularly encountered on television talk shows, in newspapers and news programs, in magazines, and in feature films.

☐ The Social Context of the Recognition of Abuse Trauma

One of the major developments that stirred awareness of child abuse was the rise of the women's movement in the 1970s. Feminist socio-political analysis was instrumental in directing attention to the frequency with which women and children were subjected to victimization and violence. In the 1970s and early 1980s, groundbreaking works by authors who were strongly influenced by feminist scholarship on the nature and damaging effects of rape (Burgess & Holstrom, 1974), woman battering (Walker, 1979), and child sexual abuse (Herman, 1981) emerged, following each other in rapid succession. These investigators set in motion a decisive shift in society's awareness of violence perpetrated against women and children. In a way that is difficult for those whose formative years came after 1980 to appreciate, acts of violence that once seemed rare are now recognized as commonplace, and their consequences, which once were minimized, now generate a degree of compassion and responsiveness more consistent with their severity and destructiveness.

Another primary contributor to recognition of the pernicious consequences of child abuse was much less obviously and directly related to child maltreatment—the aftermath of the Vietnam War. The traumatic effects of combat experience had been repeatedly documented in the professional literature throughout the succession of armed conflicts in this century. With the passing of each war, gains in understanding and treating combat-related syndromes had slipped into oblivion (Herman, 1992a; van der Kolk et al., 1996). In the years following the Vietnam War, however, the situation differed from that of earlier post-war periods in several respects. For one thing, various conditions distinguished the war in Vietnam from earlier wars. One of the most significant among these conditions was that a tour of duty in Vietnam was restricted to one year (Bourne, 1978). For this and other reasons, psychiatric casualties in Vietnam were appreciably lower than they had been in previous wars. It gradually became apparent, however, that the psychological consequences of combat exposure among many Vietnam veterans only began to emerge after their tour of duty ended. This delayed reaction was probably largely due to the isolation experienced by many Vietnam veterans. As opposed to the hero's welcome afforded homecoming soldiers from World War I and World War II, soldiers coming back from Vietnam were often ignored or derided for their service due to the unpopularity of the war. Further contributing to their segregation were the individualized schedules created by the twelve month tour of duty system, organized so that each soldier returned separately, usually unaccompanied by comrades (Bourne, 1978).

The unpopularity of the war, the extensive experience of "stress disorders" among Vietnam veterans, and discontent with what they perceived as a lack of responsiveness to their combat-related distress moved veterans to remain vocal about the psychological toll combat had taken on them. Rather than allowing themselves to be silenced by stigmatization, they lobbied to have their post-combat difficulties taken seriously (Figley, 1978a; Herman, 1992a). As a result, combat-related stress disorders came to be acknowledged as a legitimate field of study in the professional literature (Figley, 1978a).

In a manner with little precedent, these two movements represented the refusal of disempowered groups, women in the former case and combat veterans in the latter, to allow the psychological damage inflicted on them by social injustice go unheeded and without reparation. Instead of accepting the prevailing social view that such impairment was a sign of weakness, they insisted that their difficulties be acknowledged as an expectable reaction to horrific experiences. Their efforts contributed to the formation of a unique psychiatric diagnostic category, posttraumatic stress disorder (PTSD; Figley, 1978b; Haley, 1978). This diagnosis was distinctive in that it included among its criteria the explicit statement that etiology was attributable to *circumstances extraneous to the person being diagnosed,* that is, a traumatic event: "a recognizable stressor that would evoke significant symptoms of distress in almost everyone" (American Psychiatric Association, 1980, p. 238). The implication of this criterion was that PTSD did not primarily reflect that there was something defective about the person being diagnosed, but rather that there was something inherently destructive about the situation to which she or he had been exposed.

The codification of the diagnostic syndrome of PTSD and its adoption in 1980 into the *Diagnostic and Statistical Manual of Mental Disorders* (DSM-III, American Psychiatric Association, 1980) was largely guided by the work of investigators of responses to combat experiences in Vietnam (Figley, 1978b; Haley, 1978; van der Kolk et al., 1996). It was not long, however, before extensive commonalities were noted between the reactions observed among Vietnam veterans and those catalogued by investigators studying rape, child physical abuse, woman battering, and child sexual molestation (Herman, 1992a; van der Kolk et al., 1996). The symptoms of PTSD are often grouped into three major categories: (a) intrusive reexperiencing—images, thoughts, sensations, and dreams that spontaneously impinge upon awareness, usually in response to cues that serve as reminders of the trauma; (b) numbing and avoidance—attempts to circumvent situations reminiscent of the trauma along with emotional and sensory "shutting down"; and (c) arousal—a generalized state of agitation marked by characteristics such as hypervigilence, heightened startle response, and irritability. All three classes of symptoms were included in the diagnostic criteria for PTSD in the *DSM III-R* (1987), and were retained in the *DSM-IV* (1994). The presence of the first two of these three symptoms groupings was highlighted in the writings of Mardi Horowitz (1969, 1970; Horowitz & Solomon, 1978). Horowitz emphasized that this pattern of intrusion and numbing manifests regardless of the particular type of traumatic event experienced. The symptoms of reexperiencing and shutting down, therefore, were as characteristic of abused women and children as of combat veterans. The conclusion seemed obvious. Whether it occurred on the battlefield, in the streets, or in the privacy of domestic settings, exposure to violence seemed to have essentially identical psychological repercussions.

☐ Abuse, Trauma, and Memory

From early on, therefore, the study of child abuse and its long term effects has been closely linked with the concept of trauma and the syndrome of PTSD. It has seemed axiomatic, since child abuse was recognized as a form of trauma, that treatment approaches for adult survivors of child abuse should approximate those for survivors of other forms of trauma. This perception was bolstered by the "rediscovery" of Freud's (1959/1893, 1959/1896; Breuer & Freud, 1955/1895) early works on the role of trauma in the etiology of psychopathology. Even before the inception of the diagnosis of PTSD, this initial period of Freud's psychological theorizing had been referred to by some as his "trauma model" (e.g., Loevinger, 1976; Miller, 1984). In the 1980s and early 1990s, a variety of authors writing about child sexual abuse in particular (e.g., Bass & Davis, 1988; Blume, 1990; Briere & Conte, 1993; Courtois, 1988; Herman, 1981; Herman & Schatzow, 1987) and trauma in general (e.g., Herman, 1992a; Waites, 1993) revisited Freud's trauma model. They noted that almost a century earlier, Freud (1959/1896) had attributed many neurotic symptoms, especially hysterical ones, to the traumatic effects of child sexual abuse. He also pointed out similarities between hysterical neurosis and what was then referred to as "traumatic neurosis"—neurotic symptoms that manifested in response to physical injury, that is, trauma (Freud, 1959/1893). In all likelihood, Masson's 1984 book, *The Assault on Truth: Freud's Supression of the Seduction Theory*, which predated the other works by only a few years and was cited in most of them, helped to fuel this trend. Masson alleged that Freud had abandoned his trauma theory, or, as it was labeled by Freud himself, "seduction theory," not on the basis of evidence, but because it was met with incredulity and disdain. Masson's thesis, reflected in the title of his book, was that Freud's "personal failure of courage" (p. 189) led him to abandon and obscure the truth in response to a hostile sociopolitical climate.

It is true that seduction theory was based on the contention that hysterical symptoms had their origins in childhood sexual abuse. In Freud's (1959/1896) own words:

> Sexual experiences in childhood consisting of stimulation of the genitals, coitus-like activities, etc. are therefore in the final analysis to be recognized as the traumata from which proceed hysterical reactions against experiences at puberty and hysterical symptoms themselves (p. 202).

However, Freud (1959/1896) insisted that a history of childhood sexual abuse itself was not a sufficient cause of hysteria. Integral to his seduction theory were the processes of loss and subsequent recovery of recollections of abuse trauma.

> We have heard and acknowledged that there are many people who have a very clear recollection of infantile sexual experiences and yet do not suffer from hysteria. This objection really has no weight at all, but it provides an occasion for a valuable comment. People of this type *should* not (according to our understanding of neurosis) be hysterical at all, at least not in consequence of scenes which they consciously remember. In our patients these memories are never conscious; we cure their hysteria, however, by converting their unconscious memories of infantile scenes into conscious recollection (p. 207). . . . From this you perceive that it is not merely a question of the existence of the infantile sexual experiences, but that a certain psychological condition enters into the case. These scenes must exist as *unconscious memories;* only so long and in so far as they are unconscious can they produce and maintain hysterical symptoms. (p. 208)

With the revival of Freud's trauma model, therefore, came general acceptance not only of the concept that psychological symptomatology in adults could be traced to sexual abuse in childhood, but also of the notion that it was not simply the abuse experience, but the obliteration of memories of abuse from conscious awareness, that was the key etiological factor. The result was that some therapists, following the lead of Freud's trauma model, assumed that the lifting of amnesic barriers through encouraging retrieval of abuse memories was critical to recovery from the effects of child sexual abuse. This conviction was bolstered by research investigations providing evidence that loss and subsequent recovery of abuse memories occurs among at least a substantial minority, and possibly the majority, of adult survivors of childhood sexual abuse (Briere & Conte, 1993; Herman & Schatzow, 1987; Loftus, Polonsky, & Fullilove, 1994; Williams, 1994). Empirical evidence supporting the existence of the phenomenon of loss and subsequent recovery of traumatic memories continues to accumulate. In a review of 25 studies of traumatic memory, Scheflin and Brown (1996) concluded that the preponderance of the data supports the existence of amnesia for childhood sexual abuse and the accuracy of recovered abuse memories.

Despite these findings, the notion of amnesia with later retrieval of abuse memories has generated tremendous controversy. Those disputing the existence and validity of this phenomenon (e.g., Loftus, 1993; Ofshe & Watters, 1994; Wakefield & Underwager, 1992; Yapko, 1994) argue that what are alleged to be recovered recollections of abuse are actually false memories, implanted by therapists. They contend that clinicians subscribing to the belief that amnesia for abuse is common among survivors of childhood molestation unwittingly employ suggestive and leading questioning in a manner that encourages the elicitation of responses consistent with their expectations.

Existing data are inconsistent with the claim that in the majority of instances, recovered memories are false recollections implanted by therapists. In a general population study by Elliott and Briere (1995), participants with a childhood sexual abuse history reporting recovered memory were no more likely to be in therapy than those reporting continuous memory. In what was apparently a different set of analyses of the same general population sample (Elliott, 1997), participants with recovered memories were also asked what cues had led to retrieval. Out of a choice of 13 categories, psychotherapy was the least likely to have triggered recall (14%) among survivors of all forms of trauma. More specifically, among survivors of childhood molestation, psychotherapy was the second least common impetus for recall identified (also 14%). In a clinical sample, Leavitt (1997) compared the suggestibility of women who had recovered memories of childhood sexual abuse to that of women without a history of sexual molestation. A highly significant difference was found between the two groups, but in the direction of clients with recovered memories of sexual abuse being *less* suggestible than the other women. Taken together, these findings are inconsistent with the claim that recovered memories of abuse frequently are the result of leading questioning of especially suggestible therapy clients.

☐ Distinguishing Recollection from Recovery

Unfortunately, the contention about the existence, accuracy, and implantation of abuse memories has, in some ways, detracted attention from the critical practical question of whether encouraging retrieval of traumatic memories is a productive strategy for intervention. Particularly in the midst of the initial emerging awareness of childhood sexual abuse and its disabling effects in the 1980s and early 1990s, Freud's trauma theory was much more widely accepted than it is now. Some authors stressed that amnesia for abuse is common, that many survivors have absolutely no recollection of having been abused, and advocated actively seeking out abuse memories (Bass & Davis, 1988; Blume, 1990).

Careful reading of most experts on treating childhood sexual abuse, however, shows that most of them never advocated making memory recovery the sole or even principle strategy for treating survivors. Instead, they warn against permitting the processing of abuse material to threaten the client's stability of functioning and sense of well-being (see, e.g., Briere, 1989; Briere & Conte, 1993; Dolan, 1991; Herman & Schatzow, 1987; Herman, 1992a). Consider, for example, the approach Courtois (1988) took in addressing this issue. She wrote that "usually, repression lifts during the course of therapy and memories return" (p. 178). The wording here seems to implicitly convey that memory recovery is not the purpose or strategy of clinical intervention, but rather a by-product or accompaniment of therapeutic progress. The idea that the exhuming of abuse memories is not the crux of treatment is further clarified as Courtois continued, advising:

> The incest story may have to be recounted in pieces, taking into account the gradual giving way of repression of memories and insuring that the emotional impact is both tolerable and manageable. The therapist needs to closely monitor this process with a client. A recitation in great and exhaustive detail is necessary for some survivors, but not for all. For some, a general recitation of the facts suffices. (p. 179)

Perhaps the most compelling indication that Courtois is not advocating memory retrieval as a central therapeutic strategy is the almost complete absence of the topic from her book, which is about the psychotherapeutic treatment of incest survivors. The closest approximation to the subject is a single section consisting of two paragraphs titled "Recounting the Incest," from which the quotations above are excerpted.

Interestingly, understanding that encouraging recovery of traumatic memories is likely to be damaging, rather than therapeutic, seems to have existed in the early literature on treating postcombat reactions in Vietnam veterans. In Figley's (1978a) influential edited volume, *Stress Disorders Among Vietnam Veterans*, Egendorf (1978) distinctly cautioned practitioners against proceeding in a "cart before the horse style" (p. 246) by actively encouraging memory retrieval and abreaction of combat trauma. He acknowledged that resurfacing recollections of combat and accompanying intense affective reactions are phenomena often accompanying the process of trauma resolution. Egendorf warned, however, that these are collateral signs rather than the causal agents of healing in survivors of trauma.

The findings of a general population study by Elliott and Briere (1995) are particularly pertinent to the issue of memory retrieval as an intervention strategy with survivors of child abuse. Levels of posttraumatic stress symptoms of participants with no reported trauma history were compared with those of survivors with continuous recall, those with delayed recall that occurred more than 2 years earlier, and those with delayed recall that had occurred within the past 2 years. The latter group had the highest level of posttraumatic stress symptoms, but there were no appreciable differences in symptoms found between those who had recovered memory for trauma more than 2 years earlier and those with continuous memory. All three groups of participants with reported histories of trauma had significantly higher symptom levels than those without a trauma history. This pattern of findings suggests that while retrieval of traumatic memories temporarily exacerbates symptomatology, it does not, in the long run, result in resolution of symptoms. The data further indicate that, in the short term, recall of traumatic material exacerbates rather than ameliorates symptoms.

Particularly in the absence of adequate preparation, practitioner-facilitated recall can be counter-productive and destabilizing (Gold & Brown, 1997). Once traumatic memories are accessed, the spontaneous emergence of further traumatic recall in the form of terrifying flashbacks, nightmares, and panic attacks can be initiated. Rather than culminating in trauma resolution, the overwhelming and involuntary nature of intrusive recall is likely to lead to a sense of personal powerlessness and hopelessness about being able to overcome the incapacitating impact of the trauma. Most authors who do recognize uncovering memories as one possible component of therapy for adult survivors of trauma, therefore, emphasize that this is not a process that should be promoted in the beginning stages of treatment (Briere, 1996; Brown & Fromm, 1986; Courtois, 1988; Gill, 1988; Herman; 1992a; Kluft, 1982; Phillips & Frederick, 1995; Putnam, 1989). Before traumatic material can be addressed in a constructive manner, it is essential that the skills needed to cope sufficiently with the distress that is aroused by it are firmly in place. This initial phase of treatment has repeatedly been referred to as one of establishing "safety" (Herman, 1992a; Phillips & Frederick, 1995) or "stabilization" (Brown & Fromm, 1986; Phillips & Frederick 1995; Putnam, 1989). Only once this process has taken hold, can the survivor reasonably be expected to master past trauma, and develop a perspective that keeps it from interfering with current daily living. As Herman (1992a) and Phillips and Frederick (1995) have noted, this is a position that can be traced at least as far back as the writings of Janet (1889/1973) over a century ago.

Most of the works cited in the previous paragraph devote substantially more attention and explication to interventions for developing safety and stabilization than to methods for retrieving and processing traumatic material. They all urge that the former task take priority over the latter. Nevertheless, there have been clinicians who have failed to fully comprehend the risks involved in making traumatic experiences the focus of treatment (Pope & Brown, 1996). In some of the most tragic instances, well-meaning therapists who adhere to the conviction that healing can only occur with confrontation of traumatic material, engage in increasingly forceful attempts to exhort the client to endure retrieving and facing traumatic memories (Gold & Brown, 1997). If we return to the origins of contemporary awareness of child sexual abuse in the modern feminist movement's concern with empowerment, the paradox inherent in this stance becomes sadly apparent. Rather than validating the client, the therapist who assumes this posture ends up recapitulating the interpersonal pattern of coercion and subjugation that characterized the abuse itself. As Brown (1996) attested in her feminist analysis of the recovered memory controversy, such an approach is conspicuously at odds with the pivotal role in feminist therapy of affirming "a client's privilege to define what is real, set personal boundaries, and make personal choices" (p. 14).

This is not merely a philosophical stance, but an intensely practical matter as well. Integral to the experience of ongoing abuse in childhood is the development and deeply ingrained conviction of vulnerability, powerlessness, and culpability in one's own victimization, and of the unreliability and untrustworthiness of others (Briere, 1996; Courtois, 1988; Janoff-Bulman, 1992; Waites, 1993). Therapy for adult survivors that incorporates review of traumatic material without taking into account the pervasive mistrust of self and others created by ongoing child abuse can easily compound rather than resolve clients' difficulties. Survivor clients are susceptible to experiencing the distress and turmoil that can be aroused by revisiting traumatic material as a recapitulation of the original abuse. In these circumstances, the therapist is likely to be perceived as being a punitive perpetrator, and survivors are prone to blame themselves for failing to benefit from a procedure that they have come to expect should resolve their problems (Gold & Brown, 1997).

From this vantage point, the issue of whether recovered memories are accurate is supplanted in importance by even more fundamental questions: How adequately does the PTSD diagnosis capture the long term effects of child abuse? To what extent does ongoing child abuse approximate and differ from other forms of trauma? How applicable are treatments designed for PTSD to adult survivors of extended child maltreatment? Is it advisable to make traumatic memories, whether continuous or delayed, the central focus of treatment for adult survivors of child abuse? The remainder of this section will address these questions in the course of outlining a framework for conceptualizing child abuse, its long term effects, and treatment that encompasses, but extends beyond, the abuse trauma model.

2
CHAPTER

Family: Beyond the Trauma Model

For a variety of reasons, trauma-focused therapy may not be a reasonable, feasible, or effective strategy for addressing the long-term effects of child abuse in adult survivors. In reviewing the literature on the immediate and long-term effects of child sexual abuse (CSA), Finkelhor (1990) challenged the notion of equating child sexual abuse with other forms of trauma. He questioned whether it is reasonable to conceptualize child sexual abuse as "a form of PTSD" (p. 328), and on that basis to assume that its effects can be adequately treated using the "PTSD therapies" (p. 328). Finkelhor identified several possible flaws in this deduction:

1. The symptoms manifested by survivors of childhood sexual abuse routinely extend beyond those comprising PTSD.
2. The PTSD diagnosis underscores affective symptoms, but does not adequately address the cognitive distortions commonly observed among sexual abuse survivors.
3. The findings of several studies suggest that the majority of survivors of child molestation do not exhibit PTSD symptoms.
4. Childhood sexual abuse is unlike other forms of trauma, in that it: (a) often occurs without overt physical threat or violence; and (b) *is less of an 'event' than a situation, relationship or process..."* that *"often continues for a period of time* [italics added]" (p. 329).

The third of these four points, that most sexual abuse survivors do not develop PTSD symptoms, is probably the most disputable. In a literature review on the long-term effects of childhood sexual abuse conducted over a decade ago, Browne and Finkelhor (1986) concluded that depression, rather than PTSD, is the syndrome most commonly exhibited by survivors. Finkelhor (1990) also pointed to investigations in which the majority of adults sexually abused as children did not manifest symptoms of PTSD. However, this may be attributable to the fact that these studies did not employ clinical samples. Participants who did not exhibit PTSD may have been asymptomatic in general. Rowan and Foy (1993) reviewed studies of the prevalence of PTSD symptoms and diagnosis among survivors of childhood sexual abuse. They concluded that findings were sufficiently supportive of a connection between child molestation and the subsequent development of PTSD symptoms to warrant further research in this area. Nevertheless, they acknowledged that existing investigations were, in general, marked by poor methodology, and therefore produced findings that were inconclusive.

Subsequently, the same authors, with two other colleagues, conducted a study of PTSD among child sexual abuse survivors that corrected many of the design weaknesses of previous research (Rodriguez, Ryan, Rowan, & Foy, 1996). Chief among these revisions was assessing degrees of child sexual abuse, rather than simply dichotomizing this variable as having been present or absent in the reported histories of participants. A clinical sample was employed, and the measures of abuse history and PTSD used were psychometrically sound. Full *DSM-III-R* criteria for PTSD were met for 72% of the sample at the time of the study. An additional 14% met criteria for partial PTSD, and 86% were determined to have met full PTSD criteria at some point during their lifetimes. Moreover, the hypothesis that level of abuse exposure would be predictive of PTSD was supported; all the abuse characteristics they investigated were significantly correlated (at magnitudes ranging from .29 to .61) with lifetime PTSD symptomatology. In combination with the findings of previous studies, this appreciably weakens Finkelhor's contention that PTSD is not a frequently observed attribute of survivors of childhood molestation.

☐ The Consequences of Child Abuse: Beyond PTSD

Even if PTSD is a common consequence of child sexual abuse, Finkelhor's (1990) other criticisms of the trauma model of abuse retain considerable practical relevance. The key question, therapeutically, is not merely whether PTSD is a commonly occuring component of the clinical picture presented by survivors. What is at issue, rather, is whether treatments for PTSD are likely to be effective with survivors of childhood abuse. Finkelhor's remaining objections identify the ways in which child abuse and its long-term effects transcend the constructs of trauma, PTSD symptomatology, and the trauma-based models of treatment. His criticisms do not negate the potential relevance of trauma and PTSD to child abuse and its effects. They do, however, clarify how these concepts may fail to adequately encompass the broader consequences of abuse and the corresponding implications for their resolution.

The first two of Finkelhor's (1990) points, that adult survivors commonly exhibit many symptoms not subsumed by PTSD and are plagued by extensive cognitive distortions not directly addressed by the diagnostic criteria for PTSD, have received tacit recognition in the proposed diagnostic category of Complex PTSD (Herman, 1992a, 1992b). Complex PTSD (CP), also labeled complicated PTSD, disorders of extreme stress (DES), and disorders of extreme stress not otherwise specified (DESNOS), is a syndrome consisting of symptoms that transcend and subsume those comprising PTSD (Roth, Newman, Pelcovitz, van der Kolk, & Mandel, 1997). Between them, Herman (1992a, 1992b) and Roth et al. (1997) identified seven symptom categories of CP: (a) poor affect and impulse regulation (e.g., persistent dysphoria, problems with modulation of anger, self-destructive urges); (b) alterations in consciousness (e.g., dissociative episodes, amnesia); (c) damaged self-perception (e.g., sense of being essentially different from others, sense of ineffectiveness); (d) distorted perception of perpetrator (e.g., idealization, adoption of distorted beliefs); (e) disrupted interpersonal relations (e.g., mistrust, intense dependency); (f) loss of systems of meaning (e.g., loss of sustaining beliefs, hopelessness); and (g) somatization (e.g., chronic pain, conversion symptoms).

The development of the CP construct appears to have been strongly influenced by the clinical observation, substantiated by empirical data, that trauma is often found in the histories of individuals diagnosed with borderline personality disorder (Herman, 1992a; Herman, Perry, & van der Kolk, 1989; Perry, Herman, van der Kolk, & Hoke, 1990). Many symptoms comprising CP—difficulty regulating affect, poor anger modulation, self-injury and other impulsive and self-destructive behaviors, identity fragmentation, alternating interpersonal clinging and withdrawal, interpersonal mistrust, the conviction that no one can understand one's difficulties—overlap with those comprising borderline personality disorder (Herman, 1992a, 1992b; Roth et al., 1997). Although the very purpose of the CP construct is to distinguish this much more intricate and extensive syndrome from PTSD, the authors proposing its adoption contend that both the CP diagnosis (Herman, 1992a, 1992b; Roth et al., 1997) and borderline personality disorder (Herman et al., 1989; Perry et al., 1990) are rooted in the exposure to trauma.

Despite the postulate that both have their origins in trauma, CP is conceptualized as having a divergent etiology from that of PTSD. While PTSD can result from the experience of a single traumatic event, CP is a constellation of symptoms that is hypothesized to stem from prolonged or repeated exposure to trauma (Herman, 1992a; 1992b). Although CP is often claimed to be a possible consequence in any instance of repetitive or ongoing trauma, in her discussion of CP, Herman (1992a) made it clear that survivors of ongoing child abuse are prototypical of those manifesting this syndrome:

> The mental health system is filled with survivors of prolonged, repeated childhood trauma . . . Because of the number and complexity of their symptoms, their treatment is often fragmentary and incomplete . . . Survivors of childhood abuse often accumulate many different diagnoses before the underlying problem of a complex post-traumatic syndrome is recognized. (Herman, 1992a, p. 122–123)

At several points in another review of the major features of CP, Herman (1992b) indicated that these traits are especially typical of adults abused as children and are even more intense in this group than in other survivor populations. In a comparable statement, van der Kolk and Fisler (1994) wrote of CP, "We found that... this cluster of symptoms . . . occurred mainly after a person had been exposed to *interpersonal* trauma *at an early age*" [emphasis added] (p. 147). Similarly, in their evaluation of the viability of the CP diagnosis, Roth et al. (1997) selected *DSM-IV* field trial data from sexual and physical abuse survivors for their analysis. They state:

> The constellation of symptoms subsumed under the CP nomenclature is consistent with empirical findings and developmental models regarding the long-term impact of childhood sexual abuse. . . . A consensus is emerging which suggests the clinical utility of the CP construct for understanding and treating sexual abuse survivors. Although the theory underlying CP does not focus upon sexual abuse exclusively, sexual abuse may be a critical factor for the development of the symptoms subsumed under the CP heading. (p. 540–541)

Roth et al.'s (1997) results were consistent with the supposition that CP subsumes PTSD. Out of their entire sample of survivors of sexual abuse, physical abuse, or both types of abuse, the majority, 48%, were found to have met criteria for both PTSD and CP at some point in their lifetimes. An additional 19% were classified as PTSD only, and just 2% met criteria for CP but not for PTSD. This left 30% who did not meet criteria for either PTSD or CP. Herman (1992b) asserted, "In general, the diagnostic concepts of the existing psychiatric canon, including simple PTSD, are not designed for survivors of prolonged, repeated trauma, and do not fit them well" (p. 388). The obvious implication is that treatment for "simple PTSD" is not adequate for individuals with CP. Instead of making processing of traumatic events the centerpiece of therapy, the CP diagnosis underscores the necessity of placing primary emphasis on establishing a sense of safety and security, correcting cognitive distortions about self and others, and developing a strong therapeutic collaboration to weather and reverse the client's self-denigration and mistrust of others (Herman, 1992a).

Finkelhor's (1990) final point is especially pertinent to the model presented here. It has been well established in the research literature that the use of violence and physical force is one of the characteristics of childhood sexual abuse that has most consistently been found to exacerbate its long-term symptomatic effects (Beitchman et al., 1992; Browne & Finkelhor, 1986; Kendall-Tackett, Williams, & Finkelhor, 1993). However, it appears that in many instances of child molestation, physical coercion is not employed by adult perpetrators (Gold, Hughes, & Swingle, 1996; Rodriguez et al., 1996; Roesler & McKenzie, 1994; Russell, 1986). This is perhaps because force is unnecessary, due to the frequently appreciable difference in age and size between perpetrator and victim. Moreover, while other, less aggressive forms of duress have received little empirical attention, there is some evidence that less invasive varieties of coercion, such as offering or bestowing "rewards" to child sexual abuse victims, intensifies symptomatology among adult survivors even more than does physical violence (Lucenko, Gold, Elhai, Russo, & Swingle, 2000). In all likelihood, this is the case because being provided with rewards increases the survivors' sense of complicity in and responsibility for their own victimization.

☐ Child Abuse in Family Context

The use of coercive strategies such as rewards, and their impact on abuse survivors, highlights the relational/interpersonal components of the abuse experience overtly described in the second portion [(b)] of Finkelhor's (1990) fourth point. The trauma/PTSD model continues to be the one most closely associated with conceptualizing child abuse. The literature on child abuse and its long-term effects, therefore, is strongly dominated, both explicitly and implicitly, by this formulation. Nonetheless, a comparatively small but growing body of clinical, theoretical, and empirical literature is progressively articulating an alternate framework for understanding abuse and its effects. This vision has taken on a variety of forms. However, those authors sharing this general perspective emphasize the interpersonal and social features and atmosphere surrounding the abuse experience, rather than directing their attention mainly to the specifics of the discrete abuse event.

This is not by any means a new viewpoint. It is, however, one that has been eclipsed by the association of abuse with trauma and PTSD since the inception of contemporary scholarly investigation of child abuse. Paradoxically, recognition of the importance of the interpersonal aspects of child sexual abuse can be traced at least as far back as the work of Gelinas

(1983), whom Finkelhor (1990) credits as being the first to make the connection between sexual abuse and PTSD. Although she used different terminology; Gelinas used the older designation, "traumatic neurosis" rather than "posttraumatic stress disorder." The section of her influential article on the enduring effects of incest in childhood labeled "Chronic Traumatic Neurosis," which explained the effects of incest in terms of PTSD, is immediately followed by one titled "Relational Imbalances." The latter section begins,

> Incest victims also show the effects of the exploitative relational imbalances within the family that allowed incest to occur in the first place, to continue and to remain undisclosed and untreated. It is important to emphasize that incest is *relationally-based* sexual abuse [italics in original]. (Gelinas, 1983, p. 319)

Intriguingly, Gelinas then proceeded to make an observation that underscores the clinical and experiential relevance of interpersonal concerns, as opposed to traumatic factors, to survivors themselves.

> Patients usually seek treatment for the consequences of these relational imbalances. Though some present with symptoms related to traumatic neuroses . . . it is much more usual for a patient to seek treatment because of the secondary elaborations related to the problems in her relational life (p. 319).

She specifically attributed a substantial range of impairments manifested by survivors to the enduring impact of "relational imbalances" on adjustment, rather than to the incest itself. Almost all of these characteristics are contained in the diagnostic criteria for CP, particularly in the categories of alterations in self-perception and alterations in relationships with others. They include: (a) low self-esteem, including the absence of a legitimate sense of entitlement or having rights, and attendant unassertiveness and interpersonal passivity; (b) guilt and self-blame for their own victimization; and (c) vulnerability to interpersonal exploitation and revictimization, resulting in depression and feelings of being overwhelmed.

Empirical Findings on the Family-of-Origin Environments of Abuse Survivors

While Gelinas' article is specifically about incest, a number of empirical studies have assessed the general atmosphere of families of children who are sexually abused both within and outside the family. Alexander and Lupfer (1987) administered the Family Adaptability and Cohesion Evaluation Scale - II (FACES-II; Olson, Russell, & Sprenkle, 1983), and the

Traditional Family Ideology Scale (Levinson & Huffman, 1955) to a sample of undergraduate women. Women abused by a nuclear family member were found to come from families with more traditional values than women abused by an extended family member, by a non-family member, or who were not abused. However, while analysis of FACES-II scores revealed that the families of abused women were significantly less cohesive and adaptable than those of women who were not abused, this measure did not significantly differentiate women abused by a nuclear family member, extended family member, or non-family member.

Williamson, Borduin and Howe (1991) administered the FACES-II to adolescents identified as neglected, physically abused, and sexually abused with a non-abused control group. Their findings were consistent with those of Harter, Alexander, and Neimeyer (1988). Non-abused adolescents produced higher family cohesion scores than any of the three maltreated groups. They also scored higher on family adaptability than either the sexually or physically abused groups.

Ray, Jackson, and Townsley (1991) compared the Family Environment Scale (FES; Moos & Moos, 1986) profiles of women undergraduates: (a) sexually abused as children by a family member; (b) molested by someone outside the family; and (c) not indicating a history of abuse. Five of the eight scales comprising the FES were significantly lower among abused women than non-abused women: Cohesion; Active-Recreational Orientation; Moral-Religious Emphasis; Independence; and Organization. No significant differences were obtained between women molested within the family and those abused by a non-family member.

In another study of women undergraduates (Yama, Tovey, and Fogas, 1993) no differences in FES scores, depression as measured by the Beck Depression Inventory (BDI; Beck & Steer, 1987), or anxiety as measured by the Anxiety Scale Questionnaire (ASQ; Cattell & Scheier, 1976) were found between women reporting sexual abuse by family members and those reporting CSA by individuals outside the family. However, women with a childhood molestation history scored significantly lower on the Cohesion scale. They also scored significantly higher on the Conflict and Control scales of the FES, on the BDI, and on the ASQ, than those not reporting CSA.

Similar findings were obtained in a comparison of profiles of the normal and distressed family samples from the FES manual (Moos & Moos, 1986) with a clinical sample of child sexual abuse survivors molested within and outside the family (see Figure 1; Gold, Russo, Lucenko, & Vermont, 1998). Both survivor groups' FES scores were significantly lower than those of both the normal and distressed family samples on Cohesion, Active-Recreational Orientation, Intellectual-Cultural Orientation, Indepen-

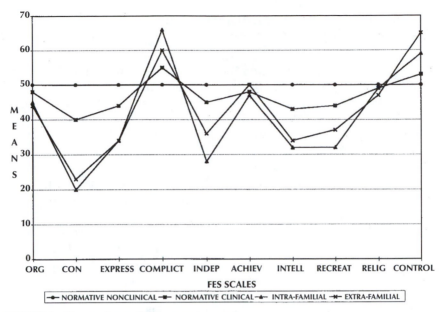

FIGURE 1. Comparison of FES mean t-scores.

dence, and Expressiveness, and higher on Conflict and Control. In addition, survivors of both intra- and extra-familial molestation scored significantly lower than the normal family sample on Organization. None of the FES scales significantly differentiated survivors of intra- and extra-familial sexual abuse.

Alexander and Schaeffer (1994) conducted a cluster analysis of women sexually abused as children by members of their households. The analysis yielded three clusters of abuse survivors. In all three clusters, survivors scored significantly lower on Cohesion and significantly higher on Conflict and Control than the normal family sample in the FES manual.

Long and Jackson (1994) used a method of employing the FES, developed by Billings and Moos (1982), to categorize families into eight types. Their sample consisted of women undergraduates who were classified into two groups: those who reported a CSA history and those who did not. CSA survivors were vastly overrepresented (100%) within the Disorganized family type, and non-victims predominated (87.5%) in the Support-Oriented family type. Disorganized families are characterized by high levels of conflict and control, and low levels of organization. Support-Oriented families are high in cohesion and expressiveness.

Family of Origin Environment and Adult Symptomatology

The research discussed thus far provides evidence that the families of origin of abuse survivors are markedly more dysfunctional than other families. In addition, the findings of another body of studies have been interpreted as suggesting that these patterns of family dysfunction may contribute to adult symptomatology independently of the impact of abuse itself. Some of the investigators who have come to this conclusion set out purposefully to test this hypothesis. Others seem to have assumed that abuse characteristics were primarily or solely responsible for adult symptoms, but arrived at the deduction, on the basis of their findings, that family environment may play an equal or greater role in long-term psychological impairment.

Harter et al. (1988) also found lower levels of family of origin cohesion and adaptability, as measured by FACES-II, among incestuously abused than non-abused college women. Abused women scored higher on social isolation and lower on social adjustment than non-abused women. However, family cohesion and adaptability and social isolation were more predictive of social adjustment than was the abuse itself.

Yama, Tovey, Fogas, and Teegarden (1992) compared the FES profiles of university women with and without a history of child sexual abuse, and with and without a history of parental alcoholism. Both abuse survivors and children of alcoholics rated their families of origin higher on Conflict and lower on Cohesion and Moral-Religious Emphasis than participants without these factors in their histories. FES scores of abuse-only and alcoholic parent-only groups did not differ significantly. Analysis of the relationship of FES scores to measures of anxiety and depression in these groups yielded results indicating that family environment may mediate these effects in cases of both abuse and parental alcoholism. The authors acknowledged that methodological constraints limited the ability to disentangle the effects of specific factors such as sexual abuse and parental alcoholism from more global influences such as family environment. Nevertheless, they did raise the possibility that their findings could be accounted for by the notion that abuse and parental alcoholism are "markers" of family dysfunction, and that it is this family pattern that is the antecedent of adult symptomotology.

Starting with a pool of 65 variables, Conte and Schuerman (1987) investigated factors that may account for the differential impact of sexual abuse on children. The majority of the variables assessed were either characteristics of the abuse itself or circumstances related to the abuse. In a multiple regression analysis, the single variable accounting for the greatest proportion of total variance in symptomatology when controlling for all other variables (10%) was "Family has characteristics of poorly functioning family." Conte and Schuerman stated that one of the implications of their findings is that they

> suggest the importance of identifying victims who live in families, regardless of whether the offender is a family member or not, who have significant problems in living or appear not to be functioning in a health-supporting way. (p. 210)

Fromuth (1986) conducted a study of college women to explore the relationship between childhood sexual abuse and adult symptomatology, and to ascertain whether abuse would provide any additional predictive value beyond that accounted for by family background. The main measure of symptomatology used was the Hopkins Symptom Checklist (SCL-90; Derogatis, Lipman, & Covi, 1973). An instrument developed by Fromuth specifically for this study in order to assess family background, the Parental Support Scale, was derived from a scale of risk factors for child abuse identified by Finkelhor (1980). Although 5 of the 12 scales comprising the SCL-90 were positively correlated with the presence of a childhood sexual abuse history, family background was correlated with 11 of the SCL-90 scales. Moreover, the existence of an abuse history only significantly increased prediction beyond that accounted for by family background on one SCL-90 scale (i.e., Phobic Anxiety). Fromuth (1986) concluded from this finding that "the relationship of sexual abuse with later adjustment is not due to the sexual abuse per se, but rather to the confounding of sexual abuse with family background" (p. 13).

Similarly, Nash, Hulsey, Sexton, Harralson, and Lambert (1993a) designed a study to evaluate whether women's abuse status would continue to be associated with current symptomatology when the effects of family environment were taken into account. Family environment was measured by the Family Functioning Scale (FFS; Bloom, 1985), and four Minnesota Multiphasic Personality Inventory (MMPI; Hathaway & McKinley, 1983) indices were used to assess psychopathology. Main effects were found on MMPI scores for both abuse status (i.e., participants with and without a child abuse history) and clinical status (i.e., participants in therapy and not in treatment). However, main effects also existed on scores of all nine FFS scales for both abuse and clinical status. The families of origin of abused participants were rated as less cohesive, expressive, sociable, ideal, and democratic, and more conflicted, enmeshed, authoritarian, and prone to blame others than those of non-abused respondents. When an FFS-derived index of family functioning was used as a covariate, the main effect on pathology for clinical status remained, but the main effect for abuse status was no longer significant. Nash et al. concluded from these findings that

Perceived family environment appears to be an important mediating variable in determining general level of adult psychological distress, so important that we found no significant residual effect for abuse per se on the extent of general psychological impairment. For some victims, sexual abuse may be a signal variable that the home environment is profoundly and broadly pathogenic. Subsequent adult impairment may be an effect not only of abuse but also of the context in which it is embedded. (p. 282)

In a rejoinder published simultaneously with Nash et al.'s (1993a) study, Briere and Elliott (1993) emphasized the limitations of covariate analysis in assessing cause-effect relationships. They compared the findings of their own study (Elliott & Briere, 1992) in which family environment, as measured by the FES, significantly differentiated participants abused by an immediate family member from those molested by an extended or non-family member. They further indicated that symptoms, as assessed by the Trauma Symptom Checklist-40 (TSC-40; Briere & Runtz, 1989), continued to distinguish abused from non-abused participants after FES was used as a covariate. However, they also reported that in the latter analysis, differences in TSC-40 scores between participants abused by immediate family, extended family, non-family, or both family and non-family members, were no longer significant. Briere and Elliott acknowledged that family dysfunction may moderate the relationship between child abuse and symptoms, but maintained that it does not necessarily account for it.

Nash, Hulsey, Sexton, Harralson, & Lambert (1993b) countered that they do not interpret their findings as being indicative of causal relationships. They stated, rather, that they were careful to word their hypotheses and conclusions in terms of mediation. They stressed that both in their own study and in that of Elliott and Briere (1992), perception of family of origin was a mediator of pathology and that the significant effect for abuse status remained when family functioning was controlled by employing it as a covariate.

Family-of-Origin Environment and Attachment

Alexander (1993) employed the model of attachment style, an individual's characteristic manner of relating to others, developed primarily in her or his family of origin, to investigate the contribution of family environment to adult functioning of survivors of childhood abuse. The Relationship Questionnaire (Bartholomew & Horowitz, 1991) was used to assess attachment style. Consistent with the abuse trauma model, in a community sample of 112 incest survivors, she found that symptoms associated with PTSD, such as intrusion, avoidance, and depression, were predicted by sexual abuse characteristics. In contrast, characterological difficulties, such as avoidant, dependent, self-defeating, and borderline traits (as measured by the Millon Clinical Multiaxial Inventory II [MCMI-II; Millon, 1987]) were predicted by attachment style but not by abuse characteristics. In discussing her findings, Alexander (1993) stated:

> although many clinicians maintain that effective treatment of sexual abuse requires a focus on the abuse, this in and of itself is not necessarily the magic key to resolving current interpersonal problems and dysfunction. Instead, a feeling of interpersonal security—established through the support of adults in childhood, a current supportive relationship, or the development of trust in a therapist—appears to be a prerequisite for even being willing to talk about the abuse. Moreover, instead of *just* being a prerequisite to the important work of remembering the abuse, the interpersonal trust and security established in a healthy therapeutic relationship may even legitimately be regarded as the goal of therapy itself for certain clients at certain points in the course of recovery. . . . (p. 359)

Alexander's (1993) findings are especially provocative in their implications regarding the differential effects of abuse itself as opposed to effects of the type of family environment in which abused children grow up. Her data are consistent with trauma theory in that they are supportive of a relationship between exposure to sexual abuse in childhood, and the manifestation of PTSD symptoms in adulthood. However, her results also suggest that the characterological types of symptoms often observed among adult survivors are related to attachment style (which is a function of family-of-origin environment), but not to abuse. Much of the distinction between "simple" PTSD and CP consists of the characterological difficulties comprising the criteria of CP. Alexander's findings, therefore, may be construed as intimating that while PTSD in survivors is largely attributable to abuse trauma, CP may be primarily a consequence of the family environment in which survivors were reared. This conjecture runs counter to Herman's (1992a; 1992b) general contention that CP is caused by ongoing or repetitive trauma itself.

Implications of Findings on Abuse Survivors' Family-of-Origin Environments

While Briere and Elliott (1993) are correct in warning that the findings of these studies do not identify causal relationships, these results do constitute substantial evidence that family environment plays an important role in mediating adult symptomatology among abuse survivors. From a clinical perspective, they point in particular to the potential value of taking interpersonal, and especially familial, forces into consideration when explaining the psychological difficulties of child abuse survivors. Taken as a whole, this body of data suggests that the families in which child abuse survivors grow up tend to be, on average, markedly more disorganized and less adaptive than other families. The pattern of dysfunction found among families of abuse survivors appears to be relatively consistent across studies and samples. The same general family structure seems to be manifest regardless of whether the abuse is committed by an immediate family member, an extended family member, or someone outside the family (Alexander & Lupfer, 1987; Gold et al., 1998; Ray, Jackson, & Townsley, 1991). Extrapolating across individual studies, in comparison to individuals not reporting a history of child abuse, abuse survivors repeatedly describe their families of origin as lower in cohesiveness, organization, adaptability, expressiveness, and moral-religious emphasis, and higher in conflict and control. A similar configuration may be present in families whose children are not abused, but who may develop at least some of the long-term psychological problems commonly associated with abuse survivors (Yama et al., 1992). Furthermore, there is some evidence that at least some of survivors' difficulties are attributable to the effects of growing up in a family system with this pattern of dysfunction, rather than being due solely to the overt acts of abuse they have experienced (Alexander, 1993; Conte & Schuerman, 1987; Elliott & Briere, 1992; Fromuth, 1986; Harter et al., 1988; Nash, et al., 1993a).

This group of studies, therefore, suggests that a particular type of interpersonal environment—one characterized by an excessive degree of conflict and control, and a deficient level of cohesion, adaptability, and nurturance—is characteristic of the families of origin of survivors of childhood abuse. The research further reflects that survivors abused in childhood by someone outside their family of origin describe essentially the same familial pattern as those whose abuse occurred within the family itself. One explanation for this is that the qualities that typify families of abused children are precisely those that are likely to mold them in a way that leaves them particularly vulnerable to being dominated and maltreated. How would we expect a child who grows up in such a family to function? A conflictual and controlling family would place strong demands on the child for unquestioning obedience. Such an interpersonal context would shape the child in the direction of developing an interpersonal style marked by unassertiveness, deference, and appeasement. A family atmosphere low in organization, cohesion, and expressiveness would leave the child with intense unmet needs for validation, dependency, and affection. These personality characteristics are exactly those that child molesters seek out in their potential victims (Conte, Wolfe, & Smith, 1989; Lang & Frenzel, 1988). A child who is unassertive and submissive is unlikely to resist sexual abuse or other forms of maltreatment. Such a child is especially easy to intimidate and coerce. A child who is emotionally needy and dependent hungers for recognition and support. Such a child is particularly vulnerable to being manipulated by the attention and flattery of an adult predator.

Family Environment as a Risk Factor for Abuse

This line of reasoning raises the possibility that the family environment not only may contribute to the pathology manifested by adult survivors, but may also be an important risk factor for child abuse. Browne and Finkelhor (1986) acknowledged both of these possibilities in their statement that "Some of the apparent effects of sexual abuse may be due to premorbid conditions, such as family conflict or emotional neglect, that actually contributed to a vulnerability to abuse and exacerbated later trauma" (p. 76). Several risk factors for abuse that have been identified in the research literature are consistent with these conjectures. In a nationwide community survey, Finkelhor, Hotaling, Lewis, and Smith (1990) found that the single strongest risk factor for childhood sexual abuse was the survivor's report of having grown up in an "unhappy family." Upon further analysis, they found that this remained a significant risk factor whether or not the perpetrator of the molestation was a family member. A related finding was that living in a household without a natural parent for an extended period in childhood placed participants at greater risk for abuse.

In a survey of college students, Finkelhor (1980) reported that "the background factors most strongly associated with sexual victimization involved characteristics of the child's parents" (p. 269). His results are highly consistent with the hypothesis that growing up with controlling, unaffectionate, and unresponsive parents increases a child's vulnerability to molestation, including that by someone outside the family. Finkelhor indicated that there was an increased risk for sexual abuse when fathers or step-fathers were unaffectionate and when they valued obedience to an unusually high degree. Similarly, girls whose mothers were unavailable, distant, or unaffectionate were found to be at higher risk for sexual victimization. One of the greatest risk factors found in this study was having a step-father. However, Finkelhor's analyses revealed that this was not necessarily because it was the step-father who was the sexual perpetrator. For example, the likelihood of being molested by a friend of the family increased five-fold for girls with step-fathers. Moreover, some of these girls were sexually abused before their step-fathers entered the family constellation. Finkelhor conjectured that single mothers who date increase the likelihood of bringing men into the home who may sexually exploit their children.

☐ Divergent Groups of "Adult Survivors"

There is yet another line of evidence that family configuration has an impact on children's vulnerability to the particularly damaging consequences of prolonged abuse. In this regard, it is especially crucial to be clear about who we are talking about when we refer to "adult survivors." From a clinical perspective, our specific interest is survivors of childhood abuse who experience appreciable long-term difficulties in psychological functioning. Consequently, it is this group that people most often have in mind when they use the term "adult survivors." However, not all adults abused as children manifest such disturbances (Browne & Finkelhor, 1986; Finkelhor, 1990; Tsai, Feldman-Summers, & Edgar, 1979). Comparison of the findings of studies of clinical and non-clinical samples of survivors consistently reveal a profound difference between these groups in the extent and duration of the abuse they report (Gold, Hughes, & Swingle, 1996; Mullen, 1993). The abuse characteristics most consistently associated with adult symptoms are early age of onset, duration and frequency (usually strongly correlated with each other), and the presence of multiple perpetrators (Nash, Zivney, & Hulsey, 1993). These same characteristics significantly differentiate clinical and non-clinical samples of abuse survivors (Gold et al., 1996; Herman, Russell, & Trocki, 1986; Tsai et al., 1979). As one might expect, survivors in clinical samples also manifest significantly higher levels of symptomatology in adulthood than do those from non-clinical samples (Herman et al., 1986; Tsai et al., 1979; Mullen, 1993).

The confluence of a high level of symptomatology and seeking psychological treatment with an abuse history having these particular characteristics, raises a critical question about the context in which such abuse occurs. How is it possible for a child to be so unprotected that victimization begins at an early age, continues for a protracted period of time, and happens repeatedly at the hands of several perpetrators? Nash, Zivney, et al. (1993) proposed that this pattern of findings

> may be an effect, not of a certain type of abuse itself, but of a particularly neglectful family environment in which such pervasive exploitation can take place. That a young child could be *continuously* abused by *more than one* perpetrator may simply be a marker variable for the presence of a profoundly chaotic and therefore pathogenic home environment. (p. 407)

Mullen (1993) cogently outlined a position very close to the one delineated here in his discussion of childhood sexual abuse (CSA) and adult mental health:

> Clinicians and victims' groups who deal daily with the long-term sequelae of severe abuse on occasion promote CSA as being the dominant, if not the

sole, origin of their clients' psychopathology. This position is often bolstered by a posttraumatic stress disorder (PTSD) model in which the blow of CSA continues to reverberate down the years creating distress and disorder. Researchers have, in contrast, become increasingly aware that CSA often emerges from a matrix of social and family disadvantage from which its effects are difficult to disentangle. CSA is not randomly distributed through the community but tends to occur more frequently to children from disorganized and disadvantaged homes. (p. 429)

The only major aspect of this statement to which one might take exception is the somewhat exaggerated dichotomy depicted between researchers and practitioners. Even if one could neatly divide empirical investigators from clinicians (many active contributors to the literature are both), neither group can be accurately characterized as uniformly affirming or rejecting the role of interpersonal context in the development of abuse survivors' difficulties in functioning. What does seem fair to say, is that the role of family and social factors has not received concerted attention in the literature on clinical conceptualization and intervention with survivors. Areas of empirical investigation are, after all, frequently initially identified as a result of observations made in the course of clinical practice. Research is indispensable in evaluating the validity and generalizability of those observations. In the final analysis, however, the function of such research is to lead us back to clinical material, in all its richness. The ultimate purpose of empirical findings is to direct attention to issues of practical relevance, to clarify understanding of those issues, and to inform clinical practice. In the following chapter, a transcript of a therapy session with a survivor of prolonged childhood abuse is employed to illustrate and clarify how the research findings just reviewed are applicable to material encountered in treatment.

Alone: Growing Up in an Ineffective Family

Increasingly over the years, both in my own clinical work and my supervision of doctoral students in their therapy with adult survivors of ongoing child maltreatment, a picture has emerged that transcends the abuse trauma model. It is informed by a consistent pattern of clinical observations that is highly congruent with the research findings on abuse survivors' family-of-origin environments reviewed in the previous chapter. There is no question that abuse has been a pivotal experience in the lives of most of these clients, one that has often had powerful and enduring traumatic effects. However, as they recount their histories, it seems clear that for most of them, overt incidents of abuse constitute landmarks that are embedded in and continuous with a much broader interpersonal landscape.

Most PTSD diagnostic models emphasize the discontinuity of trauma with everyday experience and with pre-existing beliefs (see, e.g., Horowitz, 1986; Janoff-Bulman, 1992; McCann & Pearlman, 1990). It is precisely due to this incongruity of traumatic events with previous experiences and assumptions that they are thought to have such a dramatic effect on psychological functioning. In contrast, one of the most distressing aspects of the child abuse described by many survivors in therapy, is how remarkably consistent these incidents are with the larger interpersonal atmosphere of their childhoods. This appears to be the case even when the abuse was primarily or exclusively committed by a person or several people outside of the family. The context of control and unresponsiveness which seems to typify the childhoods of many survivors may well help explain the sustained duration of their abuse and the seemingly pervasive impact of their abuse experiences.

Although each individual survivor's situation is unique, the following transcript of a videotaped session cogently illustrates many facets of the intricate interaction between overt incidents of abuse, an unresponsive and controlling family context, and adult functioning. The extensive excerpts presented here comprise most of the twelfth therapy session of Rick, a male survivor of sexual abuse who was in his mid-twenties at the time he entered treatment. Rick had five older half-siblings who, between them, had three different fathers. Rick's own biological father was married and had a family across town. Although Rick knew who his father was, his father was never involved in rearing Rick, never visited him, and never acknowledged his paternity or even admitted that he knew him.

Three men molested Rick, each acting independently, over an extended period of time. The man who abused him for the longest duration was Hank. Hank was Rick's mother's boyfriend, and the biological father of two of Rick's half-siblings. He began molesting Rick when he was 5 or 6 years old. Rick reports that when he was 9 years old, his mother came into the room while Hank was performing fellatio on him. Instead of stopping Hank or becoming angry with him, she turned to Rick and demanded, "What are you doing?". Therefore, although she had witnessed the abuse first hand, according to Rick it continued. At the age of 14 Rick complained to his mother about Hank's ongoing molestation of him. His mother initially threw Hank out of the house, but relented a week later and had him move back into the home. At that point, Rick moved out of his house and never returned, thereby ending his sexual abuse. A few minutes into this session, Rick (R) reveals to the therapist (T) his discovery that, although his mother and siblings knew that Hank was a child molester, he continued to be a "friend of the family."

☐ An Interpersonal Context of Silent Complicity

R: My sister Alice, we [he and his wife, Valerie] were talking to her, and she was saying that she went over to her father's [Hank's] house. And, that there was kids everywhere in the building that he lives at, and, she, when they went into his apartment he was in the apartment with this little girl. And there was nobody else around. You know? And um, it just, it just crushed her. You know? And just the thought of it, just made me sick. It really did. And um, I mean we all know what he's capable of, and we all know what he does. You know, and, that was what was like, I got to do something, you know? And, nobody else is going to do anything.

These people, they live there, you know, their kids are being molested, not these people that live in the building, but, you know, my, my stepsister and, all these other people, you know? She's not even my stepsister, she's my sister's step-sister. Um, her daughter was just molested by Hank, and she allows Hank to go in her house while her daughter's there. She has—I don't know if she's forgiven him or what, but I mean like, it's not her place to forgive him, it's, it's her daughter's place. You know? And there's just so much psychotic bullshit going on, and everybody lets him get away with it, you know? And I, I just can't be like that . . . The way I see it is that everybody around him is allowing him to get away with it. I'll tell you if he did that to my daughter, he'd be dead. You know, there'd be, no way, no two ways about it, he'd be alligator bait. And, you know, I wouldn't even think twice about it. But, these people, they seem to think it's ok.

T: You sound as angry at them as you are at—

R: I am angry at them. They're, they're fucking idiots. They're complete, fucking idiots. And, they remind me, you know, it's like, it reminds me of my mother. [Chuckling] Everything always reminds me of my mother, I don't know why, but, it reminds me of my mother. It's like, it's like um, you know, how could you allow this to happen to your kid, and then brush it off? And still associate, you know, with this person?

For Rick, seeing adults refuse to act when they know children are in danger is painfully evocative of his own mother's refusal to make an unequivocal effort to safeguard him against protracted molestation. Clinicians often seem surprised that survivors frequently express more anger toward those who did not protect them from abuse than from the perpetrator himself. This is a phenomenon that is common enough to have been documented by several authors (see, e.g., Bass & Davis, 1988; Briere, 1996; Herman, 1981). For example, Briere (1996) wrote:

> Issues reflecting perceived maternal failure are well known to therapists who work with female incest survivors—although the father may have been the actual perpetrator, the mother is frequently the most hated, often because she is seen as abandoning the survivor by not protecting her from abuse. As described earlier, this blaming of the mother for the father's behavior is sometimes technically unfair, although it may be psychologically "true" for the survivor. (p. 198)

This phenomenon is not exclusive to sexual abuse. One middle-aged male client reported that he and his siblings were subjected to rage-filled physical beatings by his mother throughout his childhood. In describing some of the incidents of battering, the most salient aspect of his memories was that of his father passively observing the beatings he received from his mother, while saying in a sarcastic yet listless tone, "Go ahead, go ahead, that's right, kill the boy."

It is not unusual to hear therapists voice the conviction that resentment directed toward non-offending parents or others who did not prevent or stop the abuse is undeserved, or represents displaced hostility that, in actuality, is related to the perpetrator. This follows logically from a trauma model framework, which assumes that the abuse itself is cardinal in its impact. However, this viewpoint negates a child's fundamental need to be valued and cherished enough to be protected, supported, and affirmed, particularly by parental figures and other caretakers. As subsequent portions of this transcript illustrate, the anger toward non-offending parties may also reflect the fact that failing to stop the abuse was just one of a myriad of ways in which parents and other caretakers abrogated their responsibilities to nurture, validate, and safeguard the client in childhood.

R: Never mind like, I mean he has—the audacity to, here's another, an example, another psychotic example of the family. His, um, see my brother Blake and my sister Alice—that's their real father, ok? Now he has other kids, so they have step-brothers and step-sisters, ok? Well one of their step-sisters—they were all molested by Hank, okay? And, um, one of them, her husband molested her daughter. And Hank had the balls enough, to take her to the police station, to um, to press charges on her husband, for molesting her daughter. I mean, I mean he was there, what was the hell was going through his head, when he was pressing charges on the guy for molesting this little girl when he molested the girl that he's standing right beside? You know, I mean, it just doesn't make any sense to me at all. You know, I mean what kind of power does he have over these people? You know and it's just, uh! Makes me sick, it really does. It makes me sick. And it makes me sick to think that these people know what he's capable of and they still allow these little innocent kids that live in his building to uh, like my sister said, my sister said, she was there with um, her step-sister, and—see it's a real confusing situation in my family. And, um—sometimes I get confused. Well she was there with her step-sister when she went to visit him and seen the little girl in the apartment. And, um, she said to my step-sister, she said, I mean to her step-sister, she said, um, you know, "These people don't know," you know, "who he is or what he is?" And, um, he just got done molesting this woman's daughter, and she says, "Oh no, there's no reason for them to know that." You know, I mean, what kind of an answer is that? It just, like I said it just doesn't make any sense to me. These people, they don't have any common sense at all. You know, they don't, they don't give a shit, period. You know, and um, I don't know, makes me very angry. [Laughs.]

T: But it's especially hard to see people who do know and don't do anything about it.

R: Yeah that's, that's the part that really gets me. Is the people who do know and they just don't care. I mean, are they, obviously they, they must not care. I mean, 'cause if they cared they'd do something about it. You know, so they just don't care. It, I mean, it can't just be ignorance, of the situation, you know, it can't just be—I don't know what the hell it can be.

It is especially incomprehensible that so many adults seem to be aware that children, in some instances their own offspring, are probably being abused, and yet tacitly allow it to continue. The implications grow exponentially more overwhelming as progressively larger segments of the social network are informed of what is occurring, and do not make serious attempts to stop it. The horrifying epitome of this phenomenon is the notification of authorities that children are at risk, in compliance with mandatory state reporting laws, without any substantive effect or even serious attempt by officials to intervene. In fact, this was exactly what happened in Rick's situation, when he and others alerted state officials about what was transpiring.

T: And there must have been people who knew that you were being molested by Hank.

R: Yeah I think my mother knew.

T: You told her.

R: Well I meant I think she knew before I told her. She's a fucking idiot in her own though, you know, she's out in left field somewhere [Chuckles nervously]. Doesn't make it better, but . . .

T: No, I would think in some ways it makes it worse.

Viewing his mother as ineffective and directing his rage at her for this provides little solace. In fact, it may simply serve to drive home the reality of how deprived he was of parenting in general. A few minutes later, Rick appears to change the subject. He begins to describe a seemingly innocuous incident that had occurred just a few days earlier while at a mall with his wife, Valerie. The situation stirred emotions that, although new and unfamiliar to him, were not unpleasant. At first he has difficulty articulating what he was experiencing. Gradually, as he continues, he is able to bring his feelings into focus and put them into words.

☐ Found in the Mall: A New Way of Living

R: We went to the food court, and there was this simple, I mean simple, it was a simple situation that drove me, like, it was totally alien to me though, but there was these samples of chicken, you know, and it was like Cajun chicken and then there was like New England [chicken]. And we had these samples of these chicken were like, "Mmm, you know, that's pretty good." And then, um, Valerie seen another kind, she was like, "Oh, what's that?" and you know, they told her what it was and she was like, "Yeah, all—ok, yeah, I'll have a little bit of that," and I was like, "Yeah, and I'll have some of the other," and "And we'll have a Diet Coke." And I went over and I paid for it, and we went back and we sat down, and it was just like, "Phhhuh, like wow!" You know, I mean, I sat down and I was just like, kind of like just staring out, just thinking, "You know, this is never the way it was." You know, I could never just go and do a simple thing like buy a piece of chicken, you know without counting pennies, without worrying about anything. And it's like, and Valerie was like, you know, "What are you thinking about?" And—it was just strange, it was like, it was like a strange feeling to just, to be able to go over and, you know, do something as simple as that. And not having, not even thinking about it, not saying, "Well how much is that chicken?" You know, before you buy it, you know? Just, "Okay, yeah, I'll have some of that."

T: Can—I know—

R: It was just a stu—it was, it's hard, I don't know, it's hard to explain what I'm really thinking about.

T: Yeah, it would be hard, it would be hard to explain, but do you think you could put that feeling into words?

It would be tempting, in response to the difficulty Rick seems to be having in articulating his experience, to offer suggestions and interpretations to him. There are at least two crucial hazards created by taking such an approach. One is that formulating his experience for him, implicitly and powerfully confirms his belief that he is incapable of doing this for himself. The other, much more serious threat, is that both client and therapist will be misled. In actuality, there is no reasonable way a clinician could know what experience and understanding Rick is gradually bringing into focus. With the client's willingness and written permission, I have shown this videotape to my doctoral level seminar on trauma and abuse. Without being encouraged to do so, a number of students offer interpretations of what Rick is trying to clarify and express, and inevitably they are wrong. Many of their suggestions are logical and reasonable, and I strongly suspect that if they had been offered to Rick, he would have accepted them as accurate. However, they probably would have precluded him from reaching the tremendously significant conclusions he arrives at by the end of this session.

R: I don't know, it was such a different feeling, I mean I felt—First I felt good that I could do it. Then I felt I guess like I was, like, you know, something like this—was just like missing from my life for like, all my life. You know? It was just—I don't know, it was just so different. And I've been getting a lot of feelings like that. Like—you know, just, and, it's little stuff, too. It's not like, it's not like the stuff like when we go out and we buy a brand new vehicle. For some reason it's not like that, it's the little stuff like—being able to like, walk across the street from my building, take out twenty bucks, and then order a pizza or something. You know, or just like, look around the house, and, you know, there's money laying everywhere so gather up twenty bucks and call up, order a pizza. You know, and—Or just look around my house and see where I live. You know, just—and then I get that feeling and—I don't underst—I don't know what the feeling is. It's—see, I have a hard time identifying my feelings. 'Cause I never . . .

T: No, I don't think so.

R: No, I mean like putting a word on what the feeling is, you know?

T: You said you've been getting a lot of these feelings lately.

R: Yeah—[Long pause, staring off.] I'm trying to think exactly what it was like.

T: Do you think you could just let yourself feel it?

R: [Laughs, picks up his cellular phone that has been lying beside him.] Want to order a pizza? [Laughs.]

T: Pretty intense, isn't it?

R: It is—I don't know, life is just so different, you know? And, um—I mean it's great, but it's just so different.

T: How 'bout if we take a step back from the intensity of the feelings? Are there thoughts that go with the feelings? Things like, "Life is so different"?

R: Well, there's like, like when we're at the mall, there's like a memory of, you know, like, how, I mean I just never—you know, I would never go to the mall and spend money—on these kind of things. You know, and um . . .

T: Things like?

R: Things like clothes. . . . It's just really strange, I mean it's good, it's great, I love it. You know and Valerie always says, she's like, you know, "Oh you, you know, you always . . . " see, it's hard for her to understand because of the way she grew up . . . if she wanted something she got it. And if she needed something she got it. If she needed something it was definitely there. And most of the time if she wanted something it was there. And, um—I grew up, you know—in this low class family [Laughs.], eating hot dogs and, living in houses that should have been condemned, and, you know, and then now, it's just everything—is just completely different. And it's almost hard to adjust. You know?

T: Sure.

R: But it's what I always wanted. It's what I always wanted.

T: But it's strange.

R: —to think that it's here. You know, like, [Spoken in a spooky voice.] "They're here." [Laughs.] And I'm turning into a yuppie before my very eyes—which is okay with me too. [Laughs.]

T: That's all right?

R: That's okay with me. I got nowhere to go today, I got a button-up shirt on, I'm, I got my boots on, I, I got nothing to do today. I'm going to drop my truck off. We're going to lift it up three inches and um, put new rims on and bigger tires on it, you know. Why? I don't know. [Laughs.] I don't know—It'll look little bit better. But will it look a thousand dollars better? I don't know. [Laughs.] Some of the things that I do, I don't know why I do them. You know? Maybe I just do them because I never could.

T: —or because you can now.

R: You know it's nice to think that I can just like, if I leave here, if I feel hungry, I don't have to wait till I get home and try and find something to eat. First of all, there's plenty of things to eat at home. But, I don't even have to do that. I can just like—you know I can stop at the bank and grab some money and just go and get anything I want. Any choice I want to eat. If it's Mexican, if it's American, if it's just a sub, if it's a hot dog from a stand on the side of the road, it doesn't matter. I can just stop and get it if I feel like eating it.

T: So, a lot of this is about freedom of choice.

R: I think so. Definitely. Freedom of choice. Freedom of ability to make my own choices. Like, be able to—See, and it's, and with me it's all money things, you know. I don't know. Yeah, I guess because I never had them, but—I'm pretty materialistic. [Laughs.] You know, and um—it's, it's all money things, but it all—like you said it all goes back to—you know—being able to make my own choices. [Pauses.] I guess a lot of times I think—that if I have nice things—and I'm wearing a nice watch, and I have a nice gold chain, and I'm carrying a cellular phone—you know. . . . all these things, you know, these things, then maybe I, it makes me a different person. [Laughs.] You know?

T: Different how?

R: Different—than if I look at anybody else in my family. Different than—how I used to be. Just, I think what it comes down to is I want to get as far away from—anybody ever being able to acknowledge that I came from that family—You know? And especially me—being able to acknowledge that I came from that family. [Chuckles.] I mean just as far away as I can. You know, and . . .

☐ "Maybe That's My Family": Longing and Denial

This is the pivotal deduction that neither the therapist in this case, doctoral students who have viewed this tape, nor I could have anticipated. Rick's self-proclaimed preoccupation with material things and appearances is fueled by a powerful desire to dis-identify with his family and his origins. One exception, raised below by the therapist, is Rick's maternal uncle. This uncle had established an affiliation with Rick and had been supportive of him, especially in recent years. In an earlier session, Rick told his therapist that his uncle had suggested that the two of them share the cost of buying Rick's mother a new set of tires for her birthday. The tires on her car were already dangerously worn, and she did not have the money to replace them. Rick was torn. He felt an obligation to comply, guilty about refusing to get a gift for his mother, and worried that his uncle would be angry at him if he did not agree with the proposal. Buying the tires, however, seemed to him to comprise the latest in a long series of instances of role reversal—parenting his mother. Declining to participate, though, seemed to risk losing one of the few congenial relationships he had ever enjoyed with a family member.

T: Are you including your uncle when you talk about the family?

R: Not really—But I don't see him as part of the family at all. [Chuckles.] I see him as an enabler for my mother. That's what I see. That's the way it's always been. As far back as I can remember all he's ever done is work and give her stuff.

T: And you decided you weren't going to do that.

R: Yeah, and he's still buying the tires for her. I knew he was going to.

T: That's his choice.

R: Yeah.

T: You still have yours.

R: Yeah, I'm not doing it. Fuck that. [Long pause.]

T: What's that drive to put as much distance as you can between yourself and your family?

R: What drives me to do that?

T: [Nods head.]

R: Well, they're all pretty much older than me. They're all married with kids. And they all are going nowhere. There's all, you know, the psychotic bullshit, the psychodribble that goes on. You know, the fighting between each other—I just don't want nothing to do with it. You know, and I don't want, you know. . . . when we have a kid I just don't want my kid to be subjected to that kind of life. You know? Not at all.

T: Do you think, uh, all poor families are that way with their kids?

R: No. [Long pause.] You know, I don't think I'm better than them. I don't know what I think. You know? I think that, I just don't want to be like them at all. I just don't want to be like—I don't know.

T: You don't want to be like them in what ways?

R: Well, I, first of all, I don't want to be like them in the way where they treat their kids at all. You know, and I guess I can't say every one of them because, you know, my brother Blake seems to—be the only one that really treats his kids right. But, um—you know my two sisters are like, away from their kids and, they got their own lives now, and, how the hell could you have your own life when you got, you know, three or four kids? You know and um—my brother Eric he's just in his own world and the kids are just like, around, you know and—And Alice the way she hits her kids and stuff and she is just like, she is just like my mother. As much as she hates my mother she is just like my mother—And then Mark, he's always stoned. He's always like smoking, smoking, smoking, and the kid, the kid's definitely getting high. [Laughs nervously.] You know, contact high, the kid's like, three years old maybe. You know, and he's probably stoned off his ass more than he's straight. And um, I don't know, it's just the way that they live, so dirty, and [Pause.] I don't think I ever felt like any of them feel.

T: How do you mean?

R: I don't think I ever felt—that that was even my family. You know, kind of like, you know, somebody switched the kids at the hospital, you know, and, and my family's off somewhere and, you know, living in Beverly Hills or something, you know, "What the fuck am I doing here?"

T: I bet you used to imagine that when you were growing up.

R: Yeah, I used to imagine it all the time. I used to think about it. I used to look at my friends' families and—just think that like, you know—"I think I belong in that family. I don't belong in this family." You know, like, "Maybe that's my family."

T: Well that's really weird. You say you never felt like you really were part of your family or belonged to them or fit in with them, and yet, you tell me that you're working really hard not to acknowledge that that's your family, these people who you never felt a part of, to begin with.

R: [Pause.] See I think what is, is that I grew up with them, you know, still never feeling like I belonged there—but as I grew up with them I started to act like them, and started to—I don't know—I don't know I guess I still see them as my family even though that I don't, you know, want to. I mean they are my family. As much as I don't want to have to believe that they are.

T: [Sighs.] Yeah, they are.

Rick's description of his sense of disconnection from his family exemplifies the empirical findings discussed in the previous chapter on the extremely low level of cohesion (Alexander & Lupfer; 1987; Alexander & Schaeffer, 1994; Gold et al., 1998; Harter et al., 1988; Ray et al.,1991; Williamson et al., 1991; Yama et al., 1993; Yama et al., 1992) and poor attachment relationships (Alexander, 1993; Fromuth, 1986; Long & Jackson, 1994) characteristic of the families of abuse survivors. There is a confusing dualism in his account that is clarified in more detail later in the session. On one hand, Rick felt alienated from his family. Many of his childhood memories were of being neglected, ridiculed, and excluded by them. He never felt he belonged. In addition, on some level, he claims, many of their opinions and behaviors were foreign to him. On the other hand, as he grew older he found himself modeling many of the very behaviors with which he had found fault. He often provoked physical fights, got into trouble at school, and eventually committed burglaries and other crimes. He began to abuse alcohol and drugs. He showed and felt little concern for or attachment to other people. According to his account, much of this changed when he met and became involved with his wife, Valerie. By the time he entered therapy, he was already active in Alcoholics Anonymous and had been alcohol and drug free for two years.

☐ Moving On

R: And life goes on. [Laughs.]

T: Yeah, it does. [Pause.] And it has.

R: And it has, and it will. See, I know that it just gets better from here. I know it does.

T: It's gotten an awful lot better already, hasn't it?

R: It has, it's, it's been getting better and better beyond my, you know, ever thinking, you know, how good it would get. You know they do something in the program [i.e., Alcoholics Anonymous] like, um, when you first get in the program and get a sponsor and everything they ask you to write all of the things that you want. And just put it aside. You know? And, um, you know I wrote that list and it was like, you know I want a truck, I want, you know, I want this, I want that. You know, it was all material things, which I've gotten. But then, you know, and then I look at that list now and I, and I think like, you know, I was short-changing myself, big time. You know, because I got, you know I got, first of all I got the ability to find out who the hell I am. You know, second of all, I'm, you know, married to a, to a beautiful, wonderful person, you know? I mean it's like, on a daily basis I can just like help other people and not even want anything from them, you know? And only, it's like, I know last week we were talking about like helping people and getting crazy with it, and helping people when I don't even want to help people and everything. But what I'm talking about now is, is just like helping somebody, if I'm driving down the street and somebody has a flat tire, if it's an old lady or something, I'll, I'll stop and change her tire. And I'll just drive away. You know, and, just things that I would have never done before. And it's like those are the things that I kind of like short-changed myself on that list. You know, and it's like, the way I think, the way I act—the way I feel's pretty much the same. You know, in certain areas.

T: What feelings are the same?

R: Well as far as the Hank, Hank feelings, the feelings toward my mother, the feelings of feeling inadequate, the feelings of—the confusion, still the same. You know, there are so many that are still the same, but there's so many that are, are different, like, you know, first of all feeling, feeling like that I'm here for a reason. You know, and that everything that I've gone through in my life, every place that I've been, you know, the sexual abuse, the psychological abuse, everything, has happened for a reason. And, you know, maybe that reason is something, you know, something like, you know, just being able to identify with somebody when they need to talk. You know, that kind of makes it okay. You know, it doesn't make it really all okay, but it, it kind of makes it better. You know, to think that—it's just an experience. You know, so I mean these are the kind of ways that, I just never thought that way before. You know, so . . .

T: How do you think you came to that?

R: I think accepting. Accepting, to a certain degree, what's going on.

T: Something about the way you put, "to a certain degree" there.

R: Yeah, well, I don't accept everything. [Laughs.] You know, I don't, I still don't accept a lot of the stuff, that has happened. I still don't accept the way my mother is. You know, and that keeps coming up here in our discussion. [Laughs.] Her ears must be ringing. I hope, anyway. [Laughs.] Um—I don't know. So I guess I say acceptance to a degree. You know, accepting that I am what I am, and I've been where I've been. [Pause.] Sometimes even that I've done what I've done, you know, accepting that. You know and thinking that just because, you know without—that's why I said earlier about what I did, you know, I made sure to say that I'm not proud of that. You know, because I'm not. You know and just like the things that I did when I needed to get high. You know, so that I didn't have to feel these feelings. You know, I robbed houses, I did all kinds of things. I stole cars, I did everything—so that I could get high, so that I wouldn't have to feel my feelings. And, you know, accepting that I did those things—and knowing the reason why I did them. The reason why I did them wasn't because I was just a, a prick, you know. The reason why I did them was because I had to do them so that I wouldn't feel these feelings. You know, so I mean there's just so many things, so many different ways that I think now.

T: So are you clear on the reason why you did this this week?

☐ Undeserving: The Enduring Family Legacy

The therapist is referring here to an act which Rick himself acknowledged was exemplary of the type of behavior the rest of his family engaged in routinely—one of hostile revenge. In the previous week, he had tried to publically expose and humiliate Hank. Although somewhat embarrassed about his behavior, especially because of his awareness that it was similar to the things the rest of his family would commonly do, he felt an obligation to let his therapist know about it. The therapist now encourages Rick to explore more closely the motives behind his actions. Examining his reasons for doing what he did helps to further clarify one of the pervasive effects that his family-of-origin environment continues to have on his current functioning—a lack of a sense of legitimate entitlement.

R: Yeah.

T: And what's that?

R: It's because I don't want them little kids to be molested, at that house. Or that building, or whatever. I think I did it a little bit for me too. [Laughs.]

T: And why's that?

R: The enjoyment of knowing that maybe he'll be embarrassed. . . . I say that a large part of it, like mostly, it was because of the kids, but you know, maybe it wasn't. Maybe it was 50–50. [Chuckles.] You know, maybe it was, maybe it was even mostly because of me. Maybe the only way that I do things for me is if I can say that I'm doing it for somebody else.

T: What's that about?

R: I don't know what that's about. [Chuckles.]

T: It's not okay to do things for you?

R: [Pause.] I don't know. See, I think that's all about, it, it all goes back to the childhood thing where—I just never felt that I was that important. You know, I didn't think that I was important enough, to go through the effort, to do something to make me feel better, make me look better, make me—be better. You know, I just never thought that it was—that it was important. You know, it's easier for me to do something, like even when I, when I got sober, I got sober for Valerie. I would never have gotten sober for myself. You know, I don't definitely don't think I'd be in this room right now, if I didn't meet Valerie. You know it was easier for me to go to Alcoholics Anonymous to get sober, to stay sober, for her, than it was for me. About eight months after I was sober then I changed that around and then it was for me, you know? But uh, I don't know how that change occurred. I don't know exactly what happened. All I know is I, I don't know did I tell you that before? About she was on a job interview, and um, and I used to always think, "I wonder if Valerie's getting drunk right now?" 'Cause she never used drugs, you know? So I was like, "Oh, what would I do if Valerie's getting drunk?" You know? And I was like, "We'd have a party!" You know? We'd, we'd get fucked up together. You know? We'd have a great time. And then there was this one night she was out on an interview—I was about eight months sober—And, um, and I thought again, I thought, you know, "What would I do if Valerie was drinking?" And then like, I was, then all of a sudden, I don't know where it came from, I don't know what happened, I don't know why I changed my mind or how I changed my mind but it was like, "I'd put her to bed and I'd take her to a [Alcoholics Anonymous] meeting in the morning." And I mean it hit me like such a shock, like I was looking around the room, "Who said that?" You know? [Chuckles.] "Who was that guy?" But you know that was the point in my program, in my sobriety that—everything just turned around. You know, and it was like, "Even if Valerie goes back out [i.e., begins drinking again]," you know, "I can stay sober." You know, "And I can stay sober for me." And that was a big turning point in my program. So, I don't know why we started talking about that, but . . . [Laughs.]

T: So you don't have a whole lot of experiences that led you to believe that it was okay to do things just for you.

R: No. [Pause.] What would be an experience like that? I don't even . . .

T: Having other people do things for you? Like you deserve it?

R: [Chuckles to himself.]

T: What?

This line of questioning leads Rick to reveal just how deficient his upbringing was. The lacunae in his childhood—not only emotional deprivation, but also neglect of basic physical needs—can easily be obscured when therapists direct the focus of exploration to overt acts of abuse. The kinds of omissions in parenting that Rick identifies here illuminate, in a concrete and compelling way, the nature of the family environment in which he and many other survivors of protracted childhood abuse were reared. Once again, there is a striking correspondence between the extent of the deprivation described by Rick and the magnitude of the empirical differences observed between the family environments of abuse survivors and of individuals not reporting an abuse history (Alexander & Lupfer, 1987;

Alexander & Schaeffer, 1994; Gold et al., 1998; Harter et al., 1988; Ray et al., 1991; Williamson et al., 1991; Yama et al., 1993; Yama et al., 1992).

R: I don't know. [Laughs.] I just don't—I was just trying to remember back like when I was a little kid, you know, and somebody doing something for me—I don't even remember having a birthday party. I mean that's the extent of somebody doing something for me. I don't even, I mean, I, I'd like to say, "Oh, well it happened, I just don't remember it." But I really don't remember it, I don't know if it happened or not. You know, I'd like to think that it did and I just forgot. But um, I don't know. Um, my mother never, I mean she would never even take us to the eye doctor's, to the dentist, you know, we never went for a physical, you know, we never did the things that a parent does for their kids, as far as health reasons. I mean, and, I never, was taught how to take care of myself, you know, like brush your teeth every day. Brush your teeth in the morning, brush your teeth before you go to bed. Maybe even brush your teeth in the middle of the daytime sometimes. You know, I never . . .

T: So how'd you learn it?

R: I just did it because I got out of there at an early age, and it was, you know, and the people I was living with were doing it, I was like, "Oh, I guess I should be doing that." I don't know, so I mean like, that's like, I mean if you try and think about the smallest thing that a parent would do for their kid—that's the smallest thing that I could think of that a parent would do for their kid, is to take them to the dentist. And it never happened. You know, so, it just makes me think that, I mean, if she wouldn't do anything as small as that, or as simple as that, you know, what would make her do anything else? [Pause.] Can you tell I hate her? [Chuckles.]

☐ Family and Identity: The Entanglement of Attachment and Separation

T: It would be simple, I think, if that was the whole story.

R: I would like to hate her.

T: It feels better.

R: Yeah. Hmm, I don't think I do though, the fucking bitch. [Laughs.]

T: Maybe that's what you're so angry about.

R: [Pause.] I think I should. [Pause.]

T: What do you mean, should?

R: I mean I should hate her. I'd like to hate her. I don't love her—Maybe I do love her. [Laughs nervously, picks up a tissue from a box on side table and dabs at his eyes, which are tearing up.]

T: Wouldn't that be a bite?

R: Yeah, wouldn't that suck? [Pause.] I don't see how it's possible.

T: What's that?

R: How I could love her. I mean, I don't see how it's possible. I don't have any good memories of her. She's selfish, she's uh, she's just like so much, all rolled up in one little fat ball.

T: She's fat?

R: Yeah, she's a fat lard ass. [Laughs nervously—Long pause, staring off.]

T: You ever call anybody else that?

R: A fat lard ass? You're looking at him. [Chuckles nervously—Pauses again, staring at the floor. Eventually, looks up at the therapist.]

T: What's going on?

R: I was thinking that um—sometimes I think my thoughts are so silly—but um, I was thinking that, if I call her a fat lard ass, and I call myself a fat lard ass, and I don't call anybody else a fat lard ass, and I hate her, but I might love her, and I hate myself, but I might love myself.

T: Is that what you think is silly?

R: What?

T: Is that what you were thinking was silly?

R: Yeah.

T: I don't think so—I think you're right on target.

R: [Pause. Sighs deeply. Chuckles.] Want to know what I'm thinking now?

T: Want to tell me?

R: I don't want this to be the right thing. [Chuckles.] I just tell you that before saying it. [Laughs.]

T: [Smiling.] Thanks for letting me know.

R: [Laughs.] Ah, but you can tell me if it's right. So, if all that's true, then, in order for me to love myself, I've got to love her?

T: [Sighs.] Well—

R: Or in order for me to like, not hate myself, I've got to like not hate her?

T: Mmm—you know, I don't think—

R: —I think hate's a strong word. I keep interrupting. [Chuckles.]

T: Go ahead.

R: I think hate's a strong word. 'Cause it's not like I hate myself, because I don't. I like myself. I don't—I don't know if I love myself, and I guess—maybe I don't hate her either. I don't like her. I don't like what she does. I don't like what she's about. And I don't want to love her. So, I don't know.

T: And you don't want her to be part of you.

R: No, I don't. You know what I really don't want? Is every time I go over to her house—first of all she's such a hypocrite, and, um, you know it's like when I leave if somebody's there, she wants me to give her a hug. And it's like—uh!—And I do it, but it's just like, real quickly. "Yeah, okay." But it's like, ugh, you know. I thought about telling her, too, "Don't ask me anymore." [Laughing nervously] I don't want to hurt her feelings. I don't know. So do I? Do I have to, um, love her to love myself?

T: [Sighs.] I don't know.

R: [Laughing.] I knew you were going to say that.

T: I didn't know I was going to say it. But I think you have to come to terms with—

R: —with her?

T: Yeah.

R: [Long Pause.]

T: How you end up feeling about her is how you end up feeling about her.

R: [Sighs.]

T: But I think if you try and pretend that she doesn't exist or she's not your mother or you're not her son, it's likely to create problems.

R: So I have to acknowledge the fact that she is my mother.

T: [Nods.]

R: That's easy enough.

T: You were telling me earlier though that you don't want to acknowledge that any of those people are your family.

R: Yeah, well I know they are, but I don't like to think that they are. So maybe acknowledging that they are, it was the—

T: —and acknowledging that you don't like that.

R: Huh?

T: And acknowledging that you don't like that they are, but that's different from pretending that they're not. [Pause.] Might as well pretend that the abuse never happened.

R: Hmm, it's all easier said than done.

T: Much.

What Rick has been struggling to articulate is difficult, not primarily because he has trouble expressing himself, but because it is a conceptually complex and emotionally confusing issue. He is faced with the challenge of embracing and coming to terms with the duality mentioned earlier. He felt while growing up, and continues to feel, rejected and removed from his family. At the same time, he is emotionally attached to them, still would like to experience a connection with them, and has, for better or worse, in many ways modeled and identified with them. To deny his affiliation with them is to disavow and devalue important aspects of himself. To acknowledge that they are in actuality his family, however, requires accepting and coming to terms with what they did not provide him, especially emotionally—that in at least some respects will never be remediable. Similar attachment conflicts among abuse survivors are reflected in the empirical findings of Alexander (1993) and described in the conceptual writings of Alexander (1992), Barach (1991), Koch and Jarvis (1987) and van der Kolk and Fisler (1994).

R: [Stretches, cracks knuckles. Pause.]

T: Well, we're out of time.

R: Mm-hm.

T: Is there anything before we finish up?

R: Is there anything I should do during the week?

T: I think you earned a, a break. Seems to me you worked pretty hard today.

R: I can live with that. [Chuckles.]

☐ The Core Issue: To Be Cherished

The account Rick gives in this session, and the issues that he spontaneously raises, typify the central concerns of adults who experienced prolonged, severe abuse as children. Rick is tormented by the puzzle of how it is possible that the very people who were supposed to nurture him, guide him, and protect him seemed to have so little concern for his welfare. What does their apparent disregard for him suggest about them, and about the reliability and trustworthiness of people in general? What does it say about him, about his heritage, and about his personal worth? While molestation definitely had a devastating and enduring impact on his development and is clearly of tremendous significance to him, he seems to be even more pervasively preoccupied by these fundamental questions about identity, society, and life.

It is noteworthy that the severe, ongoing sexual abuse by several perpetrators to which Rick was subjected was, in each instance, committed by someone outside the family. Despite this, however, we can recognize from his depiction of the prevailing atmosphere in his family of origin that his molestation and the fact that it was able to continue for so long at the hands of several individuals was inextricably intertwined with the larger fabric of his childhood. If, as therapists, we allow ourselves to be transfixed by the drama and intrigue of the overt incidents of abuse experienced by our clients, we risk mistaking those particular strands for the entire tapestry of their lives. If this occurs, we are almost certain to gloss over what may be their deepest and most abiding concerns.

We see Rick, in this session, grappling with the implications of continuing to subscribe to the simple equation he first arrived at as a young boy—that financial privilege guarantees children a stable and loving family life, protecting them against neglect and abuse. It may seem tempting to share Rick's childhood belief that maltreatment of children and the environment that promotes it are found exclusively in economically impoverished families. There is some empirical evidence that poverty increases a child's risk for abuse (Finkelhor, 1980; Moeller, Bachmann, & Moeller, 1993; Mullen, Martin, Anderson, Romans, & Herbison, 1996).

Just as assuredly, however, ongoing child abuse is not the exclusive province of financially disadvantaged families. For an example of this, we need to look no further than Rick's wife, Valerie. Rick compares the economic circumstances in which she grew up with his own. Materially, he insists, she wanted for nothing. Yet what he does not mention here is that economic security did not protect her from abuse. She was subjected to severe paternal incest throughout much of her childhood.

Despite popular stereotypes, the attainment of monetary security in no way guarantees immunity from either ineffective family functioning or child maltreatment. There is no question that childhood abuse and neglect occur in middle class, upper-middle class, and the wealthiest of households. In fact, clinical observation suggests that in some highly affluent neighborhoods, the over-valuation of material trappings and excessive emphasis on academic, career, and financial achievement—at the expense of devotion to quality parenting—actually increase children's risk of neglect and abuse. It is deeply disturbing to encounter individuals who fail to comprehend that materially indulging and attempting to secure privileged treatment for their children does not adequately prepare them for productive adult living. Neither do these types of advantages constitute a satisfactory substitute for the investment of time, attention, and guidance which effective parenting requires. In the midst of an atmosphere of material abundance, the vivid contrast of the emotional deprivation that is intrinsic to both ineffective family functioning and to child abuse adds a distinctive poignancy to the mistreated child's plight. As Rivera (1996) eloquently observed, the most profound and wrenching issues for our clients often are not those pertaining to the more salient characteristics of overt abuse, but those associated with the subtler interpersonal features of family context.

Some of the most painful stories I have heard—from survivors of even the most brutal and unremitting sexual abuse in childhood, as well as people who have had the good luck not to have been subjected to this kind of horror as children—had to do with other ways in which they were not heard, seen, respected, or loved. . . . children who lived in a home that looked OK, with parents who seemed OK and had a life that appeared fine and even privileged, but who never felt special, never felt cherished, never in their whole lives ran in the door knowing someone was waiting there who thought they were the most wonderful, precious children in the world. (pp. 18–19)

Unprepared: The Legacy of an Ineffective Family Background

As dramatic, reprehensible, horrifying, and damaging as discrete instances of abuse may be, viewing them through the frame of their surrounding interpersonal context transforms their apparent significance. Some trauma-based models would suggest that abusive incidents are traumatic because they are anomalous or discrepant with previous experience and prior cognitive assumptions (e.g., Horowitz, 1986; Janoff-Bulman, 1992; McCann & Pearlman, 1990). Instances in which an atmosphere exists that allows maltreatment to continue for protracted periods of the child's development contradicts this claim. In the context of such an interpersonal environment, it is difficult to conceive of circumscribed abusive events as being paramount defining moments in identity formation and long-term functioning. Instead, they seem to be occasions for a morbid confirmation of an already evolving self-image of being helpless, inept, isolated, unlovable, despicable, undeserving—in essence, of being irredeemably and fundamentally flawed.

☐ Beyond Survivorship: A Broader Perspective

One of the assets of the abuse trauma model and the PTSD diagnosis is that they explicitly identify external events—traumatic incidents—as the source of survivors' symptoms and compromised coping abilities. In doing so, the trauma model intrinsically helps to counteract abuse survivors' erroneous perception of being responsible for their own inadequacies and misery, and challenges the tendency of others to "blame the victim" (Herman, 1992a). As van der Kolk and McFarlane (1996) put it, "unlike other forms of psychological disorders, the core issue in trauma is reality" (p. 6).

As helpful as the external attribution of problem causation may be in decreasing the unproductive consequences of self-blame, excessive emphasis on the traumatic events in their lives can be detrimental to adult clients who were repeatedly abused as children. The term "survivor" was advocated and adopted in order to avoid the connotation of helpless submission connected with the term "victim." It can be a useful and respectful way of designating people who have been abused. In the context of treatment, however, the use of any label such as "victim," or even "survivor," almost inescapably carries the implication that the most important thing about such clients, their cardinal characteristic, is their abuse history. Emphasis on the term "survivor" can unwittingly encourage both clients themselves as well as their therapists to see their lives, and even their identities, as being shaped and defined, above all, by their experiences of childhood victimization. To appropriate a term from feminist analysis, a focus on survivorship "privileges" abuse experiences, casting them as uniquely decisive episodes in the person's life history. In the process, other possible influences on current functioning, including beneficial circumstances and inner strengths, as well as debilitating forces other than trauma, are subject to being obscured.

An excessive focus on abuse trauma can become especially problematic when therapists impose on clients their conviction that incidents of abuse *must* have had a momentous and enduring impact on character development and psychological functioning. The research literature does not, by any means, support that this is always and inevitably the case (Finkelhor, 1990; Tsai et al., 1979). More importantly, some clients themselves hold the belief that circumscribed abusive events may not be strongly related to their current difficulties—and they may well be correct. In some instances, for example, the onset of certain symptoms can be identified as considerably predating overt abuse, and can be reasonably attributed to other factors. In other cases, the problems that bring the individual into treatment may be much more clearly attributable to current circumstances than to remote historical events. It can be extremely problematic, therefore, when therapists fail to consider these alternate possibilities and assume, once they find out that a client has an abuse history, that this abuse unquestionably lies at the root of the presenting complaints. For those who were subjected to instances of overt maltreatment, and who grew up in an interpersonal environment that was controlling and invalidating, a dogmatic stance on the part of the therapist can tragically come to constitute a reenactment of the very coercion that permeated the backgrounds of these individuals (Gold & Brown, 1997). Many people with an abuse history are vulnerable to allowing their realities to be defined by others. Moreover, in the absence of a clear sense of self, an emphatic focus on abuse trauma can easily foster the perception that a history of victimization is the single most important thing about themselves, engendering the adoption of survivorship as a core aspect of their identities.

Revisiting and reframing the circumstances that characterized their formative years can be a crucial aspect of therapy for survivors. It can be a key component of the therapist's role to assist clients in reformulating their understanding of their own histories and in challenging their resultant maladaptive beliefs about themselves and others. However, the more intently the therapist insists that abusive events are the cause of current difficulties, the more likely it is that clients will negate and avoid expressing their own convictions about the sources of their problems. Especially for people who grew up surrounded by an atmosphere of coercion and invalidation, it is essential that clients have ultimate jurisdiction over determining what elements of their experiences are subjected to examination, and the pacing of that process (Courtois, 1991). Ultimately, the *clients* must identify which life experiences contributed to the problems that led them to seek treatment, and they must come to these conclusions in their own time, based on the strength of their own judgment. Otherwise, particularly because of their previous interpersonal experiences of subjugation and the resulting self-doubt, therapy can easily lapse into being one more in a long line of instances of passively bending to someone else's authority.

The transcript of Rick's therapy session in the previous chapter vividly portrays the reason for this principle. Rick mentions that confusion remains a salient aspect of his experience. He is self-doubting enough that it would be easy for an overly zealous clinician to unwittingly appropriate the exploratory process and influence its outcome. Note, for example, how toward the end of the session Rick comments, "sometimes I think my thoughts are so silly." One suspects that if the therapist had not prompted him, he may not have risked revealing what was on his mind. A bit later in the session, he says, "I don't want this to be the right thing. . . . but you can tell me if it's right," as if the clinician could know better than Rick himself what is right and true for him. During the course of treatment, Rick repeatedly admitted that he was hesitant to give voice to his feelings because he doubted that what he said would be true, since his feelings seemed to him to be constantly changing.

Nevertheless, the therapist makes an effort to ensure that the introduction, examination, processing, and flow of material remains primarily under Rick's own direction. Some survivors are so unsure of themselves and so fearful of being attacked that they are unable, at least in the early stages of treatment, to take the lead to the degree that Rick does. They may actually experience themselves at times as being mute—not unwilling to speak, but literally almost without a voice. With clients such as those, the therapist has to be even more vigilant to refrain from inadvertently deciding for them what is worth attending to, and to guard against unwittingly shaping the conclusions at which they arrive.

Rick is typical of survivor clients in another crucial respect. When allowed a measure of control over the direction of treatment, he acknowledges the existence and importance of his abuse experiences, but does not focus on them exclusively. When permitted to convey and develop his own story, on his own terms, he has as much or more to say about the impact of his family life on his current functioning as he does about his sexual abuse. His ambivalence toward his mother—his fury at her for tacitly allowing his molestation to continue, for failing to provide many of the fundamental requisites of parenting, and for expecting attention and support *from* him without providing it *to* him, as well as his underlying yearning for affection, validation, and affirmation from her—was a prevalent theme in the session presented here and throughout the entire course of his therapy.

In the course of the treatment process, he eventually was able to identify the fact that, in his mind, his molestation was explicitly tied to the issue of seeking recognition from his mother. Throughout therapy, he had shared anecdotes demonstrating how her attention and emotional investment were devoted almost completely to whatever man was in her life—to the relative exclusion of concern for Rick and his siblings. Rick also indicated that Hank, his first sexual perpetrator and the one who abused him over the longest period of time, would criticize and reject him when the rest of the family was present. However, when the two of them were alone in the house, he would silently approach Rick, fondle him, and perform oral sex on him. As terrifying and confusing as these recurring instances of molestation were for Rick, they stood out for him as being among the pitifully rare occasions when an adult would actively seek him out. They also constituted the only time when Hank seemed to want him around. Rick explained, however, that his own primary interest was not in receiving Hank's approval. Rather, since his mother seemed to be dedicated to Hank above all else, Rick maintained the fantasy that if he could manage to please Hank, this would somehow win him his mother's love and acceptance.

Several authors have invoked attachment theory to explain the impact of family environment on abuse survivors (Alexander, 1992; Barach, 1991; Koch & Jarvis, 1987; van der Kolk & Fisler, 1994). As a group, they argue that disrupted and disturbed attachment to parental figures leads to interpersonal styles that leave children at particular risk for abuse. These "attachment styles" are characterized by many of the same difficulties commonly manifested by abuse survivors: anxiety, confusion, dependency, fear of abandonment, social inhibition, unassertiveness, and avoidant and preoccupied personality styles (Alexander, 1992, 1993). This is particularly understandable when one considers that the absence of a secure attachment figure in early development appears to be associated with an impaired ability to modulate affect, behavior, and interpersonal relationships—all key attributes of Complex PTSD (van der Kolk & Fisler, 1994). The disordered attachment styles manifested by survivors of child abuse, therefore, are hypothesized to both contribute to the occurrence of abuse and exacerbate its adverse long-term effects (Alexander, 1992; Barach, 1991).

☐ Inadequate Transmission of Essential Living Skills

It is arguable, however, that disturbances of attachment only constitute one major class of the effects of family background on abuse survivors. In order to better appreciate the impact of this type of unresponsive and controlling family context, it is necessary to set aside the specific issue of abuse for a moment and consider an infinitely more fundamental matter—the purpose of the family system for the child. In most of its variations, the abuse trauma model aims to account for the disturbances in adaptation that are created by extreme circumstances. Consequently, it presumes that prior to the occurrence of the trauma, functioning was intact. According to this model, exposure to trauma, engenders PTSD—intrusive reexperiencing of the traumatic event, avoidance of reminders of the trauma, and generalized autonomic arousal. Prolonged or repeated traumatization is seen, within this framework, as resulting in the much broader and more pervasive impairment in functioning that constitutes CP.

Abuse trauma theory, like many etiological models of psychopathology, seeks to explain *disruption* of psychological functioning. In effect, it implicitly assumes the existence, before the onset of the trauma, of intact adjustment. What if however, before the onset of the trauma adequate functioning was not established to begin with? What if the child who ends up being abused grew up in a family that never provided her or him with the tools necessary for adequate psychological adaptation in the first place?

Recognizing the adverse impact of growing up in a controlling and unresponsive family environment entails confronting a reality even more distasteful than that suggested by the maltreatment of children in the form of overt abuse. It means acknowledging that even before the occurrence of explicit acts of abuse, some children never even had access to the tools needed for effective psychological functioning. It requires under-standing that being able to cope with day-to-day living is not a given, not something anyone is born with, not the default condition.

Managing effectively as an adult, particularly in contemporary society, is a remarkably demanding, complex achievement. It calls for mastery of an unfathomably diverse and vast array of knowledge and skills, as ex-tensive as the acquisition of language fluency and as specific as familiarity with how to write a check, as concrete as understanding how to boil wa-ter and as abstract as being capable of accurately reading facial expres-sions, as advanced as mastering how to form a friendship and as funda-mental as knowing to regularly brush one's teeth. Instruction in the intricate and subtle performances that comprise the fabric of day-to-day living does not, for the most part, occur verbally, directly, or in a class-room. Instead, these skills are largely conveyed implicitly, often via mod-eling, and primarily in the context of the family. Probably both because they are so pervasive, and because they are unspoken, transmitted tacitly and by example, it is easy for them to escape our attention. We take them for granted, assuming that they are innate, the background and reper-toire of just about everyone.

The transmission of these myriad skills constitutes what is probably the single most important function of the family unit—to prepare its offspring for the tremendously intricate task of independent adult living. If we lis-ten carefully to adults who grew up with prolonged abuse, we will hear that many of them grew up without sufficient familial instruction in adap-tive living skills, and that this deprivation usually predated the onset of overt abuse. The absence of a secure attachment relationship is frequently a critical contributor in the failure to establish adequate adjustment, but it is rarely the only one. There is another major category of deficits in the early family experiences of survivors that account, above and beyond the disruptive impact of abuse, for many of their adaptive impairments—in-adequate transmission of essential living skills.

In the transcript found in the previous chapter, Rick mentions and in-directly refers to several of the adaptive living skills which he was never taught while growing up at home: dental hygiene, grooming, and other forms of basic self-care; recognizing choices and options, decision-mak-ing, and implementing decisions; self-expression, self-assertion, and iden-tifying and labeling feelings; and addressing and productively resolving interpersonal conflict. It is commonplace to hear such reports from cli-ents with protracted abuse histories. Many of these clients mention child-hood experiences such as: never having been taken to see a physician or dentist, even when they were injured or sick; having been deprived of an adequate amount of food and receiving minimal nutrition, even when the families were solidly middle class or upper-middle class and could readily afford it; and being left alone to fend for themselves or to care for younger siblings, even when parents were not working or were in a financial position to hire babysitters. Unless they were fortunate or resourceful enough, as was Rick, to "adopt" friends and families outside their families of origin, they often are not even aware of many of the sorts of things they should have learned from their families, but were not taught. For example, not knowing that in other families parents monitor whether their children have homework and help them learn how to organize and discipline themselves to do it, children in this type of family environment may simply believe that they are stupid and lazy. Not realizing that in other families parents purposefully set out to teach their children how to manage and budget money, these children may conclude that they are irredeemably irresponsible and reckless. Not understanding that social interaction is a learned skill, intentionally modeled and promoted by parents, such children are prone to consider themselves inherently socially awkward and inept. One particularly striking phenomenon is how often these patterns are described by people whose families of origin were not disadvantaged in terms of social class or income.

An additional factor that can interfere with the acquisition of effective living skills is that these families not only fail to model adaptive behavior, but often model distinctly maladaptive forms of coping. It is not uncommon for survivors of abuse to have grown up in families in which parents, siblings, and other family members regularly engage in drinking alcoholically, substance abuse, domestic violence, compulsive spending and gambling, binging, restricting, and purging, compulsive sexual behavior, and other unproductive and injurious forms of stress-reduction, self-soothing, and responding to problems. In an interpersonal environment such as this, children not only fail to learn effective methods of resolving difficulties and managing distress, but adopt, consciously or unwittingly, the faulty strategies represented by compulsive and self-destructive behaviors. Moreover, due to the deficient transmission of social skills within the family, as they expand their social contacts outside the family they are at increased risk for associating with others of limited social facility who are likely to engage in and reinforce these ineffective modes of coping.

It is interesting to note that in the transcript in the previous chapter, Rick refers to all three of these forms of ineffective family functioning. He recognizes that he was deprived of basic social learning, giving as examples never having been taken to a doctor or dentist, and never having been taught how to brush his teeth ("I was never taught how to take care of myself.") He also acknowledges that he modeled patterns of behavior that were maladaptive and even destructive ("As I grew up with them I started to act like them.") Most poignantly, he describes how he continues to grapple to come to terms with the awareness that although this was in fact his family, he never felt attached to them ("I never felt I belonged there.")

It is important to emphasize that the reasons for these three forms of ineffective familial functioning—disturbed attachment, deficient learning, and faulty modeling—can vary widely. Although in some cases it appears that the family willfully and intentionally neglected and deprived the client as a child, this is far from universally the case. Certainly, financial status and social class can contribute to such deprivation by limiting the supportive resources available to the family and therefore to the child. Sometimes other external circumstances, such as the death or disabling illness of a parent, or the dissolution of the parental relationship, contribute to the failure to adequately prepare the child for adaptive living. Often, the family fails to effectively teach the developing child the skills of adaptive functioning because of the parents' own history of deprivation and consequent limited child-rearing skills. Unfortunately however, regardless of the reason, whether purposeful, circumstantial, or some combination of the two, the result—inadequate preparation for adaptive living—is similar.

☐ Two Related Pathways to Impaired Adjustment

Consider the implications and consequences of growing up in an ineffective family environment. As other authors have suggested, for many survivors, such an environment probably predated, and in all likelihood facilitated the occurrence of explicit abuse (see, e.g., Alexander, 1992; Finkelhor, 1980; Long & Jackson, 1991; Ray et al., 1991). In reviewing the research literature in Chapter 2, this effect was discussed in terms of the prevalence of control and inexpressiveness in the family-of-origin environments of survivors, and how this molds the qualities of submissiveness and emotional neediness that leaves her or him especially vulnerable to domination and exploitation. Here we are examining the same phenomenon from a slightly different but entirely compatible vantage point (see Figure 2).

As a consequence of growing up in an ineffective family unit, the child's individual adaptive capacities are stunted by insecure attachment, deficient social learning, and modeling of unproductive and self-destructive modes of coping. The effects of these factors are observable in the form of various gaps and warps in emotional, interpersonal, and instrumental capacities. A child growing up in such a context can be expected to be severely restricted in both actual competencies and self-confidence. Socially, this is likely to manifest in the form of difficulty developing relationships with peers and with adults. Interpersonal awkwardness and

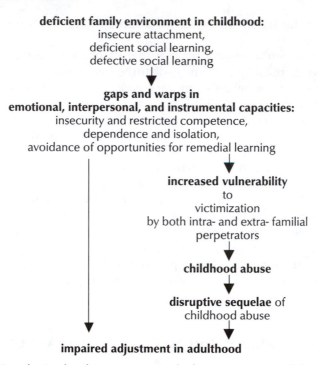

deficient family environment in childhood:
insecure attachment,
deficient social learning,
defective social learning

**gaps and warps in
emotional, interpersonal, and instrumental capacities:**
insecurity and restricted competence,
dependence and isolation,
avoidance of opportunities for remedial learning

increased vulnerability
to
victimization
by both intra- and extra- familial
perpetrators

childhood abuse

disruptive sequelae of
childhood abuse

impaired adjustment in adulthood

FIGURE 2. Hypothesized pathways to impaired adjustment among adult survivors of prolonged child abuse.

deficient social skills make it unlikely that others will seek out the child's company. On the child's part, an extremely negative self-image and a core sense of shame fuel avoidance of anything beyond casual interaction, out of fear that self-disclosure will inevitably lead to rejection. As a result, although the child may maintain some relatively superficial acquaintanceships, she or he is at high risk to remain emotionally isolated, to continue to be deprived of social support, and to have minimal access to experiences that would correct the existing gaps and distortions in social learning. Once this cycle is set in motion, therefore, it tends to perpetuate itself, severely restricting the possibility of remedial social learning, perpetuating and exacerbating existing skills deficits, and progressively magnifying the conviction of being hopelessly inept and unworthy of others' attention or affection.

This downward spiral of isolation and insecurity that develops as the child's social interactions expand beyond the family compounds the intense yearning for validation and support and the vulnerability to manipulation that is already set in motion by being reared in a controlling and emotionally unresponsive family context. The intensification of these trends, in turn, leaves her or him even more susceptible to being victimized and abused. Where overt incidents of abuse do occur, they further aggravate already high, existing levels of mistrust of self and others, further exacerbating the tendency toward insularity and the avoidance of self-disclosure. This pattern can activate an alternating cycle of interpersonal withdrawal and revictimization that, without the intervention of professional assistance or fortuitous life circumstances, may persist into early adulthood and beyond.

☐ Why Trauma-Focused Treatment is Inappropriate for Survivors of Prolonged Child Abuse

Serious reflection about the pervasive deficits in functioning that result from growing up in a family that does not adequately prepare its offspring for the complexities of effective adult living should make it evident why trauma-focused treatment is unwise. Trauma is, by definition, destabilizing, thereby overwhelming adaptive capacities. When trauma is confined to a single or limited set of events, and the victim's adaptive coping capacities were well developed and intact before exposure, trauma-focused treatment is highly likely to be effective and relatively brief. An adult, for example, who enjoys the support of a primary relationship and a surrounding social network, is gainfully employed and financially secure, and was able to effectively manage the stresses of daily living before being subjected to trauma, may nonetheless experience full-blown PTSD following exposure to trauma. Symptoms such as flashbacks and nightmares, interpersonal withdrawal and avoidance, and insomnia and irritability may be severe enough to seriously disrupt premorbid social and occupational functioning. However, for clients such as these, trauma-focused forms of treatment, such as prolonged exposure (PE; Foa & Meadows, 1997; Foa & Rothbaum, 1998), stress innoculation training (SIT; Resick, Jordan, Girelli, Hutter, & Marhoefer-Dvorak, 1988), eye movement desensitization and reprocessing (EMDR; Shapiro, 1995), and traumatic incident resolution (TIR; French & Harris, 1999; Valentine, 1995) can appreciably diminish PTSD symptomatology resulting from a single traumatic incident in relatively short-term treatment. PE, in particular, has been empirically assessed in outcome studies and found to reduce symptoms to a level below criteria for a PTSD diagnosis in an appreciable proportion of clients at termination of treatment, with even greater improvement at 6-month follow-up (Foa & Meadows, 1997; Foa, Rothbaum, Riggs, & Murdock, 1991).

To return to the issue of recovered memories raised in Chapter 1, none of these treatments has, as its aim, the retrieval of blocked memories of trauma; however, they do entail attending to traumatic material already available to the client. In this respect, these treatments reflect a growing sophistication. As the study and treatment of trauma-based disorders has progressed, so has the recognition that resolution of trauma does not require the recovery of traumatic memories that are not already readily accessible.

Individuals exposed to circumscribed trauma as adults who possess adequate coping skills are equipped to benefit from, rather than be further distressed by, addressing traumatic material retained in memory. The situation is vastly different, however, for survivors of ongoing childhood abuse. In the case of individuals exposed to prolonged maltreatment as children, we are rarely dealing with people who once attained stable, effective adult functioning and then lost it. Whether due to the disruptive consequences of the abuse itself, the lack of adequate attachment and social learning resulting from growing up in an ineffective family, or, as argued here, from a combination of these factors, in most instances adult survivors of prolonged maltreatment never established solid adaptive functioning in the first place. Treatment approaches centered primarily around confrontation of traumatic experiences, therefore, are highly unlikely to be productive. In fact, they are very likely to exacerbate rather than resolve distress and dysfunction (Gold & Brown, 1997).

Adults with adequate adaptive skills that have been disrupted by the impact of a single traumatic event enter treatment with an array of personal capacities (e.g., coping skills, judgment, a sense of efficacy) and environmental resources (e.g., social support, financial reserves) that are no where near as likely to be accessible to survivors of extended child abuse. The former group, therefore, even if they are highly symptomatic initially, have firmly rooted strengths to draw upon that greatly bolster their capacity to face and productively process trauma. The latter group, however, lacks these advantages. Consequently, even the routine stressors of daily adult living tax their capacities and can be destabilizing. It is unreasonable to expect that they are in a substantially better position to productively assimilate traumatic experiences than they were when those events originally occurred. Constructively addressing and resolving the extraordinary pressures inflicted by traumatic experience requires, at minimum, sufficient personal strengths and external resources to effectively navigate the exigencies of day-to-day functioning as an adult. This is the central goal toward which treatment grounded in an interpersonal conceptual framework guides us. Without these capacities, addressing trauma can only be expected to create further deterioration in already deficient coping abilities. Therapy that fosters the development of these capacities, on the other hand, simultaneously repairs much of the damage done both by abuse per se and by the unsupportive and controlling interpersonal context that is likely to have accompanied it.

CHAPTER

Impact: Intersecting Varieties of Abuse and Deficient Family Context

To a large extent, thus far I have been referring to child abuse in relatively global terms. In many instances, I have discussed child sexual abuse interchangeably with child maltreatment in general. There are a number of considerations that have led me to take this approach up to this point. The most central is that, over the past two decades, child sexual abuse has by far been the most widely written about and researched form of child maltreatment. From an empirical viewpoint, we simply know immeasurably more about child sexual abuse, its effects, and its relation to family context than we do about other types of child maltreatment (Briere & Runtz, 1988a, 1990; Mullen et al., 1996).

A second reason that much of my focus in previous chapters was on sexual molestation is that in contrast to child physical abuse, psychological abuse, and neglect, which most extensively occur within the family context, child sexual abuse often is committed by someone outside the family circle (Mancini, van Ameringen, & MacMillan, 1995; Mullen et al., 1996). This makes it possible, by comparing maltreatment by intra- and extra-familial perpetrators, to conceptually distinguish and empirically measure the differential effects of overt sexual abuse and global family context. This task is much more difficult in the case of physical abuse or neglect. Particularly in the instance of less concrete forms of maltreatment such as emotional neglect, the type of maltreatment and the larger family context intersect to a degree that makes them almost indistinguishable.

☐ Beyond Sexual Abuse

Although I have purposely been referring to child abuse and CSA inter-changeably up until now, too often the equation of the two concepts seems to occur unwittingly, due to lack of conceptual clarity. Other types of child maltreatment have been overshadowed as a consequence of the intense interest and controversy surrounding child molestation in recent years. In actual practice and in the clinical literature, vastly greater atten-tion has been directed toward the treatment of adult survivors of child-hood sexual molestation than toward adult survivors of other forms of child abuse. Most models of therapy for adult survivors are explicitly ori-ented toward those who were sexually molested as children, rather than those who were subjected to other varieties of maltreatment. It is essen-tial, both conceptually and empirically, to differentiate various modes of child abuse and their divergent effects. Researchers increasingly warn practitioners that preconceptions about the importance of sexual abuse may detract from the recognition of other clinically pertinent factors. Mullen et al. (1996), for example, cautioned that

> The message for therapists is that when evaluating the relevance of child-hood abuse to beware an exclusive, and potentially exaggerated focus on the traumas of sexual abuse which may obscure both the relevance of other forms of abuse and the unfolding of other damaging developmental influ-ences. (p. 20)

A primary purpose of this chapter is to assist practitioners in avoiding these pitfalls by reviewing the existing research literature on the differen-tial and overlapping long-term effects of various forms of child maltreat-ment. This, in turn, will provide a foundation for maintaining conceptual differentiation between the divergent impact of these disparate categories of abuse, and of aspects of family context, here and in subsequent chap-ters.

The interpersonal context model presented here does not seek to mini-mize the long-term damage generated by overt child abuse, but rather to clarify that the effects of explicit abuse are often accompanied by other forms of maladjustment not directly attributable to discrete acts of mal-treatment. These latter effects often result from a family context that fails to provide the developing child with the tools needed for effective daily living. The more accurately we can classify difficulties that are commonly associated with one form or another of child maltreatment, the more clearly we can differentiate from them other problems in adjustment that are traceable to a deficient family context and consequent lacunae in social learning. This can be an invaluable corrective to the flawed assumption that addressing the destructive impact of overt abuse will resolve all of the client's symptoms and difficulties. To the extent that certain problems manifested by survivors reflect gaps in social learning due to a deficient family environment, no amount of trauma-focused treatment can reasonably be expected to rectify them.

☐ Varieties of Abuse: Divergent and Convergent Effects

There are surprisingly few studies that investigate the differential and convergent sequelae of a number of types of abuse. Briere and Runtz (1990) assessed the relationship of self-esteem, disordered sexual behavior, and aggression in adulthood to childhood sexual abuse, physical abuse, and psychological abuse (i.e., verbal denigration) in a sample of women college students. They hypothesized that problems in sexual functioning in adulthood would be most strongly related to a history of child molestation, low self-esteem would be related to child psychological abuse, and aggressiveness would be related to child physical abuse. Their findings were supportive of these differential effects. They conjectured that low self-esteem reflects internalization of degrading parental statements and that aggressiveness results from concluding, on the basis of personal childhood experience, that physical assault is acceptable social behavior. Drawing on a conceptual framework presented by Finkelhor and Browne (1985), Briere and Runtz attributed the higher levels of sexual dysfunction found among survivors of molestation to its distorting influence on the developing child's sexuality.

In a randomly selected community sample of women, Mullen et al. (1996) compared the psychological functioning of adults reporting childhood sexual, physical, and emotional (i.e., psychological) abuse with women from the same sample who did not meet criteria for any of these forms of abuse. They found that all three forms of abuse increased the likelihood of psychological, sexual, and interpersonal difficulties in adulthood. In all three types of child maltreatment, psychological problems consisted "almost exclusively" (Mullen et al., 1996, p. 17) of anxious and depressive symptomatology. Similarly, the prevalence of eating disorders was higher in participants reporting any of the three forms of childhood abuse, although it was higher among those with sexual and psychological abuse histories than those who were physically abused. Consistent with the findings of Briere and Runtz (1990), low self-esteem was found to be most strongly associated with psychological abuse, and sexual problems were most common among sexually-abused participants. There was no measure of aggression in the Mullen et al. study, so the association of this variable with a childhood physical abuse history could not be tested. Mullen et al. emphasized, however, that although these differences were statistically significant, they were not of substantial magnitude. They indicated, therefore, that their findings do not support the theory that these three varieties of child maltreatment are related to appreciably differential outcomes. They concluded that it is important for clinicians to recognize that any form of child maltreatment may be important in understanding adult symptomatology, and they further stressed that neither should the contribution of family context variables (which were also assessed in this study) to psychopathology be ignored:

> Factors such as growing up in a nuclear family, having a confiding relationship with one's mother or female caregiver, and reporting having had at least one close confident among one's childhood friends were all associated with lower rates of most of the negative outcome variables. (p. 15)

Similarly, abuse was more frequently reported by study participants whose parents separated, had frequent arguments, or were physically violent toward each other, and who identified themselves as having been shy in childhood or not having had a close friend before age 11. Conversely, abuse was less frequently reported by those who indicated that their parents were physically demonstrative to each other and toward the children.

Widom and colleagues conducted a series of prospective studies in which individuals with substantiated reports of neglect, physical abuse, and/or sexual abuse in childhood were followed up in young adulthood, and compared with a demographically matched sample of research participants without a history of childhood abuse or neglect. Both abuse and neglect were found to be related to higher levels of PTSD (Widom, 1999). In addition to the somewhat unexpected finding of a relationship between neglect (as distinguished from overt abuse) and PTSD, a number of family of origin difficulties, such as parents who were arrested or who had drug or alcohol problems, were found to be independently related to increased risk for PTSD. Widom (1999) noted that:

> Abused and neglected children often come from multiple problem families, and these results reinforce the need to disentangle consequences specifically associated with childhood victimization from other risk factors. . . . Forms of family dysfunction . . . may contribute substantially to PTSD. (p. 1227)

In another prospective study of similar design, adult violence was found to be related to both childhood abuse and neglect (Weiler & Widom, 1996). However, the findings suggested that the relationship of abuse and neglect to violent behavior was mediated by psychopathy. Alcoholism was found to be related to neglect, but not to either sexual or physical abuse among women; neither abuse nor neglect were significantly associated with alcoholism among men (Widom, Ireland, & Glynn, 1995). Prostitution was significantly related to neglect and sexual abuse, and less strongly related to physical abuse among women (Widom & Kuhns, 1996). Higher levels of prostitution among abused and neglected men than among control men approached, but fell short of attaining, statistical significance.

Wind and Silvern (1992) compared the adult symptom levels of women employees at a state university reporting sexual abuse, physical abuse, both types of maltreatment, and no abuse in childhood. Abused women scored significantly higher on all measures of pathology—the Beck Depression Inventory (BDI), Coopersmith Self-Esteem Inventory (CSEI; Coopersmith, 1981), and a checklist of negative experiences in adulthood (NE)—than did nonabused women. In addition, on two items regarding sexuality, the abused women were more likely to endorse a history of promiscuity and less likely to indicate that they enjoyed sex than were the nonabused group. When the nonabused women were compared on these variables with only those women with a history of CSA, the latter group was found to be significantly higher only on NE. Women who reported both physical and sexual abuse had the highest symptomatology on all measures. No significant differences were found on any symptom measures between participants who reported having been sexually abused, physically abused, or both sexually and physically abused. Wind and Silvern (1992) concluded that, "These findings suggest a highly generalized response to abuse regardless of its specific physical or sexual nature" (p. 276). In attempting to explain the contrast between their results and those of Briere and Runtz (1990), who did find differential effects for sexual and physical abuse, Wind and Silvern pointed out that they examined internalizing symptoms, while Briere and Runtz found differences on the externalizing behaviors of aggressive and sexual acting-out.

Rosen and Martin (1996) conducted a large scale comparison of symptomatology among men and women in the military with histories of childhood physical-emotional abuse, sexual abuse, emotional neglect, and physical neglect. The Brief Symptom Inventory and a separate scale of dissociation (Briere & Runtz, 1988b) were used to measure adult psychopathology. On all scales, the largest effects found were for physical-emotional abuse, with sexual abuse also yielding significant effects, but of a lesser magnitude. Effects for emotional neglect and for physical neglect were only found on selected scales.

In a study of female and male college undergraduates, Loos and Alexander (1997) examined the differential effects of parental physical abuse, verbal abuse, and emotional neglect. Emotional neglect and, to a lesser extent, physical abuse were both predictive of social isolation and loneliness in adulthood. Both physical and verbal abuse in childhood were related to higher levels of anger and aggression. There were indications that parental verbal abuse was even more strongly associated with anger and aggression than physical abuse, but that even infrequent physical abuse was predictive of elevations in anger and aggression. Similarly, even "harsh" physical parental discipline of insufficient proportions to be considered abusive was found to be predictive of anger and aggression in adulthood. Unlike Briere and Runtz (1990), Loos and Alexander failed to find a relationship between verbal (i.e., "psychological") abuse and self-esteem, but did find an inverse relationship between self-esteem and emotional neglect.

Gauthier, Stollack, Messé, and Aronoff (1996) investigated the differential effects of childhood neglect and physical abuse on adult attachment styles as measured by the Adult Attachment Scale (Collins & Read, 1990) and symptomatology as assessed by the Symptom Checklist-90-Revised (SCL-90-R; Derogatis, 1983). They hypothesized that since neglect, as opposed to physical abuse, consists of the relative lack of parental involvement, it would have the greater impact on symptoms and attachment. Neglect was found to be positively related to the Global Severity Index (GSI) of the SCL-90-R and to the anxious attachment styles of avoidant and resistant attachment, while negatively related to secure attachment. The only significant finding for physical abuse was a positive relationship to avoidant attachment.

Bryer, Nelson, Miller, & Krol (1987) studied psychological symptomatology as measured by scores on the SCL-90-R in female psychiatric inpatients who reported child sexual abuse, physical abuse, both sexual and physical abuse, or no abuse. Remarkably, over 70% of the participants acknowledged having experienced some type of childhood abuse. Each of the three groups of abused women scored significantly higher on eight of ten SCL-90-R scales than the non-abused women, with those subjected to both sexual and physical abuse scoring the highest.

A comparison of levels of dissociative symptomatology as measured by the Dissociative Experiences Scale (DES; Bernstein & Putnam, 1986) and general symptomatology as assessed by the various sub-scales of the SCL-90-R among women psychiatric inpatients with and without histories of child abuse was conducted by Chu and Dill (1990). Out of 98 study participants, 37% denied any child abuse history, 28% acknowledged a history of child physical abuse, 23% both physical and sexual abuse, and 12% a history of child sexual abuse only. Analysis of DES scores yielded significant main effects for physical abuse and sexual abuse and a significant interaction effect, with the strongest effect being that for physical abuse. On the SCL-90-R, significant main effects were obtained on the GSI and on several individual symptom scales for physical abuse, but not for sexual abuse.

Williamson et al. (1991) compared the effects of physical abuse, sexual abuse, and neglect on adolescents. Three groups, each of which consisted of adolescents who were subjected to only one of these types of maltreatment, were compared with a fourth, nonabused control group. Higher levels of symptomatology, as measured by the GSI of the SCL-90-R, (Derogatis, 1983), were found among sexually abused participants than in neglected or nonabused groups. Physically abused and neglected adolescents did, however, report significantly higher symptom levels than the nonabused group. Given that the GSI is a composite measure of overall symptomatology, it is not surprising that more differential effects were not found across maltreatment groups. Scores obtained on the Family Adaptability and Cohesion Evaluation Scales - II indicated that levels of cohesion were higher in the families of nonabused adolescents than in the three maltreated groups. Levels of adaptability were also higher in this nonabused group than in the physically or sexually abused groups. Family adaptability scores of the physically abused adolescents were lower than those who were neglected or sexually abused.

A sample of female patients in primary care internal medicine practices reporting childhood sexual abuse, childhood physical abuse, and both sexual and physical abuse in childhood, was assessed for psychological and physical symptoms (McCauley et al., 1997). No significant differences were identified between the three groups in level of psychological symptomatology. However, participants with histories of both sexual and physical abuse were found to have a higher number of physical symptoms than those who indicated they had experienced childhood physical abuse only.

A study on risk factors of homelessness (Herman, Susser, Struening, & Link, 1997) is of particular interest for its relevance to the relative contribution of childhood abuse and family context to adverse outcomes in adulthood. A telephone survey of a national random sample identified whether respondents had been homeless as adults, and whether they had experienced physical abuse, sexual abuse, or lack of parental care (i.e., neglect) in childhood. Among those who had been homeless, 66% reported lack of parental care, 47.8% physical abuse, and 14.7% sexual abuse in childhood, compared to 13.3%, 5,5%, and 9.3% respectively among those who had never been homeless. A combination of both lack of care and abuse was found among 53.9% of participants with a history of homelessness, as opposed to only 4.8% for those who never had been homeless.

☐ Clinical Implications

Taken as a whole, this group of studies suggest that to some extent sexual abuse, physical abuse, verbal-emotional abuse, and neglect have differential effects (Briere & Runtz, 1990; Gautheir et al., 1996). However, an equally critical implication of this body of literature is that these divergent forms of child maltreatment generally result in similar types and levels of impairment (McCauley et al., 1997; Mullen et al., 1996; Wind and Silvern, 1992). For the most part, it appears that what distinguishes the impact of different types of abuse are relatively specific aspects of functioning, such as sexual adjustment or aggressive behavior. More global dimensions, such as overall level of symptomatology or distress, seem to be less differentiated across different varieties of child maltreatment.

A related trend among those studies that compare the effects of different varieties of child maltreatment is how little support they provide for the relatively strong emphasis practitioners have placed on sexual molestation. In some of these investigations assessing the relative impact of child sexual abuse and child physical abuse, no difference was found between participants who reported sexual abuse, physical abuse, or both types of maltreatment in childhood (McCauley et al., 1997; Wind & Silvern, 1992). In others, physical abuse was found to be related to higher levels of psychological symptomatology than sexual abuse (Chu & Dill, 1990; Rosen & Martin, 1996). None of these studies, however, yielded stronger generalized symptomatic effects for sexual than for physical abuse.

Moreover, the results of those studies which examined neglect and other aspects of family environment (Gauthier et al., 1996; Herman et al., 1997; Mullen et al., 1996) suggest that these factors can make an appreciable contribution to difficulties in functioning in adulthood, above and beyond that accounted for by overt abuse. Similar conclusions can be drawn from the empirical investigations reviewed in Chapter 2, which were designed to assess the contribution of family environment to child abuse survivors' adult functioning. The findings of several of these studies indicated that family-of-origin environment may be more strongly related to at least some dimensions of psychological maladjustment in adulthood than child abuse per se. These dimensions include social adjustment (Harter et al., 1988), characterological difficulties (Alexander, 1993), and general psychological symptomatology (Fromuth, 1986; Nash et al., 1993a).

All of these findings highlight the degree to which forms of child maltreatment other than sexual molestation warrant more attention than they have thus far received in clinical practice. Innumerably more clinically oriented books, professional journal articles, treatment programs, and conferences have been devoted to the adverse impact of child sexual abuse than child physical abuse. These indicators strongly suggest that clinicians are much more likely to be alert and responsive to child sexual abuse or its impact than to other forms of child abuse or to deficits in family-of-origin environment. While the research literature supports the assumption that child sexual abuse is related to substantial problems in adjustment in adulthood, it does not confirm that an emphasis on this form of maltreatment to the relative exclusion of others is warranted in clinical settings. What it does appear to indicate strongly is that considerably more awareness and sensitivity to the destructive long-term effects of physical abuse, verbal abuse, neglect, and deficient family-of-origin environments is in order among practitioners. An appreciation of the potential relevancy of these factors to a wide range of difficulties in adult adjustment is needed to better inform the way in which both assessment and treatment are routinely conducted.

The presence of childhood maltreatment and a family background marked by ineffective transmission of adaptive coping abilities in clients' histories is easily obscured by the diversity of symptom pictures that can develop from these circumstances. The ability to detect these elements in a client's background and to recognize their relationship to current problems in living can be further impeded when the type of abuse involved is emotional or even overt physical assault as opposed to sexual molestation. While many mental health practitioners have become highly aware of the adverse impact of childhood sexual abuse on adjustment, recognition of the repercussion of other forms of maltreatment and of deficient family context is much less prevalent. The connection of the difficulties of the woman whose situation is described here to childhood maltreatment and an ineffective family environment, for example, was far from immediately apparent.

Patricia, a woman in her mid-thirties, entered therapy about two weeks after she began to suffer from symptoms so severe that they threatened to interfere with her continued employment. Upon awakening, she would experience intense anxiety and dread, often accompanied by excruciating headaches and nausea that would sometimes lead to vomiting, all of which were increasingly preventing her from going to work. She reported that during a two week period her mind was racing when she tried to fall asleep at night, she awoke frequently, her appetite was suppressed, she engaged in a great deal of self-recriminative thinking, and she felt fearful and apathetic. Medical examinations had not identified any organic basis for her physical symptoms. Initial exploration failed to reveal a clear precipitant for the sudden onset of these difficulties.

Gradually, it emerged that the acute somatic symptoms upon awakening only occurred on work days, and that Patricia had grown increasingly dissatisfied with her job, and in particular by the way she was treated by her supervisor. She was consistently placed on undesirable shifts and assigned the least agreeable duties on the staff, but she had not been able to effectively assert herself and remedy the situation. It became apparent that she was extremely angry about her circumstances at work. However, when she was a child her mother forbade the expression of anger, and in fact would become physically abusive when the client did allow her angry feelings to show. Consequently, she had learned not to display anger, or even to openly express disagreement. From childhood onward, therefore, she had suffered from headaches and nausea in response to situations that provoked angry feelings.

Patricia described an extremely conflicted and enmeshed relationship with her mother that persisted in the present. During her growing up years, she reported, her mother had kept her isolated from peers by insisting that she had to meet and approve of her friends, and then unfailingly finding fault with them. As a result, her social skills, comfort in social situations, and her capacity for intimate relationships were appreciably compromised. Her social life was very limited and she had two marriages that were unsatisfactory and ended in divorce.

In addition to placing restrictions on her social life in childhood and adolescence, her mother pushed intently for academic achievement, teaching her to read and write as a preschooler. In fact, the client was unhappy not only with her job, but with her profession, which she had entered at her mother's insistence. Her mother had also demanded throughout childhood and adolescence that the client engage in a meticulous level of household cleaning and organizing.

Patricia's account suggested that her father was an alcoholic, workaholic, and largely absent from the household. It appeared that his minimal involvement in the family was, at least in part, a passive attempt to avoid discord with his wife, and that this only served to exacerbate the intensity of the conflict. Patricia stated that while she passively complied with her mother's demands, her brother openly rebelled. From adolescence onward, he had a history of alcoholism, substance abuse, delinquent behavior, and marginal academic and work adjustment. The combination of physical abuse by her mother, insufficient connection with and support by her father and brother, and being blocked from developing peer relationships created considerable gaps in Patricia's capacity to identify and voice her own wishes, resulting in extremely low self-esteem.

Several months after treatment was initiated, Patricia had grown assertive enough to take leave of her job and find more suitable employment. When she took this step, her acute distress and physical symptoms remitted immediately. During the course of therapy, she eventually was able to productively express anger and assert herself appropriately, and consequently to disengage from her over-involved relationship with her mother. She gradually developed her capacities for effective interpersonal and work adjustment. Once these abilities were developed, and as she recognized the tremendous degree to which she had subordinated her own wishes and abrogated major life decisions to her mother, Patricia eventually decided it was time to deliberately establish an independent adult life structure. With considerable trepidation, she decided to make a major geographic move away from the city in which her parents and brother lived to a part of the country and a climate that better suited her personal preferences. She later told her former therapist, with tremendous vibrancy and enthusiasm, that "The best thing I did was leave. . . . Life's a ball." Despite initial apprehension and various setbacks, she successfully adapted to the new location, developed a gratifying social life, made an excellent work adjustment, has now been very happily married for several years, and describes having extremely warm and fulfilling relationships with her husband, her step-children, and her step-grandchildren.

As Patricia's case illustrates, in working with clients we need to be more vigilant not only for sexual abuse, but also for histories of physical abuse, verbal abuse, physical neglect, emotional neglect, and a deficient family environment, and to consider whether or how these other circumstances may be related to clients' presenting complaints. Another noteworthy aspect of her situation is one that is commonly overlooked. The same conditions of disturbed family environment in which Patricia was reared— being drawn into conflicts with her mother and between her parents, subjected to criticism and hostility, and encouraged to forgo her own interests and defer to her mother and other family members—continued to operate in her daily life to actively reinforce and perpetuate her negative self-image and maladaptive behavior and lifestyle. Too often clinicians do not adequately appreciate the degree to which abuse and ineffective family environment may not only be relevant as historical factors, but may persist in the present. This often takes the form of revictimization in adulthood due to the replication of disturbed familial patterns of interaction in current relationships. Surprisingly often, not only maladaptive family-of-origin relationships, but even overt incidents of abuse by family members continue well into or throughout adulthood. In situations such as Patricia's, intervention that is purely symptom-focused is highly unlikely to be effective, because it fails to take into account how current maltreatment and family disturbance act to reinforce and maintain present difficulties.

One of the practical implications for an individual who has been subjected to multiple forms of child abuse is that there is a substantially additive adverse effect on both psychological and physical well-being (Felitti et al., 1993; Mullen et al., 1996; Wind & Silvern, 1992). In addition, it is crucial that we explore the general family-of-origin environments of our clients, and conceptually address how they, in combination with any overt history of abuse, may be related to the clients' current difficulties. Explicitly recognizing the differential and additive impact of a broader spectrum of current and historical abuse and disturbed patterns of family environment than that represented by childhood sexual abuse alone is one of the specific issues the family/social context model was designed to address.

6
CHAPTER

Society: Beyond Family Context

As is the case with many psychological phenomena, our understanding of the difficulties in functioning experienced by individuals who endured ongoing childhood abuse shifts dramatically, depending on the level of analysis we assume. The most basic perspective is to view survivors, whether of child abuse, combat, or other forms of trauma, solely in terms of the problems they present. The variety and intensity of symptoms and difficulties in interpersonal and adaptive functioning manifested by many survivors, when observed independent of any surrounding context, can strain the bounds of credulity and empathy. To a greater degree in the past, but even in the present day, survivors may be seen as fabricating or exaggerating their symptoms, indulging in self-pitying bids for attention, or attempting to manipulate others to escape responsibilities that they are presumed to be entirely capable of handling. This viewpoint is typi-fied by the phenomenon that has commonly come to be referred to as "blaming the victim" (Ryan, 1971)—discrediting victims by attributing negative characteristics and motives to them. This process has probably occurred in every type of interpersonal trauma to which people have been subjected. It is illustrated by accusing soldiers with "shell shock" of being cowards and returning them to the front as soon as possible (Herman, 1992a), by insisting that women victims of rape enjoy being sexually as-saulted (Brownmiller, 1975; Chesler, 1998), and by branding accident or crime victims who attempt to obtain compensation for their injuries as opportunistic malingerers (see, e.g., Gasquoine, 1998; Uzzell, 1999).

☐ Levels of Analysis

I am not, of course, arguing that individuals never malinger, exaggerate the adverse impact unfortunate incidents have had on them, or suffer from instabilities that make them especially defenseless when confronted with traumatic events. It is imperative that we assess each individual's situation in light of the clinical evidence, empirical knowledge, and range of conceptual possibilities at our disposal. To reflexively and uncritically accept claims of traumatization ultimately benefits no one, least of all the genuine trauma survivor. My point, rather, is that the consistent refusal to seriously consider the possible reality of the trauma and its potentially devastating impact is equally harmful. Such a stance is particularly destructive when it is rooted in a self-serving but covert desire to avoid acknowledging unpleasant truths about the universal vulnerability of human beings to the repercussions of tragic occurrences. The transition from seeing survivors' psychological difficulties in isolation to appreciating them in the context of their traumatic histories entails more than mere intellectual understanding. It requires that one confront disturbing realities that are a palpable threat to assumptions at the core of one's world view (Janoff-Bulman, 1992). It means tolerating the emotional recognition that horrible things happen in the world, that such occurrences can arise unbidden and unforseen, and that no one, including oneself, is immune to them.

☐ Individual Problems in Adjustment

There is a powerful temptation to retain a view of survivors' symptoms that is disengaged from their traumatic etiology in order to avoid acknowledging and accepting the truth that for all of us, safety and security are tenuous. To forestall coming to this conclusion, it is enticing to remain preoccupied with identifying and cataloguing survivors' difficulties, to dispute the veracity of their complaints, or to see their problems as a sign of weakness. Maintaining this position often leads people to react with what may seem to be well-meaning responses that nevertheless, can sound devastatingly callous and demeaning to those who have endured traumatic events. It can lead to offering advice such as the admonition to "just forget about it," or conjectures that those exhibiting posttraumatic symptomatology "must not have been very stable" before the traumatic incident occurred. Likewise, accusations that affected individuals "relish the role of victim" are often motivated by the emotional distancing and intellectual incomprehension that result from a refusal to acknowledge that anyone, no matter how well functioning, is vulnerable in the face of over-whelming circumstances.

☐ Traumatic Antecedants of Current Problems

As soon as one transcends a focus on immediate symptoms and takes into account their relationship to the events that precipitated them, one's point of view is radically transformed. When they cease to be viewed independently of the tragic circumstances that engendered them, the emotional, interpersonal, and adaptive difficulties manifested by survivors can no longer be seen as marks of a flawed personal or moral character. Instead of reflecting on the survivor, they are instead revealed as a reflection of what she or he has endured. When we genuinely and unflinchingly absorb the experiential significance and implications of a traumatic event, manifestations of survivors' impairment become transformed from puzzling and exotic "symptoms" to comprehensible reactions to excruciating circumstances.

It is precisely this alteration in perspective—toward an understanding of survivors' difficulties that is informed by recognition and appreciation of the context of their traumatic experiences—that has been precipitated over the last two decades by the work of researchers, writers, and practitioners specializing in psychological trauma. As Judith Herman (1992a) explicitly warns, however, knowledge of the connection between trauma and psychological impairment has been secured in the past, only to be lost. Appreciation of the traumatic context can easily be forgotten once again. The strength of individual and societal disincentives to recognize the existence and ubiquitousness of trauma constantly threaten to eclipse our accumulated knowledge about trauma and its psychological effects. Disturbingly, people generally seem much more prone to "blame the victim" in situations in which the trauma is one of interpersonal violence than when it takes the form of a natural disaster (Herman, 1992a). While people often spontaneously rally to assist those who have been endangered by floods, earthquakes, hurricanes, or tornados, they frequently apathetically ignore the plight of victims of rape, war, political atrocities, or hazardous, exploitive working conditions. In the most extreme instances, almost invariably in cases of interpersonal violence rather than of catastrophic natural disasters, the existence of the traumatic event itself may be vehemently denied, even when it has been witnessed or documented on a broad scale. Consider, for example, efforts to dispute or minimize the occurrence of the Holocaust (Gleberzon,1983–1984; Price, Tewksbury, & Huang, 1998; Yelland & Stone, 1996) the My Lai massacre (Hamilton, 1986; Kelman & Hamilton, 1989), or countless rapes (see, e.g., Chancer, 1991) and others violent atrocities (see, e.g., Fischman, 1996; Nichols, 1982).

☐ Abuse Trauma in Family Context

Adding the context of family background to that of trauma represents a further transition toward deepening our understanding of the causes of survivors' compromised functioning and the identification of potential remedies for their difficulties. Although any of us is vulnerable at any time to exposure to trauma, those who grow up in family backgrounds that fail to transmit effective living skills are rendered even more susceptible to trauma, particularly in the form of interpersonal victimization and violence. A key example of this is the vulnerability of children who grow up in such a family to sexual molestation by someone outside the family, as discussed in Chapter 4. Moreover, such individuals, by virtue of being reared in an atmosphere that does not provide adequate resources for social learning, are left with substantially fewer adaptive coping mechanisms with which to overcome the debilitating consequences of trauma than people reared in more fortuitous circumstances. At best only marginally able to manage the demands of day-to-day living, they are even more likely than other traumatized individuals to be overwhelmed when experiencing the intrusion and arousal components of posttraumatic symptomatology. In effect, those of us least equipped to handle trauma are most likely to be exposed to it.

Similar interpersonal patterns arise when an appreciation of the indispensibility of family context to adequate preparation for effective and rewarding adult functioning is absent. In a process that strongly parallels the inclination to "blame the victim" seen in the case of trauma survivors, individuals who have been deprived of adequate resources for developing stable emotional attachments and productive coping and daily living skills are frequently subjected to scorn. They are condemned and stigmatized, punished and rejected, all ultimately for bearing characteristics and inadequacies that are themselves a consequence of prior deprivation and neglect.

A prime example of this is the way in which individuals with borderline personality disorder are commonly perceived and treated, even by the very mental health professionals whose role it is to help them. Recognizing the erratic and unproductive behavior of clients with borderline personality disorder as being an indication of never having learned essential interpersonal and adaptive skills because of an inadequate and intolerant family environment can lead to the generation of effective methods for remediation of these difficulties (see, e.g., Linehan, 1993). Divorced from the perspective provided by family context, these clients are almost inevitably seen as being intentionally and reprehensibly irritating, capricious, and uncooperative. The irony is that in response to difficulties stemming from deprivation and rejection, they are once again abandoned and vilified. Borderline personality disorder is, of course, just one variation in a spectrum of patterns of difficulty that can develop in response to an inadequate family background. However, the contempt to which individuals with this disorder are exposed is similar to that elicited by all forms of "pathology" resulting from deficient families of origin when the role of this context in the creation of these difficulties goes unrecognized.

Case conceptualization that draws exclusively on the trauma context cannot reasonably be expected to lead to effective treatment for individuals whose families of origin do not provide adequate training in adaptive living skills. On the contrary, in many cases intervention approaches informed solely by a trauma perspective will be harmful to these clients because they are ill-equipped to productively confront traumatic material. Consequently, they are highly likely to experience increased distress and dysfunction when urged to do so. One of the most disturbing consequences when practitioners do not sufficiently appreciate the presence of coping skills deficits is the tendency to berate the client for failing to benefit from trauma-focused treatment (Pearlman & Saakvitne, 1995). In these circumstances, therapists have been known to intensify their exhortations that the survivor work even more diligently to uncover and unflinchingly face traumatic recollections. This can culminate, ironically and tragically, not only in further deterioration in functioning, but in a recapitulation of the type of coercive interchange that characterized the original abuse and the kind of gross insensitivity that characterized the family of origin atmosphere (Gold & Brown, 1997).

Integration of the contexts of trauma and family environment, on the other hand, can establish a vastly broader point of view and substantially deeper understanding of survivors and their difficulties than can either framework by itself. Awareness of the relevance of the context of family of origin alerts practitioners to the ways in which an individual client's social learning history alternately augments or attenuates her or his capacity to effectively cope with trauma. This recognition can immeasurably enrich clinicians' conceptual understanding and enhance the sophistication and effectiveness of their treatment planning. The resulting expanded perspective sensitizes practitioners not to presume that all gaps in functioning and maladaptive patterns observed in survivors are attributable primarily or solely to traumatic incidents. By thoroughly assessing whether present difficulties are traceable to deficiencies or warps in social learning, therapists are better equipped to identify those areas that are most likely to respond to skills training and other remedial treatment approaches. Difficulties stemming from skill deficits will at best be unresponsive to trauma-focused treatment, and at worst will be exacerbated by it. Therapy that draws on an integrated appreciation of both family and trauma contexts, on the other hand, can lead to much more sophisticated and effective intervention planning than could either perspective alone. The incorporation of a family context perspective facilitates awareness and implementation of this broad range of approaches without sacrificing the advantages of treatment informed by trauma models.

☐ Analysis at the Level of Social Context

However, it is essential to concede that even the integration of family context with trauma-centered therapy does not sufficiently encompass the broad matrix of causal forces surrounding survivors' symptoms and deficits in functioning. The limitations of a family context perspective for understanding the impact of abuse trauma on someone who grew up in an ineffective family of origin come sharply into focus when we consider the issues of responsibility, culpability, and blame for the survivor's difficulties. A commonly expressed concern about therapies that highlight the role of family background in the development of psychological problems is that they can easily lead individuals to attribute responsibility for their problems to family members and blame past events for their current difficulties (see, e.g., Alter, 1997; Robinson, 1990; Yaeger-von Birgelen, 1996). It is largely for this reason that I avoid using the popular but heavily judgmental term, "dysfunctional family." This phrase has come to be widely associated with blaming one's problems on a willfully malevolent, rejecting, or neglectful family of origin. From a practical point of view, inculcation in a vantage point that attributes causation of contemporary difficulties primarily to historical familial forces can readily (although not inevitably) leave the individual feeling stuck, powerless, hopeless and even more isolated than before. To the degree that problems are seen as having originated in previous, unalterable circumstances, clients are susceptible to concluding that solutions are now beyond their sphere of influence. In fact, this is a fallacy that can arise whether current problems are traced to deficiencies in family of origin or abuse trauma, since both perspectives invoke, as causal explanations, past situations for which one did not have responsibility. Even if one did not have control over or responsibility for the circumstances that created a problem, this does not mean that one is powerless to overcome it now.

There are, however, at least two other potential complications that can emerge from a conceptual perspective that assigns blame for psychological problems to family of origin. The first of these is that blame often not only connotes holding responsible, but also implies purposeful or intentional infliction of harm. It overlooks the fact that often a survivor's family background, even if it was a deficient environment for social learning, was not necessarily malevolently so. Often the truth is much less stark and absolute. Parents and other family members obviously cannot transmit knowledge and skills that they do not possess themselves. Frequently this is, to a considerable degree, the case. The family environment is inadequate in preparing its offspring for effective adult functioning not as a result of intentional deprivation, but more simply due to the ignorance and gaps in social and coping skills on the part of parental figures.

This observation quickly leads us to the second limitation of a family context perspective. How do we account for the deficiencies of parenting agents who are simply and guilelessly inadequate rather than malevolent? The most obvious answer is that they themselves grew up in unsatisfactory family environments. If we stay within the confines of family context in tracing causation, this almost inevitably leads us to an infinite regress. How can we account for the failure of parents and other family members to effectively teach the skills required for adaptive living? The most obvious and frequently encountered explanation is that they themselves were not taught these abilities, and therefore could not reasonably be expected to be equipped to pass them on, or that emotional difficulties rooted in their own families of origin interfered with their capacity to effectively parent. Since this same conclusion can be applied to each preceding generation in turn, a model that stops at the level of family context rapidly culminates in a conceptual void. Due to these limitations, this perspective ultimately fails to yield a convincing understanding of causation, a satisfying attribution of accountability, or a useful approach to resolving psychological difficulties.

But what other explanation could there possibly be for the inability of a family to adequately prepare its offspring for effective functioning in adulthood than the repeated failure of each generation to transmit adaptive living skills to the next? The answer lies in understanding family functioning itself in a contextualized fashion. Just as an individual does not function independently of contexts such as trauma and family, families do not exist as self-contained systems. For a comprehensive model that sufficiently addresses these conceptual and practical concerns, therefore, we must move beyond the contexts of trauma and of family to the even more extensive context in which families systems are embedded and in which interpersonal violence occurs—society as a whole. This contextual shift requires an appreciably more extenisve conceptual transition than those we have considered up to this point. It necessitates that we grasp that, just as all the elements discussed thus far—the individual and her or his symptoms, traumatic events and interpersonal violence, and family context and social skills acquisition—cannot be sufficiently understood in isolation from each other, none of these elements can be fully comprehended apart from the larger social context in which they exist.

Neglecting to grasp this fact promotes a tendency to find fault with and castigate "dysfunctional families" in a manner which is analogous in many respects to the phenomenon, on the level of the individual, of "blaming the victim." Just as it is unrealistic to expect an individual to function effectively without the emotional support and instrumental learning transmitted through the family system and other socializing agents, it is unreasonable to believe that a family can fulfill its role adequately without access to the resources and support of the larger society. It is not a new observation that families in which abuse occurs tend to be characterized by isolation from surrounding social systems (Gaudin & Polansky, 1986; Gelles, 1987; Roscoe & Peterson, 1983). However, often it is the family that is understood to sequester itself from the larger society. Given our cultural assumptions, it is difficult for us to consider that society may play a role in keeping families segregated from the rest of the community.

☐ Society: Holding Ourselves Accountable

The implications of examining the part society plays in the generation, perpetuation, and exacerbation of problems in adjustment, exposure to trauma, and deficient family systems are vast. They call into question some of our culture's most fundamental assumptions about society itself and about the roles and responsibilities of individuals and families within the greater social context. As a nation, we claim to be supportive of "family values," but how closely have we examined what that phrase, usually drawn upon for political purposes, really means? The term "family values" is often used to suggest that families function best when they are left alone to manage themselves, without the constraints of outside interference. Although this particular term has been coined and invoked with increasing frequency in this country in the recent past, it reflects a much older societal assumption that parents are sovereign, know what is best for themselves and their offspring, and can and should function free from government or other external influences (Stacey, 1996).

There is, however, a flip side to this sort of "freedom." Our culture places tremendous value on self-sufficiency and self-reliance. Just as individuals are esteemed for taking care of themselves rather than relying on others, effective families are glorified as being self-contained, self-regulating, autonomous entities. Hidden behind the aura of dominion implied by the term "family values" is the expectation and demand that families be self-sufficient. Not only should they be liberated from the constraints of outside forces, they should be capable of functioning without depending on external supports and should be independent of outside influences.

This conception of family values is particularly dangerous in a society in which families are increasingly isolated and segregated from the larger community. As important as parental and family influences are in learning to become an effectively functioning adult, they cannot prepare the individual adequately without drawing upon extra-familial supports. After all, much of adult living—working, shopping, worshiping, recreational pursuits—entails competent interaction with people and institutions outside the family. With increasing frequency, mobility and shifting employment opportunities lead nuclear families to relocate, removing them from stable, dependable, and consistent contact with extended family, friends, neighbors, schools, places of business, religious congregations, and other socializing forces in the surrounding community. Physical barriers, in the form of walled and gated communities, and social ones, such as racial discrimination and economic hurdles, insulate "privileged" families from their surroundings and exclude "disadvantaged" ones from opportunities. In both instances, however, the flexibility and adaptability of family members is diminished by curtailing their range of interpersonal and social experience.

As a society, we subscribe to and propagate the myth that "the good life" is restricted to those who enjoy the stature of financial, political, and social advantage. But these "privileges" do not protect families from emotional disconnectedness, personal doubt and insecurity, or interpersonal alienation. In many ways, it could be argued, these qualities are fed and perpetuated by the pressure to achieve, maintain, and protect the trappings of social and economic status. The resulting atmosphere creates a society in which individual competitiveness, acquisitiveness, and immediate self-interest are valued considerably more than cooperation, affiliation, and the welfare of the larger society. As a consequence, the institutions that form the social context for effective child rearing—well-run schools, safe neighborhoods, quality child care, affordable health care, and so on—progressively come to be seen as commodities to be hoarded by the economically privileged, rather than as necessities for a productive society. We therefore allow these institutions, which are essential to a society invested in helping families to rear children who reach adulthood fully equipped to meet the challenges of adult living, to become increasingly inaccessible to the average family.

The truth is, survivors of prolonged abuse and of ineffective families are very much like the rest of us. The difference between them and others is not one of type, but of degree. For how many among us can honestly assert that we have a solid handle on living well? How many are justifiably content with our parenting abilities, intimate relationships, family connectedness, social adeptness, capacity for coping with stress, occupational adjustment, or responsible management of finances? How much do any of us really know about the skills necessary for effective functioning in these areas? Why do we persist in evolving an applied psychology grounded in a framework of pathology, while neglecting to systematically investigate the components of effective living? We would like to believe that living well is to be expected, and that it is the failure to function effectively that requires explanation. This conviction fails to take into account the tremendous complexities of adult functioning, especially in modern society. Living that approaches anything approximating the state of the art is a rare achievement indeed.

Who, then, in the final analysis, is to blame for adults who cannot function adequately in society, and for the families which failed to prepare them for daily living? Society as a whole is to blame. In other words, we all are to blame. By leaving families to their own devices, we abandon children by putting them at risk for inadequate preparation for adulthood and for ongoing abuse. We abandon them again as adults when we choose to perceive their complaints as illegitimate rather than face the reality of trauma, when we hold them solely accountable for their problems in living rather than acknowledge the chaotic and neglectful circumstances in which they grew up, and when we ignore that as a society we have neglected our responsibility to provide many children and their parents with the necessary resources for effective family functioning.

If this strikes the reader as mere polemics, consider the circumstances described by Rick in the therapy session transcribed in Chapter 3. When he was a child, he, his siblings, and several other children in the neighborhood were sexually assaulted on an ongoing basis by Hank. Now, years later, Hank continues to molest children, including the offspring of several of his former victims. According to Rick's account, many people in the vicinity know about Hank's past and current pedophilic activities, but no one acts decisively to stop him. When Rick assumed the responsibility of contacting the State Attorney's Office, notifying them of the past and continued sexual abuse committed by Hank, and volunteering to travel to that state at his own expense to testify against him, no action was taken.

By the time he reached the upper elementary school grades, Rick was so anger-ridden by the failure of adults to provide him with basic recognition and responsiveness to his emotional needs, to guide him and attend to his basic physical needs, and to protect him from sexual abuse, that he was regularly picking fights with other children. No one tried to find out why he was doing this. Instead, he was simply punished. He was expelled from several schools, eventually dropped out of school, became heavily involved in drug abuse, and began supporting his addiction by stealing. It is interesting that in his therapy session transcribed in Chapter 3 he appears to attribute much of the initial impetus for his recovery from substance abuse and his entrance into therapy to the influence of the woman he eventually married, Valerie. (It is also noteworthy that she herself is a survivor of paternal incest). Sometimes all it takes to help a disenfranchised person to embark on the process of healing and integrate into the larger society is a connection with a single caring individual. Not everyone, however, is as fortunate as Rick.

Susan, an exceptionally bright and engaging woman, had in a previous course of therapy had been diagnosed with Dissociative Identity Disorder. During that treatment, she had done extensive journaling about her fragmented identities and their relationship to her past history, and had given these entries to her therapist. However, when she terminated treatment, her therapist refused to return her writing to her. When several subsequent mental health professionals tried to assist her in retrieving her written material, they were unsuccessful in either obtaining it or securing an explanation for why it was being withheld. This experience compounded her already considerable level of interpersonal mistrust.

When she embarked upon the subsequent course of therapy described here, Susan was in her late thirties, married, and had an adolescent daughter. She described a childhood characterized by growing up with contemptuous, hostile, and physically abusive parents. By her (strikingly emotionless) report, there were times when her father would fly into a rage so acute that he literally would chase her down and attempt to kill her. Like Rick, she depicted growing up in community in which, rather than receiving sympathy and concern, she felt ostracized and abandoned.

During treatment her husband, who periodically would become physically violent toward her, revealed to her that he was seeing another woman and intended to divorce her. Once he moved out of the house, he was minimally involved with both Susan and their daughter. Apparently largely in response to her sense of abandonment by her father, Susan's daughter, who was bright and had been an excellent student, began neglecting her schoolwork and associating with increasingly more marginal and delinquent peers. Of necessity, Susan's therapy became increasingly focused on helping her manage her daughter's behavior, rather than on improving her own functioning. On those occasions when it became necessary to seek residential treatment for her daughter, the staff of these facilities were quick to accuse her of being an over-involved mother and to imply that this was the primary reason for her daughter's difficulties. This allegation was highly inconsistent with the assessments of Susan's therapist and her daughter's outpatient therapist, who were impressed by Susan's rationality, caring, and determination to see her daughter through this difficult period.

Susan's problems were compounded when the divorce left her with meager financial resources and no health coverage. Her psychological difficulties, particularly her memory impairment and compromised distress tolerance, made it unfeasible for her to maintain employment. Although she was relieved that she was eventually able to help her daughter stabilize sufficiently enough to become employed and self-supporting, live independently, and attend college, her own situation progressively worsened. Her circumstances became even more precarious when she became physically ill, experiencing severe chronic pain and greatly restricted mobility. The alimony on which she supported herself was barely adequate to meet her basic needs, but was of a sufficient amount that it barred her from qualifying for Medicaid coverage. Several physicians she consulted implied that her difficulties were "all in her head," some making this pronouncement over the phone before they had even examined her. The one or two who quietly affirmed the reality of her condition were unable to provide her with treatment because of her lack of financial means. Susan currently vacillates between resigning herself to a continued decline in her medical and financial condition leading to eventual homelessness and mobilizing to attempt to seek out resources to help prevent this outcome.

As Susan's situation dramatically demonstrates, people who grow up abused, neglected, disregarded and abandoned as children are as adults at extreme risk for continued invalidation and mistreatment by society at large. A substantial and growing literature on revictimization suggests that individuals who are abused as children are at substantially increased risk for violent victimization in adulthood (see, e.g., Messman & Long, 1996; Neumann, Houskamp, Pollack, & Briere, 1986; Wyatt, Guthrie, & Notgrass, 1992). For the most part, this literature conceptualizes the phenomenon of revictimization as a vulnerability to assault attributable largely to the personal qualities of the survivor (e.g., unassertiveness, resignation, expectation of negative treatment by others, low self-esteem) which are engendered by childhood victimization.

This is a legitimate viewpoint, but a limited one in at least two major respects. For one thing, although this perspective acknowledges the causal role of abusive treatment in the genesis of revictimization, it places the locus of causation for continued maltreatment primarily within the individual, in the form of traits acquired as a result of prior victimization. For another, by defining victimization specifically in terms of interpersonal violence, it fails to capture the more subtle ways in which survivors of prolonged child abuse are subject to mistreatment, disregard, and neglect by the larger society. While Susan did manifest many of the traits commonly ascribed to revictimized individuals, it seems clear that her social status—as a woman, an unemployed person, and a person with limited financial resources—contributed to her being treated in a marginalized and dismissive fashion. Paradoxically, our society's emphasis on self-reliance, coupled with the propagation of inequities based on gender, ethnic background, financial status, and other social classifications, converge to restrict the access of already deprived and maltreated individuals to resources that would help them attain effective, self-sufficient functioning.

This is the social context in which survivors of prolonged abuse grow up and in which they later live. It is the social context that continues to surround them when they come to us for therapy. It is within this social context, which so frequently views them with derision and contempt, that we practitioners must work. It is this social context which we must appreciate, of which we must be mindful, and which we must be dedicated to changing if we are to be optimally helpful in promoting our survivor clients' well being.

TREATMENT IN CONTEXT: FOUNDATIONS OF THE THERAPEUTIC MODEL

The deficits in interpersonal functioning and the complex past and current life circumstances of many individuals with a history of prolonged child abuse pose special obstacles to the establishment of a productive course of treatment. Restricted social skills, dependent longings, and wary mistrust displayed by many survivors can act as formidable impediments to the development of the collaborative alliance between practitioner and client that is a crucial foundation for effective psychotherapy. In addition, the intricate web of past deprivation and maltreatment, current adverse conditions and disadvantages, and personal limitations and conflicts constitutes a daunting challenge to the construction of a coherent conceptual formulation to guide the treatment process. In the absence of the context of a productive therapeutic alliance and a clearly articulated conceptual framework, specific interventions are at best compromised and at worst rendered completely ineffective. This section discusses the interpersonal and conceptual challenges frequently encountered in working with survivors of prolonged child abuse, and offers strategies for surmounting them. It also provides an overview of the structure of the contextual therapy approach to treating survivors of prolonged child abuse, and the rationale supporting it.

CHAPTER

Collaboration:
Forming a Therapeutic Alliance

Due to a series of self-perpetuating and mutually interacting influences, adults with a history of prolonged childhood abuse (PCA) often enter therapy having had extraordinarily little experience with productive, collaborative interpersonal relating. A good deal has been written about how abuse trauma warps and attenuates capacities for effective interpersonal interaction (see, e.g., Courtois, 1988; Herman, 1992a; Freyd, 1996). Both the anguish and sense of betrayal that abuse engenders promote abiding feelings of mistrust of others and disdain of oneself that can forcefully block the formation of mutually gratifying, reciprocal, stable relationships.

☐ The Anticipation of Distain

However, if we think of PCA as most commonly occurring within a particular type of ineffective family context, a more intricate picture emerges. Family backgrounds which foster the conditions that contribute to ongoing intra- or extra-familial abuse are highly unlikely to promote strong and consistent capacities for attachment or to model effective social skills. The limited capabilities of individuals reared in these types of family environments to engage in effective interpersonal relating, therefore, are largely traceable to factors that predate and are much more pervasive than the occurrence of overt incidents of abuse.

Consequently, the level and type of social impairment manifested by adults with a PCA history are often considerably more profound and extensive than would commonly be seen in, for example, cases of single incident trauma occurring in adulthood. There is a palpable difference between someone whose capacity for stable interpersonal relating was intact before being disrupted by trauma, and someone in whom these capacities were never strongly established in the first place. In the former instance the requisite skills are already present. Confidence in self and trust in others existed before the trauma occurred. The primary task necessary to establish gratifying and productive interactions with others is to access and revive these preexisting resources. The latter scenario, however, has entirely different implications. For someone who grew up in a family marked by emotional disengagement, vehement conflict, and interpersonal control, the capacity for attachment is at best tenuous and the patterns of social relating that have been learned are likely to foster conflict rather than affiliation. In these cases one of the cornerstones of efficacious psychotherapy, the formation of a collaborative working relationship between client and therapist, is itself a central challenge.

Where an inadequate family background figures prominently in a client's history, overt episodes of abuse are pitifully congruent with previous experience. Abuse, for such individuals, punctuates and is emblematic of a much more extensive historical narrative of negation, objectification, and subjugation. The explicit and conspicuous maltreatment embodied in discrete incidents of abuse compellingly substantiate what has already been conveyed by the pervasive family atmosphere in which the child has been immersed. Deeply entrenched convictions of being hopelessly and irredeemably contemptible, defective, unlovable and unworthy, already present, become even more rigidly fixed by overt acts of abuse. Firmly implanted expectations of being emotionally rejected, abandoned, reviled and accosted by others, long established, are simply verified and further ingrained by overt maltreatment. For such individuals, a profound sense of desolation and aloneness is a core aspect of the experience of daily living.

Deprived of models of effective and comfortable social interaction, surrounded instead by examples of contentious and chaotic interpersonal relating, contemptuous of self and wary of others, such children frequently develop patterns of behavior that inadvertently maintain and compound their social deficits. Their social awkwardness and ineptness invites avoidance by adults and derision by peers. Their desperation for nurturance and belonging may fuel an overbearing, clingy interpersonal style that ultimately serves to drive others away. Their unmet needs for affection and acceptance make them easy targets for exploitation and manipulation. Their hunger for attention leads them to act up in disruptive ways that invoke punishment and rejection. Their mistrust and apprehensiveness around others keeps them separate and deprives them of opportunities to remediate the gaps in their interpersonal repertory. Their extreme sensitivity and lack of interpersonal savvy leads them to misinterpret social cues and respond inappropriately, promoting further estrangement from others. In this way, a mutually reinforcing and self-perpetuating cycle of accumulated interpersonal injury and mounting social incompetency gradually and steadily intensifies from childhood through adolescence and into adulthood.

By the time they reach the therapist's office, PCA survivors usually have developed a deeply rooted conviction that both their own families and society as a whole view them with disdain. Too often there is convincing evidence that this is in fact the case. Sometimes there is no such indication. Almost inevitably, however, this conviction powerfully mirrors the low regard in which such individuals hold themselves. They have little reason to expect interpersonal relationships to be marked by cooperation and good will, have had minimal if any experience of being nurtured and supported, and have developed an interpersonal style and a set of beliefs about interpersonal relationships that are likely to work actively against the formation of a collaborative partnership.

Nevertheless, clients with a PCA background do not present with a homogeneous interactional style. Some appear distant, unemotional, and guarded. Others seem hostile and rageful. Still others come across as desperate and clingy. Many are anxious and self-denigrating. Most will fluctuate between these modes of interaction.

☐ Fear of Abandonment

While overt behavioral style varies widely from one individual to the next, underlying preoccupations and experiences of self and others are often uncannily consistent. By far the most common and central among these is the perception of the self as being reprehensible and unlovable. This self-image usually seems closely tied to the impression of being unloved by parents. It is as if the PCA survivor concludes, "Who could possibly know me better than my parents? Who could possibly be expected to love me if they did not? If my parents didn't hold me in high regard, how can I possibly expect anyone else to? I must be fundamentally vile and unlovable."

Closely related to this view of self is an intense fear of and presumption of inevitable abandonment by the therapist. Some clients express this concern overtly. "It is just a matter of time before you will get sick of me and send me away." Others convey it only slightly less directly, by repeatedly begging for reassurance. "Please promise me that you won't get rid of me. Can I count on you to always be there, no matter what?" In extreme cases I have heard clients say things such as, "I was afraid to come here today. I was sure I would find the door to your office bolted and a sign posted indicating that you had moved away." They then volunteer that this fear is an expression of their assumption that the clinician has grown weary and impatient with them, and, lacking the courage to tell them to leave, has decided that the only solution is to close up the practice and relocate.

Very often, however, the concern and presumption of the inevitability of abandonment by the therapist, although present, will not be expressed directly or verbally (at least not until advanced stages of treatment). The expectation of abandonment is largely constructed from real life experiences of being deserted and rejected when unmet dependency and affectional needs overwhelm others and lead them to cut off interaction. Combined with the impact of a history of coercive and abusive interpersonal experiences, the fear of abandonment affects and restricts the development of the therapeutic relationship in myriad ways—some of them blatant, others extremely subtle.

One particularly complicating manifestation of these effects is a form of unassertiveness and tacit compliance that can be very difficult to detect and circumvent. Many survivors of PCA have learned, both from their family backgrounds and from overt instances of abuse, to interpret questions that ostensibly offer choices as commands. For example, the inquiry, "Would you like to tell me about that?" is likely to be heard not as a question to which one possible response is "No," but as an order—"Tell me more about that!" Consequently, while in the practitioner's mind options are being offered, from the client's perspective directives are being issued. In many instances, it will not even occur to the client to object to or be resentful about receiving commands, based on the assumption that the therapist knows what is best for her or him.

If the clinician is not alert to this possibility, this form of miscommunication can continue unnoticed indefinitely. In order to avoid this, it may be necessary to discuss explicitly the possible presence of this pattern when the practitioner suspects that it is operating. In addition, it can be useful periodically, when offering a choice, to preface the question with a reminder such as, "I'm about to ask you one of those questions to which 'No' is a perfectly acceptable answer." This certainly will not guarantee that the client will feel free to respond candidly in any particular instance. Over time, however, it will help to encourage a different way of viewing choice and interpersonal relating.

An associated pattern of interaction is the exercise of an extreme degree of caution in communication. On the basis of past experiences, most commonly beginning with the family of origin, there may be a tremen-

dous concern that expressing feelings, sharing perceptions, making requests, or revealing certain kinds of information may risk arousing the
anger or annoyance of the therapist. This, in turn, raises fears of abandonment. The result is often an intense effort to censor these types of
communication through omission, misdirection, and minimal and misleading responses to direct questions.

Frequently, the presence of this phenomenon will not come to the attention of the therapist for quite some time. Usually it will first begin to
emerge at a point in treatment when the client has developed sufficient
trust to take a chance and hesitantly broach those areas that until then
have been avoided. This may take the form of questions designed to "check
out" perceptions and beliefs with the therapist such as, "Are you angry at
me now?", "Does what I just said sound silly to you?", and so on. Alternately, when a sufficient degree of comfort is reached, there may be direct disclosure of certain topics and types of information that have been
purposely avoided until that point. While the acknowledgment of this
pattern, in whatever form it takes, represents a turning point in the therapeutic relationship, it should not be mistaken for a sign that the obstacle
it represents no longer exists. The level of wariness and self-protection
that sustains this type of behavior can only be expected to subside gradually. To help accelerate this process, it is crucial for the practitioner to
exercise attentiveness for instances in which these self-imposed restrictions are breached, in order to verbally encourage and behaviorally reinforce them.

A similar expression of the fear of abandonment is making attempts to
placate and please the clinician. This tendency can assume a variety of
forms. One of the most insidious of these is a willingness to "perform
well" by deciphering and conforming to the therapist's expectations. When
present, this tendency can make survivors of PCA particularly susceptible
to leading and suggestive questioning by the clinician. Although in some
instances this type of compliance may be intentional, it is more often
subtle and unwitting. The tendency to allow others to define and interpret their experience is usually compounded by the presence of an inor-
dinate receptivity to doubting their own perceptions, judgements, and
feelings. This vulnerability to mistrusting their own experience is attributable to growing up in a family environment in which having their reality questioned and negated was a commonplace occurrence (Linehan,
1993).

Their proclivity to accommodate to the perceived expectations of others underscores the importance of open-ended questioning in the treatment of PCA survivors. By framing exploratory inquiries in broad terms
that allow for a range of possible answers, practitioners can appreciably
reduce the likelihood that they are unwittingly conveying expectations

that these types of clients may feel compelled to fulfill. This approach requires that therapists learn to resist the temptation to allow their working hypotheses to shape excessively the wording of their questions. One of the best safeguards against this inclination is to understand clearly that when it comes to exploration of subjective experience—feelings, recollections, perceptions, and the like—the clinician's role is not to educate clients, but to be educated by them. It is presumptuous and potentially misleading to believe and convey that one can identify or understand those subjective experiences better than the client her or himself. It is inevitable, and in many ways useful, to formulate working hypotheses that guide the direction of inquiry in a session. However, the more open-ended the questioning is, the less likely responses are to be tainted by the practitioner's preconceptions, and the more confidence both therapist and client can place in the data produced. For example, asking in regard to a particular incident, "Was that distressing?" may be read as an indication that the clinician believes it was or should have been. This may be taken as a cue that the "right" answer is an affirmative one. It would be more useful to ask, "How did you feel about that?", or, even more broadly, "What was that like for you?"

A considerably more overt but much less frequently observed indication of concern with pleasing and placating the therapist is behavior that has traditionally been referred to as "seductiveness." While this term may accurately capture the surface appearance of behaviors ranging from coy flirtatiousness to explicit invitations to engage in sexual activity, it is grossly misleading. The term "seductive" is too easily interpreted as denoting that the motivations and intentions behind these actions are sexual in nature. Although sometimes seen in clients who have been subjected to other forms of maltreatment, such as physical abuse, sexual suggestiveness is most often observed among survivors of extensive molestation in childhood. These are usually individuals who felt ignored or rejected by their families of origin. Often they report very few childhood recollections of feeling wanted or even of capturing the attention of adults outside of their experiences of sexual abuse. Consequently, they come to believe that the only value they hold for other people—quite literally—is as objects of sexual gratification. On the basis of this conviction, it is a small step for some survivors to conclude that offering themselves sexually will keep their therapist from losing interest in them.

It is enormously helpful for therapists to recognize that although they are sexual in appearance, these behaviors are not primarily sexually or romantically motivated. One of the greatest difficulties for many therapists in responding to these behaviors, in addition to the discomfort and anxiety promoted by our culture about sexual matters in general, is the concern that clients will feel rejected and rebuffed by the refusal to comply with their requests for sexual intimacy. In fact, although clients may be surprised by their own reaction, they are much more commonly relieved. At the same time, they are likely to be puzzled. It may be difficult to believe that the therapist will not sexually exploit them, even if "invited" to do so. However, calm and steadfast assurance that sexual contact of any kind simply will not occur at any time, under any circumstances, facilitates the client's realization that what was really sought was the therapist's continuing presence, interest, and support.

Another common but quite different response to fear of abandonment by the clinician is to consciously maintain an emotional distance. In rare instances, a client will explicitly announce the intention to avoid becoming attached to the therapist. This is usually expressed in terms such as, "I just want you to know that I never get so close to anyone that I can't cut them off without a moment's notice, and you're no exception." More typically, however, the intention to maintain an emotionally safe level of detachment remains unspoken. In either case, it is generally best to accept and respect this stance, which is ultimately an attempt at self-protection. The resulting sense of safety allows the client to risk continued involvement in therapy, and eventually leads to a gradual easing of the insistence on remaining emotionally aloof.

An even more extreme form of protection against the possibility of abandonment—a constellation of behaviors designed to disguise emotional attachment by giving the appearance of actively pushing the clinician away— is fortunately relatively rare. I am referring here to an abrasive style that, upon careful examination, appears unrelated or grossly disproportionate to the therapist's behavior. Ranging from mildly disparaging comments to overt expressions of hostility, criticism, and contempt, this stance can be particularly confusing to the practitioner and difficult to respond to productively. It is essential that the clinician maintain sufficient objectivity to be open to validating legitimate expressions of anger. PCA survivors grew up in a family and social context in which authority figures rarely, if ever, acknowledged the validity of warranted displays of anger by apologizing and accepting responsibility for their hurtful or offensive actions. The therapist's willingness to do this can have an enormously positive impact on the survivor's view of the legitimacy of his or her own anger and the utility of expressing it appropriately.

However, when angry outbursts and demeaning comments seem to constitute a global style that appears independent of slights or disrespectful behavior on the part of the clinician, they represent an entirely different phenomenon. When this is the case, they often constitute attempts to ward off the development of an emotional attachment to the therapist, which is perceived as a dangerous prelude to vulnerability to being hurt and abandoned. It is also usually a form of "testing" behavior designed to assess the genuineness and durability of the clinician's commitment. The ability to recognize when hostile behavior is motivated by fears of attachment and efforts at self-protection is invaluable in helping the practitioner to respond to them in a constructive manner, and to avoid reacting in an unproductive or harmful manner. At times, it may be best to ignore low level jibes in order not to reinforce them. In response to more intense and dramatic demonstrations of hostility, however, expression of perplexity about the hostile statement or behavior and sincere inquiry about what provoked it can help to avoid the development of a needless and potentially detrimental confrontation. In some instances, this approach may even provide the client with the opportunity to recognize and acknowledge the self-protective and testing functions of this interpersonal stance. However, if the excessive and unprovoked hostile displays continue, it will be necessary for the therapist to calmly establish limits about what she or he is willing to tolerate in order to work effectively with the client. Otherwise, these outbursts are likely to escalate and make productive collaboration impossible.

☐ Dependent Longing

Among the most frank, overt, and dramatic expressions of the contemptuous self-image and associated terror of emotional abandonment experienced by many PCA survivors are behaviors reflecting an urgently experienced longing to "cling" to the therapist. Sometimes clients with a PCA history will explicitly give voice to the wish that the practitioner could always be present with them, or will disclose that the separation during the intervals between scheduled sessions are painful to endure. Some convey these feelings with great intensity and poignancy, while others who experience excruciating shame for having such feelings will only disclose them hesitantly and haltingly.

In rare instances, these dependent feelings are communicated in a way that is prone to be misread as a sense of entitlement. In these cases clients may vehemently insist that the practitioner be available by phone or even in person, at any hour of the day or night—whether in response to a life-threatening emergency or to transient pangs of loneliness, anxiety, or other types of distress. I have even seen a few extreme situations in which, despite attempts to maintain appropriate boundaries, a client took extraordinary measures to contact the clinician outside of session by, for example, deceptively or illegally obtaining unlisted home phone numbers and calling late at night "just to chat." These expectations appear to come from individuals who grew up without a conception of privacy and autonomy because their own personal boundaries were routinely invaded or consistently ignored. As irrationable as this stance may seem, it can be very difficult to modify, especially when previous therapists have legitimized and reinforced it by capitulating to these unreasonable types of demands. It is essential, in these instances, for the practitioner to calmly but unequivocally establish the limits of her or his availability and the rationale for these boundaries. This includes making it clear that self-care is as essential for the therapist as it is for the client. Having a respite from one's work is a necessity in order to sustain the emotional resources and presence required for effectiveness in session.

☐ Navigating Obstacles to a Collaborative Alliance

Whether openly acknowledged, obliquely revealed, or concealed beneath a convincing display of detachment, the interacting forces of a loathsome self-image, fear of being rejected and abandoned, and excruciating feelings of dependency constitute pivotal influences on the PCA survivor's perception of and interactions with the clinician throughout much of the course of treatment. Appreciation of this configuration of experiences can be an invaluable aid to the clinician in avoiding misinterpretation of the intentions behind the client's interpersonal behavior. Interactions that would otherwise seem capricious, offensive, hostile, unfathomable, or that may have gone entirely unnoticed, can be recognized as expressions of profound distress, efforts at self-protection, or manifestations of turbulent conflict between unmet needs and intense guardedness. This awareness, in combination with an appreciation of the constricting effects of the contexts of family of origin and society on the PCA survivor's social skills, is necessary for navigating toward a therapeutic relationship characterized by collaborative interaction.

The ways in which the sensitivity fostered by this understanding directs the practitioner's interpersonal approach will differ appreciably, depending on the client's overt style of presentation. In most instances, one of these three styles—coolly detached, cautiously tentative, or frankly dependent—will predominate. However, these are obviously abstract generalizations and not purely distinct types. Usually, a single client will exhibit a shifting combination of these three modes at various points in the course of treatment, requiring the therapist to adjust her or his interactional style accordingly.

In the case of the client at the detached end of the spectrum, this conceptual framework alerts the therapist that the surface appearance of disconnectedness is likely to be a reaction to repeated experiences of betrayal and hurt that have forged a deep sense of distrust toward people in general. While in some individuals this wariness may be expressed through overt guardedness, in others it may be convincingly masked by a display of calm disconnectedness or even of superficial affability. Recognition of the possible presence of underlying dependent longing can help the clinician to understand that these individuals may be just as sensitive to perceived slights and rejections as those who are more overtly dependent. Equally importantly, it helps draw the practitioner's attention to subtle signs that the client is in fact emotionally engaged in the therapeutic relationship, and to unobtrusively act in accordance with this involvement. These indicators will aid the practitioner in the diplomatic establishment of a therapeutic bond guided by appreciation of and respect for the protective function that maintaining the appearance of detachment serves. As this alliance evolves, it can gradually make it possible for the client to acknowledge, address, and resolve the emotional impact of past betrayals. As a consequence, the pattern of assuming an interpersonal stance of detachment in extratherapeutic relationships can eventually be relinquished.

The other extreme end of this spectrum, that of explicitly expressed dependency, calls for a radically different stance on the part of the clinician. Instances such as those considered earlier, where the client seems distant, require drawing on conceptual understanding as an aid in mobilizing empathic responsiveness. Conversely, in situations where the desperate longing for soothing of unmet dependency needs is manifest, the therapist needs to rely on critical reasoning to moderate the temptation to react out of emotion in ill-advised and potentially harmful ways. In response to compassionate awareness of the enduring sense of abandonment, isolation, and betrayal experienced by the PCA survivor, it can be tremendously enticing for the practitioner to attempt to use the therapeutic relationship as a vehicle for satiating the client's unmet needs. This approach may appear logical and rational on the surface. If many of the difficulties experienced by survivors are attributable to interpersonal deprivation, then why not repair the resulting deficits by providing what has previously been unavailable to them? This is the reasoning behind the conclusion that what these clients need most from the therapeutic relationship is a "re-parenting" experience. Demonstrations of affection, reassurances that she or he will always be available and will never leave, and declarations by the therapist of positive valuation of the client as a person may appear to be the remedy that is most obviously indicated. Even treating the client as "special" by not setting the limits on one's time and availability can at times appear to be a rational method of responding to her or his dependent longing.

Although on a superficial level these deductions seem logical and may appear reasonable to the practitioner, they are in fact fundamentally flawed and inescapably destined to lead to a disastrous outcome. Acting on these beliefs initiates the unfolding of a destructive interactive pattern that the client is likely to have experienced in innumerable other relationships. Most PCA survivors, including those who express their dependent feelings overtly, experience considerable caution in trusting that someone else may genuinely care about them and be willing to fulfill their emotional needs, due to past injuries and betrayals. When someone finally does seem to have these qualities, and they respond by letting their guard down and allowing themselves to be emotionally vulnerable, a flood of urgent longing—for reassurance, soothing, and interpersonal contact—is unleashed. Partly due to the strength of these needs, and partly as a consequence of never having learned how to moderate them, a situation develops in which both members of the interaction end up feeling overwhelmed.

In those instances where the object of these dependent longings perseveres in trying to fulfill them rather than immediately retreating, the outcome is the opposite of that which she or he would have anticipated. Paradoxically, attempts to assuage the dependent needs by being responsive to them are ineffective. Instead, these efforts only result in exacerbating the intensity of expression and experience of dependency. While their immediate effect may be calming, very soon dependent feelings resurface. Assuming that the only way to soothe them is to have contact with the therapist, the client's desperation for contact with her or him intensifies, and the sense of neediness, unrealistic expectations, and urgent demands accelerate. Eventually, as all efforts to accept and respond to these emotional needs fail to appease them, feelings of exasperation, resentment, and hostility are likely to emerge and escalate on both sides of the interaction. The almost universal outcome is that the person who was trying to fulfill the survivor's dependent needs withdraws and severs contact entirely.

Lamentably, this scenario only serves to reinforce the PCA survivor's prior convictions of being unlovable, reprehensible, and insatiably needy. The resulting sense of shame, hopelessness, and despair compounds her or his already pervasive experience of distress and longing. The damage created by this pattern of interaction is considerable in any type of relationship, but is especially severe when it occurs within the context of therapy. The contrast between the authority, dedication, knowledge, and skill attributed to the therapist and the doubt and denigration that permeate the experience of self dramatically increase the likelihood that the PCA survivor will take primary or sole responsibility for the poor outcome of the therapeutic relationship. Not only is treatment aborted, but, if the survivor does subsequently risk resuming therapy with another practitioner, it will be with an extreme level of guardedness and mistrust that will only subside very gradually, over a prolonged period of time.

☐ Dependency and Power

How can we account for this phenomenon? Why is it that attempts to fulfill the PCA survivor's frustrated dependency strivings only result in augmenting them? I believe the explanation for this paradox can be found in the recognition that dependency is a matter not only of emotional connection, but also of instrumental power. The more intense and pervasive dependency feelings are, the more strongly held is the conviction of being incapable—incapable of meeting one's own emotional needs, of reducing one's own distress, of fending for oneself in daily living—in brief, incapable of self-care. This is probably why we commonly speak of dependency *needs*. The urge to rely on others, especially when accompanied by the disbelief that one is capable of taking care of oneself, is perceived as a need—something absolutely essential for survival. It is a feeling which, although valid as an experience, cannot be relied upon as an accurate reflection of the facts. The felt longing to rely on someone *emotionally* can be difficult to differentiate from the erroneous belief that one is not capable of *behavioral* self-sufficiency.

It is precisely this distinction, however, that helps to explain why efforts to resolve the client's dependent urges by satisfying them only result in the perpetuation and augmentation of dependent longings and behaviors. While each attempt to ease dependent feelings by responding to them may provide momentary reassurance and relief, it simultaneously leads to the intensification of experienced distress by increasing the client's conviction of helplessness. This is because efforts to meet the client's dependency needs are experienced, subtly but potently, as a form of confirmation of her or his own inability to successfully practice self-care. The resulting downward spiral of interaction brings to mind the saying that "It's cruel to be kind." Despite irreproachable intentions, responding to survivors' dependent feelings by trying to satiate them is most likely instead to engender greater misery by reinforcing perceptions of the self as being helpless, needy, and vulnerable. Consequently, rather than being soothed by the therapist's willingness to nurture them, they grow progressively more reliant on her or his support and assistance as they increasingly come to feel and believe that they need it to survive. Attempting to fulfill their dependency needs simply serves to reinforce and strengthen them.

An appreciation of the issue of power and its inextricable connection to emotional deprivation, therefore, is essential to the successful formation of a collaborative working relationship in therapy with PCA survivors. Despite the intensity of feelings associated with a history of emotional deprivation, what these clients need is to be treated not as helpless children, but as adults who by surviving extraordinarily adverse circumstances, have already demonstrated the potential to endure the stresses and challenges of daily living. Even though some survivors may themselves believe that a "need-fulfilling" type of relationship is what they need in order to overcome their difficulties, this type of interaction is actually disrespectful of clients' strengths and antithetical to the development of effective adult functioning. In the midst of the intensity of distress and the urgency of expression of dependency feelings by survivor clients, it is easy to lose sight of the indications of resiliency and resourcefulness that sustained them through experiences of extreme adversity.

This is not to suggest that empathic support is not a reasonable component of the therapeutic relationship. Recognition, acceptance, and validation of survivors' feelings, experiences, and longings is a helpful and essential aspect of treatment. It is imperative, however, when responding to dependency, that the practitioner be clear on the distinction between empathic acknowledgment of dependent urges, and efforts to ease these feelings by unwittingly treating the client as someone who is incapable of self-soothing and self-reliance. This is a difficult balance to maintain. It requires that the practitioner listen to, witness, and share in the pain, thereby demonstrating caring *for* the client, while resisting the temptation to try to soothe that pain by attempting to do things for the client, thereby taking care *of* her or him.

More generally, leading with listening rather than doing (i.e., intervening) is a vital general principle in working with PCA survivors, and a cornerstone of developing a genuinely collaborative therapeutic relationship. The therapist's attitude of receptivity, of wanting to be educated and informed by the client of her or his experiences, beliefs, and treatment objectives, is beneficial for several reasons. Survivor clients, not only because of the abuse they have experienced, but often as a result of the global family of origin and social context in which they have lived, rarely have had substantial opportunity to feel attended to, heard, taken seriously, and validated. A demeanor of receptivity on the part of the clinician implicitly and powerfully communicates a position of respect, regard, and valuation that is likely to be more affirming and empowering than any direct, deliberate intervention. This form of interchange, more than any other factor, can be effective in gradually eroding the deeply held convictions of being unlovable, reprehensible, and ineffectual that commonly plague the PCA survivor. Participation in this type of interaction requires the practitioner to have a solid appreciation of the critical role the survivor client's expertise plays in the ultimate success of the therapeutic enterprise. While the clinician must bring extensive professional knowledge and skill to the treatment situation, her or his failure to recognize and respect the preeminence of the survivor's lived experience is at best misguided and at worst arrogant and destructive. In brief, we cannot possibly know how to productively intervene until we have adequately understood the background, experiences, and perspective of the individual we are seeking to help.

This statement, taken in isolation, may appear too obvious to mention. However, disturbingly often, practitioners, when faced with the scope of the PCA survivor's suffering, difficulties, and uncertainty, respond by imposing their own agenda, solutions, and assumptions in a way that is unproductive and potentially damaging (Gold & Brown, 1997). A clinician's cognitive understanding of a survivor's situation may be accurate. A particular form of intervention may be sound and its effectiveness may be substantiated by empirical data. However, when conceptions and solutions are arrived at and applied without active consultation with the client, a larger, more consequential influence is at work. Treatment which is primarily or exclusively under the control of the therapist affirms the survivor's convictions of powerlessness, incompetence, and dependence on others. For this reason, wherever possible, it is crucial that the clinician be mindful of the importance of leaving as much of the process of therapy as possible under the direction of the client.

☐ The Need for Structure

This approach is very different from entirely abrogating control of the therapeutic process to the personal preferences and momentary wishes of the client. The objective, after all, is the evolution of a cooperative alliance in which there is active participation by both parties. The attainment of a collaborative relationship involves constant critical thinking, at numerous points in the treatment process, about how to maintain an optimal balance between empowering the client to take the lead and providing her or him with structure, support, and guidance.

Structure, a set of parameters that define the nature, extent, and limits of the treatment situation, which is essential in any therapeutic relationship (Cherry & Gold, 1989), is especially vital in working with PCA survivors. Clearly delineated guidelines provide the survivor with a sense of predictability and therefore of safety that has often been glaringly lacking in other social contexts. In contrast to the frequently ambiguous and chaotic organization encountered in her or his family of origin, it is critical that the therapeutic environment provides a context of reliability, order, and regularity.

A collection of ground rules for treatment is equally important for the therapist. Above all, the guidelines constituting a framework for therapy help to ensure that the client's best interests remain paramount (Gold & Cherry, 1997). A series of treatment parameters can assist the practitioner in avoiding yielding to the temptation to blur the boundaries of the therapeutic alliance by treating the client as "special" and construing the extent or variety of her or his problems or history as a rationale for violating standard rules and practices. More broadly, adherence to fundamental guidelines can help the practitioner guard against permitting her or his own preferences and needs from subverting those of the client.

In order to serve these functions for both members of the therapeutic relationship, the ground rules and parameters of treatment need to be explicitly established and agreed upon at the outset. Wherever feasible, the terms of the therapeutic contract should be arrived at through negotiation and consent (Pope & Brown, 1996). Neither member of the alliance should be expected to agree to conditions that she or he is concerned may be ineffective or antithetical to the client's treatment goals. Considering that much of therapy for survivors is aimed at repairing the damage created by the coercive interactions that comprise abuse, it is foolish to believe that substantial benefit will be obtained if they perceive the conditions under which treatment will take place as having been foisted upon them. Similarly, deferring to the client's wishes against one's better judgement when negotiating the terms of the therapeutic contract is a course of action the therapist will almost inevitably come to regret. If, therefore, a potential client insists on certain conditions that the practitioner sincerely believes will be ineffective or detrimental, or uncomfortable for her or him, it is best at the outset to refer the client to other clinicians who may be willing to adopt the proposed parameters.

The very process of negotiating ground rules is a precious opportunity to establish a precedent for collaborative interchange at the outset of treatment. Taking time to discuss the rationale behind each party's point of view and to resolve disagreements in establishing a therapy framework helps to avoid an extensive range of difficulties and misunderstandings throughout the remainder of the course of treatment. These discussions can serve as a singular opportunity to begin demonstrating that differences of opinion can be resolved without coercion or rancor; that planning ahead and anticipating potential difficulties can save considerable time and avoid myriad complications in the long run; and that numerous options can be found that constitute a middle ground between each participant's initial position. These are examples of the very types of learning of which survivors frequently have been deprived by virtue of growing up in an ineffective family-of-origin environment.

An additional benefit of these types of interchanges with survivor clients is that they require the practitioner to have a well thought out philosophy of and structure for treatment. The clinician needs to exercise critical judgement in developing a set of ground rules that is appropriately tailored to each particular client, rather than imposing a uniform structure regardless of individual differences and needs. *Negotiating* the terms of the therapeutic contract, rather than unilaterally dictating them, compels the practitioner to clearly articulate the justification for each of the proposed ground rules of therapy. This is a powerful means of inhibiting the therapist from arbitrarily imposing her or his authority on the client.

As a general rule, it is more feasible to move from a tight structure to a loose one than it is to move in the opposite direction. No matter how legitimate the proposed modifications may be, if they entail increased restrictions, they are likely to inflame the PCA survivor's fear of being abandoned by the therapist by raising the concern that the intention is to gradually cut off treatment entirely. This is one of the reasons why, for example, I treat the scheduling of sessions more frequently than once a week as an exception rather than as a rule. Even though twice weekly meetings have been advocated as a standard practice in therapy with this clientele (International Society for the Study of Dissociation, 1997), it has been my experience that this schedule often tends to exacerbate dependency by reinforcing the client's self-perception of neediness and helplessness.

In general, with both my own PCA clients and those treated by the doctoral trainees I supervise, I have found that the more frequently sessions are held and the more indiscriminately available the practitioner is between sessions, the greater the likelihood that the therapeutic relationship will become chaotic and unproductive. Under these conditions, reported levels of distress climb precipitously, effective functioning is appreciably disrupted, and crises proliferate. Conversely, when the terms under which the therapist will be available between scheduled sessions are kept relatively restricted and meetings occur no more frequently than weekly, client self-sufficiency and security are usually augmented. It is incumbent upon the clinician to provide specific instructions on who to contact and how to proceed if an emergency situation arises. However, it has been my observation that when individuals and agencies other than the therapist—such as friends, relatives, crisis hot lines, day treatment facilities, or hospital emergency rooms—are identified as the ones to seek out in these circumstances, crises occur extremely infrequently. This appears to be because when contact with the therapist is established as the expected response to an emergency, it provides an incentive to experience crisis situations. Consequently, instead of increasing the frequency of sessions in response to a deterioration in client functioning, I am more disposed to meet more often than once a week in those instances where sessions are being used so productively that twice weekly meetings can be expected to accelerate progress.

☐ The Therapeutic Alliance in Family and Social Context

As these considerations highlight, the interpersonal challenges faced by the clinician working with PCA survivors are formidable. This is one of the areas in which a conceptualization of ongoing child abuse grounded in an interpersonal-social-family-of-origin context is an indispensable guide to the practitioner. Thorough understanding and appreciation of the core issues of dependency, negative self-image, and fear of abandonment, as well as their roots in an emotionally detached and conflict-ridden family-of-origin environment, are invaluable in helping the clinician to make sense of the otherwise puzzling and potentially frustrating interpersonal behavior of individuals with a PCA history.

Although a solid working alliance is not sufficient in and of itself in assisting survivor clients to achieve their therapeutic goals, it is an imperative prerequisite to effective treatment. Sadly, I know many therapists who, until a few years ago, specialized in treating abuse survivors but who now actively avoid taking on such clients. This includes many clinicians who were extremely knowledgeable, worked diligently to keep current with literature and training opportunities in abuse trauma, and who were active in training other therapists to work with this population. When asked why they now avoid the clientele with whom they previously worked so extensively, the reason they most often cite is the unpredictability of the behavior of these clients and the interpersonal difficulties they present. In many respects, their sense of futility about effectively relating to PCA survivors seems attributable to the limitations of an exclusively trauma-based model in accounting for these relational challenges and in providing a framework for productively responding to them.

While survivors' problems in interpersonal relating are certainly exacerbated by discrete incidents of abuse, they are more thoroughly explained by the interpersonal-family-social context in which PCA frequently occurs. The insecurity, mistrust, misperceptions, sensitivity and neediness that complicate their relationships with others are too pervasive and fundamental to be solely ascribed to the betrayals they have experienced at the hands of their abusers. They become much more comprehensible when viewed as a result of growing up in a family environment where basic social skills were not transmitted, destructive means of coping with interpersonal conflict were modeled, satisfactory emotional attachments were not formed, and rejecting, ambivalent, and insecure attachments prevailed. In other words, many of these interpersonal difficulties are not performance deficits—capacities that are present but are not being manifested or have been disrupted due to interfering influences—as an abuse trauma model might suggest. Instead, they represent skills deficits—abilities that were never satisfactorily developed in the first place.

A family and social context-based formulation reveals the need for a very different approach to the formulation of a collaborative therapeutic relationship than would a trauma-centered conceptual model. If the capacity for productive interpersonal relating were present but for some reason dormant, providing a therapeutic atmosphere that promotes a sense of safety and security could realistically be sufficient to allow these resources to resurface. However, if these social competencies were never fully developed to begin with, then no amount of support and reassurance will lead to their emergence. What PCA survivors need, in conjunction with a reliable and secure therapeutic environment, is a structure that will foster the remediation of deficient interpersonal relationship skills, while simultaneously correcting distortions created by invalidating and abusive familial and extra-familial interpersonal contexts.

□ Personhood: Avoiding Rigid Categorization

Having reviewed the various styles of interpersonal interaction that challenge the development of a collaborative therapeutic relationship, it is vital to caution that these distinctions will do much more harm than good if they are used to pigeonhole clients. As I have already mentioned, most PCA survivors, rather than being restricted to one or the other of these modes of interaction, will at various times—or within a single session—display aspects of a range of them. The utility in being cognizant of this spectrum of interpersonal styles, and more importantly of understanding the core experiences and associated perceptions of self and other that underlie them, lies in employing that knowledge to help surmount the obstacles they can create in the formation of a collaborative alliance. If the practitioner's recognition of these interpersonal modes leads to rigid and stereotypical perception and treatment of the client, then this framework will itself become one of the most formidable obstacles to the establishment of productive collaboration. This is because any system of classification, whether of interpersonal styles, symptoms and diagnostic syndromes, or survivor status itself, can insidiously encourage relating to the client as a category rather than as a person. As one woman diagnosed with dissociative identity disorder (formerly known as multiple personality disorder) expressed it, "I am a person. The worst thing anyone can do to me is 'thing' me." By this she meant that above all, she was not a diagnosis, a curiosity, or even a life history marked by adversity, but a human being who viscerally experienced being violated and diminished when not treated accordingly.

Therefore, it is essential to be mindful that no matter what interactional styles predominate, and no matter how restricted their resources for effective interaction, the vast majority of survivor clients will to some degree, from the very outset of treatment, demonstrate some capacity to assume a collaborative interpersonal stance. By being vigilant for these moments, the practitioner can, from the earliest phases of therapy, look for opportunities to facilitate, reinforce, and extend them. It is useful, in this regard, to remember that actions speak louder than words, and that subtle, guileless, spontaneous responses that implicitly communicate respect and regard for the personhood of the client speak the loudest of all.

This type of approach, however, is not as easily achieved as it may at first appear. On the contrary, it can be exceedingly difficult to relate to a PCA survivor client. It can be difficult to keep from relying on the unnecessary distancing and counter-therapeutic trappings of the practitioner role on one hand, and from crossing boundaries and violating parameters that are essential to effective treatment on the other. Many of these types of distinctions will require the exercise of sound clinical judgement that takes into account the specifics of the situation, the particular participants involved, and the point in the therapeutic process that has been reached. In order to make effective judgements such as these, it is crucial that they be grounded in a well-thought-out conceptual framework.

CHAPTER

Conceptualization: Constructing Order From Chaos

People are remarkably intricate and multifaceted. Life is inexpressibly complex and exacting. No matter how fortunate and well-equipped certain individuals are, managing life in an effective, productive manner is a formidable task. These statements are more or less true of everyone, and certainly no less true of individuals with a history of prolonged child abuse (PCA). Usually, however, PCA survivors' backgrounds are even more convoluted, their current life circumstances even more arduous, and their problems even more numerous and diverse than most other people's.

Some individuals seek out therapy because they are experiencing one or two readily identifiable, circumscribed difficulties. In some of these instances, it may not be necessary to develop an extensive conceptualization of the client's character and functioning and her or his life history. A more or less standardized treatment protocol developed for that particular focal problem may be adopted, with excellent results.

☐ Distinguishing the Impact of Abuse From That of Family Context

This is not a realistic approach in working with most individuals with a PCA history. PCA survivors rarely manifest only one or two clearly defined problems. Often they present with a wide range of symptoms and meet criteria for a number of diagnoses (Briere & Elliott, 1997; Courtois,

104

1988; Gold & Brown, 1999; Herman, 1992b; Herman et al., 1986). How-ever, their difficulties are not adequately characterized primarily in terms of symptoms and diagnoses. Most often, their problems extend beyond this domain into the realm of day-to-day living. Routine aspects of func-tioning, such as conducting a casual conversation with an acquaintance, managing the monthly budget, or preparing to go to work in the morn-ing, may be experienced as overwhelming and disabling. These difficul-ties are not often solely attributable to the interference of symptoms, such as anxiety and depression, but also stem from having been deprived of the opportunity to learn basic life skills. Many of us tend to take these abilities for granted. Once mastered, they are experienced as being so integral that we rarely think about them. It may not even occur to us that they are skills that have been taught to us. They seem to be "common sense" approaches to situations that are self-evident. It can be hard to appreciate, therefore, that not everyone is fortunate enough to come from a family and social background where caretaking adults (I include here teachers, coaches, religious clergy, and other members of the extra-famil-ial community) are sufficiently motivated and effectual to see to it that these capacities are transmitted to the children for whom they share re-sponsibility. In this respect, therapy for PCA survivors is not merely about resolving particular problems, but about helping them to acquire the re-sources to live a productive and fulfilling life.

A model for understanding PCA survivors that takes into account the impact of family and social context as well as of circumscribed incidents of abuse draws our attention to two categories of difficulties that may seem equivalent in appearance, but which have very different origins. Trauma can disrupt existing functional capacities (American Psychiatric Association, 1994; Waites, 1993), emotional equilibrium (Foa & Rothbaum, 1998; van der Kolk & MacFarlane, 1996; van der Kolk, 1996), adaptive cognitive assumptions (Janoff-Bulman, 1992; McCann & Pearlman, 1990), and the capability to establish and maintain secure interpersonal attach-ment (Alexander, 1992; Herman, 1992a; Waites, 1993). Similarly, indi-viduals from an ineffective family background often have restricted daily-living skills, difficulty modulating affect, distorted beliefs about and perceptions of self and others, and restricted capacities for secure attach-ment. Consequently, the long-term effects of abuse trauma and of an inadequate family-of-origin environment may be difficult to distinguish from each other. However, in contrast to exposure to trauma, being reared in an inadequate family context is associated with the failure to develop these resources in the first place. Therefore, each of these two potential sources of difficulties, abuse trauma and an ineffective family background, calls for a very different strategy of intervention. To the extent that adap-tive capacities were originally established but have been disrupted by traumatic experiences, they need to be accessed and revived. In these instances, resolving the trauma and thereby alleviating its impact can be a reasonable strategy for restoring effective functioning. Where an ineffective family and social environment failed to transmit basic living skills to begin with, however, the lacunae in adaptation need to be systematically identified and taught. No amount of trauma-focused intervention will instill abilities that were never learned.

☐ Anchoring Exploration Around Focal Problems and Goals

These distinctions powerfully illustrate that case conceptualization is not a mere academic exercise, nor an end in itself. At its most productive, it is also much more complex than selecting a clinical approach solely on the basis of philosophical preference, personal conviction, or empirical findings derived from aggregate data and applying it to the case material at hand. Development of an efficacious treatment plan, especially in cases as intricate as those of PCA survivors, is predicated on an accurate conceptualization of the origins and nature of the individual's problems, in the context of her or his unique personal history, sociocultural background, and present-day situation.

To a considerable degree, therefore, the task of conceptualizing the interlocking history, lifestyle, current life circumstances, character, functioning, problems, and social context of the PCA survivor revolves around distinguishing trauma-induced performance deficits from family context-related skills deficits. However, just as conceptual contexts such as the abuse trauma and family environment models can illuminate areas of investigation and explanation, they can simultaneously obscure and divert attention from others. Once these elements are identified in the life history of an individual, it can be easy to lose sight of the fact that other causal agents may coexist along with them. An abuse history and ineffective family system certainly do not preclude the presence of other causal and contributing factors for a client's problems. On the contrary, individuals with this type of history have a higher probability of exposure to other sources of dysfunction, such as organicity (e.g., due to physical abuse and resulting injury) and the presence of adverse life circumstances other than abuse and ineffective family environment (e.g., poverty, limited educational opportunities, gender and racial discrimination) than do those without these circumstances in their backgrounds. While these possible aspects of the client's background might be related to abuse history and family background, their potential for independently contributing to current difficulties and deficits in functioning need to be considered as well.

As a general rule, I believe it is unproductive to routinely assess for the presence of a history of child abuse at the outset of treatment. I am well aware that others may find it incongruent and perplexing, or even suspect, that someone who directs an outpatient treatment program for adult survivors of child abuse would take this position. There are, however, several reasons why I advocate this stance.

To begin with, it is generally problematic to structure exploration around possible causes rather than around focal or presenting problems themselves. Setting out on a "fishing expedition" for the presence of a childhood abuse history that is not anchored to the difficulties that brought the client to therapy appreciably increases the risk of confirmation bias. One of the more common errors practitioners make is to automatically presume, upon discovering that a client has a history of abuse, that it is this factor alone that accounts for all or most of her or his presenting problems. Conjectures about the origins and implications of these difficulties are then predicated on this assumption. Once this occurs, alternative explanations, including more proximate causes, are unlikely to even be considered.

Instead of prematurely subscribing to global assumptions of this type, it is essential that the clinician carefully gather relevant information about the onset, surrounding circumstances, course, and contingencies of each problem being addressed. When did the difficulty begin? What situations were associated with its initial occurrences? Have the nature of the problem, associated features, or the circumstances that elicit it changed over time? If there is a history of child abuse, is there evidence for a connection between that abuse history and the difficulties that are currently motivating the client to seek therapy? Is there a plausible connection between the onset, severity, duration, and nature of the abuse and the client's presenting complaints? Do the difficulties experienced by the client serve a purpose, such as relieving distress, providing a sense of security and protection, or keeping others at a distance in an attempt to ward off further maltreatment?

Another, equally important reason to refrain from pointedly searching for a childhood abuse history at the outset of treatment is that the client may not be ready to comfortably and productively acknowledge experiences of child maltreatment to the therapist, or even to her- or himself. An integral component of abuse is the experience of being coercively controlled. It is therefore essential that the practitioner avoids prematurely forcing confrontation of traumatic material. Despite the clinician's positive intent, to do so is likely to arouse the client's all-too-familiar sense of being subjugated and dominated, in a way that is destined to have a markedly counter-therapeutic effect (Gold & Brown, 1997).

One client, for example, had sought out therapy for a severe episode of major depression precipitated by a sudden and unanticipated loss. She would "interrupt" herself in the midst of her sessions with comments that appeared unrelated to the topic she had been addressing. In each instance, the interpolated comment appeared to constitute an oblique suggestion that she had been sexually abused as a child. These comments continued over a period of several weeks of treatment. When she was asked in each instance what the comment meant, she seemed puzzled and replied that she did not know.

Eventually, without prompting from her therapist, she began to re-cover memories of childhood sexual abuse. It was probably not a coinci-dence that these recollections did not begin to emerge until after the de-pression that initially brought her into therapy had been resolved and subsided. It has been my experience that generally, if allowed to control the pace of treatment, clients will acknowledge and productively address traumatic material when they are ready, without prompting or coaxing by the therapist.

When questioned, much later in the course of treatment, about what she thought would have happened if earlier she had been asked directly whether she had ever been molested as a child, she replied emphatically that she would have left treatment immediately. She added that she had done precisely this several times in the past when this material had begun to surface during therapy. (A fuller description of this case appears in Gold, 1998a).

A similar situation was handled differently in another case, resulting in a much less favorable conclusion. A woman presented for treatment out of concern that her difficulty getting along with her step-children might create discord in her marriage. She greatly valued her relationship with her husband, partly because she had previously been married to a man who had been severely physically violent toward her, and who had in many ways created chaos and hardship in her life. In the years following the separation from her first husband her life had improved dramatically. She had pursued advanced education, climbed rapidly in her profession, and built a stable and gratifying life structure for herself. The relationship that she subsequently developed with her second husband was her first experience of a stable, supportive, mutually gratifying intimate connec-tion. However, when her step-children would periodically visit she would find herself frequently losing her temper and becoming embroiled in al-tercations with them. This was strikingly at variance with her unassertiveness and hesitancy to express anger in most other situations. Despite the fact that these quarrels with the children were sufficiently distressing to her husband that she believed they might endanger her marriage, she found herself unable to restrain herself from initiating them.

The client reported that her arguments with her step-children invariably were about the same subject—their failure to live up to her standards for maintaining order and cleanliness in the house. In order to understand this pattern better, she was asked if she knew how her fervent investment in keeping the house organized and immaculate had developed. It had not occurred to her before that moment, but in response to this question she described growing up with a father who had been extremely critical, unpredictable, and physically abusive toward her, her siblings, and her mother. He would be absent from the home for days at a time, and then would suddenly reappear. When the client and her siblings would hear his key in the front door lock, they would frantically scramble throughout the house, straightening up and putting things in order. This was because when her father walked through the door he would immediately perform an "inspection" of the premises. If the condition of the house failed to meet his exacting specifications, he would fly into a rage and violently batter the client, her mother, or her siblings.

The client immediately sensed the connection between these intensely frightening experiences and her altercations with her step-children. Eventually, she came to recognize that underlying her anger at the disorder created by her step-children was intense and reflexive terror. Household disorder triggered acute anxiety conditioned by the beatings she had received as a child, which her father had justified by claiming that the house was in disarray.

Over the course of treatment, the client was able to identify and reverse many of the enduring effects of growing up with a father who had been physically abusive, temperamental, and mercurial. She experienced a deep sense of shame about her upbringing, and had worked hard to avoid thinking about it and to prevent others in her adult life from finding out about her background. As a result, she had been remarkably unaware of how the circumstances of her childhood had continued to affect her. Gradually, her general level of anxiety subsided and her self-esteem became more consistent with the impressive level of occupational and social functioning she had attained despite the disadvantages and deprivation that had characterized her growing up years.

Several months into therapy, however, with a tremendous degree of anxiety and discomfort, she revealed that there were additional aspects of her history that she had not yet divulged. Over the next few sessions her distress escalated as she hinted, but conspicuously avoided acknowledging outright, that her father had been sexually assaultive toward her. Finally, seeing that her anguish persisted and suspecting that bringing the issue out into the open in an understanding and accepting way might provide her with relief, her therapist asked her directly if her father had molested her. Although in talking around the subject it had appeared obvious to the clinician what she had been insinuating, when he openly addressed the topic she expressed shock and confusion about how he "knew" this was the circumstance to which she had been alluding.

Despite the extensive gains she had made in treatment up until that point, she decided in the next session to discontinue therapy, because she did not feel equipped to confront her incestuous history. It is possible that she might have come to this conclusion in any case. However, it is at least as likely that if allowed to pace her confrontation of this material, rather than having the practitioner, in effect, make that decision for her, she may have continued to progress. She may eventually have been able to address and come to terms with her incestuous victimization, rather than abruptly discontinue treatment.

☐ Client-Directed Exploration

As these case excerpts illustrate, exploration of experiences of child abuse in PCA survivors is most likely to be productive when it occurs under the initiation, direction, and guidance of the client. This material is highly charged, and strongly associated with a sense of helplessness and being controlled. It is usually best to leave it up to the client to determine whether and when to acknowledge and address it. Moreover, allowing this material to arise spontaneously in connection with the exploration of the origins of particular focal problems increases the level of confidence both client and therapist can place in its accuracy and relevance. This can help to reduce the likelihood of excessive attribution of causation of difficulties to abuse in a way that forecloses consideration of the contribution of alternate factors.

The same principle applies in regard to assessment for the possible presence of a global family-of-origin environment characterized by tenuous or distant emotional attachment, failure to provide adequate social learning, and modeling of maladaptive patterns of coping. Rather than search for this material in a decontextualized manner, it is preferable for the practitioner to trust that this constellation, if it exists, will surface in the course of problem-centered exploration. In those cases where it has been established that both discrete instances of abuse and an inadequate family context are related to the client's difficulties, it is important to assess how these two factors may have augmented each other and jointly contributed to the problems being targeted for intervention. Is there evidence of the existence of a general family of origin atmosphere that was consistent with the overt abuse experienced by the client? Did the abuse occur within the family? If the abuse was committed by someone outside the family, did the family context create a vulnerability to the occurrence and perpetuation of victimization? In the absence of reports of overt abuse, is there evidence of the existence of a general family-of-origin atmosphere that may have led to or contributed to the client's current difficulties due to poor attachment, inadequate social learning, or maladaptive social learning? In some instances it is this general family context that will become apparent first, perhaps including evidence for more subtle forms of maltreatment such as emotional neglect or verbal and psychological abuse, before the existence of more explicit varieties of abuse, such as physical and sexual assault, come to light. Hopefully at this point it is evident to the reader that one cannot presume either overt abuse or a more pervasive ineffectual family background to be components of the client's history purely on the basis of the nature of the current problems presented by the client. It is now widely recognized by mental health professionals that there is no difficulty or constellation of difficulties that occur exclusively in individuals with a history of childhood abuse (Alpert, Brown, & Courtois, 1996; Briere, 1996; Pope & Brown, 1996). Such a history cannot therefore be extrapolated from the particular problems a client presents.

☐ Formation and Revision of Hypotheses

Identifying and conceptually organizing these diverse factors and causes is obviously an imposing undertaking. I do not believe it is realistic, or even desirable, to attempt to formulate a comprehensive conceptual picture at the outset of the treatment process. For one thing, insisting on proceeding in this way is antithetical to allowing material to unfold naturally by empowering the client to pace and control the direction of exploration. In addition, case conceptualization is ideally an ongoing process grounded in the principles of scientific investigation (Trierweiler & Stricker, 1992). Components of the conceptual framework, once arrived at, are viewed as tentative conjectures rather than final conclusions. These hypotheses are open to revision in response to newly acquired data that disconfirm or are inconsistent with them. It is recognized that simply because an explanation is plausible in no way guarantees that it is accurate. Theories and models are employed as a guide for organizing and interpreting clinical data, but defer to and are not used as a substitute for the data themselves.

Consider the following examples:

> A woman in her early twenties presented with a long history of severe depression. She was referred to an outpatient treatment program specializing in CSA based on a single incident of sexual molestation in her early teens. It was assumed that her long standing depression must be a consequence of her CSA experience. However, she was able to date the onset of her depression at age 8, and to provide a description of the circumstances

surrounding the first appearance of her symptoms that convincingly accounted for their emergence. It followed logically that if therapy focused on her CSA history it would be unlikely to appreciably resolve her depression. Both the practitioner conducting her initial intake interview and the client herself agreed that treatment centered on her experiences of childhood molestation was not indicated.

A man in his late thirties experienced depression and disabling anxiety on a daily basis. Although bright and highly educated, he had significant problems in occupational adjustment and therefore his financial status was far from commensurate with his capability. He often felt taken advantage of and he had developed the conviction that others were invested in oppressing him and making him miserable. At about age 9 he had been sexually molested on a number of occasions by a male cousin several years older than himself. While one could make a case that his complaints were related to his CSA history, this did not seem to be the major source of his problems. Instead, he attributed his distress, mistrust, and problems in adjustment to a much more long standing and pervasive history of physical and verbal abuse by his father, and to justification of his father's behavior by his mother. Upon investigation, the maltreatment by his father appeared to be much more directly related to his impaired functioning than his more circumscribed CSA experiences. Addressing the effects that his father's criticism and physical assaults had on his beliefs about himself and others and on his general level of arousal resulted in dramatic increases in career adjustment and financial status, significant improvement in his interpersonal relationships, and elimination of rumination, panic attacks, and depression.

A woman in her early thirties was referred to a practitioner who specialized in CSA because she reported that throughout her childhood she was sexually assaulted by a number of family members. She also experienced ongoing childhood verbal and physical abuse by her father, and repeatedly witnessed him berating and battering her mother. Her major complaints were severe panic attacks that occurred several times per week and agoraphobia, which consisted of avoiding leaving the house when unaccompanied by her husband. Exploration of her current circumstances soon revealed that her husband was extremely controlling, demeaning, and possessively jealous. He would frequently question her extensively about where she was going when she would leave the house alone and upon her return would interrogate her about where she had been and what she had been doing. A few weeks after therapy began he left town for several days. The client was surprised to discover that during his absence her panic attacks abated, her general level of anxiety decreased markedly, and she was able to leave the house and go about her business comfortably. Her past experiences of physical, verbal, and sexual abuse, combined with a family atmosphere that powerfully encouraged the adoption of a subservient posture as a central aspect of her sex-role identification, were key contributing causes to her difficulties. However, the immediate circumstances of her marital relationship were clearly the primary contributors to her panic and agoraphobia.

These vignettes illustrate the importance of attending openly and carefully to the data contained in clients' reports, rather than being guided primarily by theoretical assumptions. In this regard, just as the relational foundation of therapy for PCA survivors is most productive when it is collaborative in nature, conceptualization is likely to be most accurate and useful when it is the product of conjoint investigation between therapist and client. The therapist brings to this enterprise the proficiency comprised of professional knowledge of current empirical findings and explanatory models, the professional judgment and deductive reasoning needed to apply them to the situation at hand, and the knowledge and skills required to translate the conceptual framework into appropriate forms of intervention. The client contributes the expertise and authority that is due her or him, as the participant whose experience comprises most of the data from which the conceptualization is fashioned.

☐ Conceptualization as a Collaborative Process

Having established this much, it is crucial to acknowledge that in the same way that many PCA survivors enter treatment with limited capacities for collaborative interpersonal interaction, they also initially have restricted resources for participating in conceptual collaboration. Interpersonal collaboration and conceptual collaboration each constitute, in analogous ways, both means and ends. A strong working alliance is a necessity for effective treatment of survivors. This type of relationship must be developed during the therapeutic process because most survivors have never learned the interpersonal skills necessary for interactions marked by cooperation and mutuality. Consequently, the formation of this type of interaction is itself a learning experience that develops relational capacities (i.e., an end), while also serving as a prerequisite to other types of learning (i.e., a means). Much of this interpersonal learning occurs through modeling on the part of the clinician, and through "learning by doing."

A similar process applies to learning to engage in conceptual collaboration. It is incumbent upon the practitioner to actively enlist the client's cooperative involvement in developing an understanding of her or his difficulties, their nature, and their origins. One cannot assume, as one might with other clients whose interpersonal backgrounds have not been as extensively characterized by the coercion of abuse and the invalidation of a rejecting and neglectful family background, that PCA survivors will be equipped from the outset of treatment to participate in collaborative exploration and conceptualization with the therapist. They have learned through abuse that it is better to tacitly submit than to defy those in authority. They have been taught, through invalidating reactions to their expressions of feelings and beliefs, to mistrust and ignore their own perceptions and experiences. Having been reared in a deficient family context, they rarely have developed much skill in the exercise of critical judgment and reasoning. Consequently, they are primed to accept the assumptions and conclusions of the clinician without question. Unless therapists are aware of and sensitive to PCA survivors' vulnerability in this area, it can be easy for them to indoctrinate the client with their own convictions and beliefs without even realizing that this is occurring.

In order to involve the client in conceptual collaboration, therefore, it is essential that the therapist model the component skills of effective conceptual problem solving, which the PCA survivor often has never had the opportunity to learn. Conceptual strategies such as grounding conjectures in evidence rather than relying solely on plausibility, leaving conclusions open to being discarded or revised as new information becomes available, and entertaining alternative explanations, are examples of the elements of problem solving that not only constitute sound clinical practice, but also serve as examples of transmitting skills via modeling. Perhaps the single most essential among these skills is the exercise of critical thinking and judgment. This, above all, is what the practitioner must model for the client. Therefore, acknowledging the data comprised of the lived experience of the survivor as being the ultimate determinant of conceptual deductions does not mean that the survivor's perceptions and conclusions are to be accepted without question. Rather, it is part of the role and responsibility of the clinician to help the survivor learn to critically examine her or his experiences and corresponding beliefs about them.

Particularly at the outset of treatment, it may be difficult for some survivors to distinguish dispassionate inquiry about their reports from invalidating incredulity. Take for example, the woman survivor of childhood sexual abuse who declares, "My step-father did not molest me. Beginning at the age of 14, I seduced him." From the perspective of her understanding, learning history, and conceptual framework, this may well be an accurate statement of her experience. To respond with a comment such as, "No, that could not possibly be the case. How could a 14-year-old seduce an adult man of 40?", would be invalidating, dogmatic, and disrespectful. If the therapist, in response to this type of assertion by the client, concludes that further critical examination is warranted, she or he needs to proceed by questioning in a neutral, open-minded fashion. For instance, she or he may respond, starting with open-ended inquiry and gradually becoming more specific, with the following queries: "Tell me more about that."; "How is it possible for a 14 year old to seduce an adult man?";

"Does he have any responsibility for the situation?"; "Why do you think you would have wanted to seduce your step-father?". This type of questioning will be most productive when the therapist does not have any particular (i.e., "correct") answer in mind, and instead maintains the mindset of dispassionately seeking information and wanting to be enlightened by the client. It is not essential for the client's perspective to change instantly as a consequence of the immediate interchange. In fact, it is likely to be damaging if the clinician tries to impose her or his assumptions on the client. What is more important in the long run is for the practitioner to introduce, by virtue of her or his line of inquiry, the possibility that alternative views of the same situation might exist, and to model for the client the dispassionate examination of the facts and various ways of construing them.

☐ The Multiple Functions of Conceptualization

The approach to conceptualization being advocated here is one which is multifaceted, serving several purposes simultaneously. The first and most obvious of these functions is assessment. Assessment in this approach is not primarily centered around a survey of symptoms and a search for the possible presence of diagnostic syndromes, but around identification of areas in which the client would like change to occur. It is helpful in this regard to frame inquiry of this type not by requesting a list of *problems*, but by asking the client what she or he would like to *accomplish* in therapy. Framing questions in this way orients the client toward seeking solutions rather than toward enumerating difficulties (Dolan, 1991). It helps the client begin to construct a picture of the way things could be, rather than being mired in despair about the way things currently are. It suggests that therapy is about learning new things rather than about repairing deficits. Perhaps most importantly, it implicitly conveys the idea that the practitioner believes the client is capable of achievement.

Once a focal goal is articulated, exploration concentrates on the nature of the issue involved. Does the goal pertain to behavior, thoughts, feelings, sensations, circumstances, or some combination of these? Is it centered around the reduction or elimination of existing behaviors, thoughts, feelings, etc., the development of new ones, or both? If the goal consists of reduction or elimination of a problem, when did the difficulty begin? What circumstances were associated with its first occurrence? How have the nature, frequency, and intensity of the problem changed over time? When did it last occur? What were the events (both in terms of the external situation and in terms of feelings, thoughts, sensations, and other subjective experiences) immediately preceding its most recent occurrence?

If the goal consists of the establishment of or increase in a particular behavior, was that capacity ever in place? If so, when did it diminish or cease, and what circumstances were associated with its reduction or elimination? If not, are any components of it present, or were they in evidence at some time in the past? What might account for them never having developed further?

Initiating the conceptualization process by identifying goals establishes focal areas around which the complex and extensive life histories and current circumstances of PCA survivors can be organized. In this way, exploration is guided and structured by an effort to achieve a particular objective, rather than proceeding as an expansive, haphazard search for information. This approach reduces the likelihood that either therapist or client will get caught up in exploration as an end in itself. Keeping inquiry tied to goals helps to prevent extensive, diffuse exploration of presumed causes for difficulties. Rather than examining one aspect of the client's background (such as childhood abuse history or inadequate family context) exhaustively and exclusively, this strategy encourages the consideration of the contribution of a range of factors to the evolution of each targeted area.

The ultimate aim of delineating the nature, origins, and causes associated with each focal area of difficulty obviously extends beyond assessment. The ultimate aim of conceptualization is to point to appropriate methods for achieving treatment goals. Where deficits appear to be a consequence of never having learned essential living skills, training in those abilities is indicated. In instances where capacities appear to have at one time been established but were derailed by the traumatic impact of abuse, trauma-focused interventions may prove to be more effective. In areas where the client's perspective has been shaped by the restrictive and disempowering influence of ethnic, racial, gender, or other forms of discrimination, identification and challenging of internalized social prejudices may be called for. In these respects, the content yielded by exploration serves as a foundation for developing interventions that are logically grounded in an understanding of the nature, roots, and causes of problem areas.

Simultaneously, the very process of addressing these questions often functions as a mode of intervention in and of itself. Frequently, illuminating the myriad influences that contribute to the PCA survivors' current difficulties engenders a reformulation of their understanding of the problems being examined. The recognition that gaps and warps in functioning are attributable to factors such as a history of deprivation of learning or to the disruptive effects of maltreatment helps to make them comprehensible to clients. In turn, this often effectively diminishes the clients' tendency to find fault with themselves for having these difficulties. They grow less inclined to see their problems as a reflection on them, or as insurmountable obstacles. Instead, they are more able to appreciate that their difficulties are a consequence of their life circumstances, and that they are reparable.

In addition, engaging in the conceptualization process in concert with the therapist allows survivors to master its elements and to apply them independently in their daily lives. Through direct explanation and implicit modeling, clients learn to employ the methods used in session to deduce the origins, causes, and nature of difficulties, and to arrive at sensible strategies for resolving them. As has already been mentioned, on a broader level, collaboration in the enterprise of conceptualization with the clinician in session teaches survivors critical judgement and reasoning skills that can be applied to a wide range of situations encountered in day-to-day living.

Making conceptualization an explicit component of treatment and addressing it as a collaborative effort between therapist and client offers several distinct advantages in therapy for PCA survivors. Recognizing her or his unique and indispensible contribution to this endeavor as the sole source of the data from which the conceptual framework is constructed is implicitly validating and empowering. Enlisting survivors in the process of deducing the origins and causes of their difficulties helps them to appreciate that their problems are attributable to external circumstances (e.g., in the form of overt abuse and ineffectual family of origin environment) rather than to inherent failings on her or his own part. Active participation in the enterprise of conceptualization promotes the acquisition of skills in critical judgment and reasoning, and transmits the more circumscribed ability to deduce the nature, source, and causes of difficulties in order to develop a strategy to resolve them.

Handling conceptualization as a collaborative venture also carries particular advantages for the clinician. It constitutes a safeguard against unwittingly imposing her or his assumptions and conclusions on the client. It encourages the practitioner to listen to the client respectfully and retain awareness of the client's singular authority by virtue of being in sole possession of the experiential data from which the conceptual scaffolding that guides treatment is largely constructed. Perhaps most importantly, framing this core aspect of treatment as a collaborative enterprise is consistent with and supports the development of a therapeutic relationship characterized by cooperation and mutual respect.

9

Planning: Prioritizing Treatment Goals

Grounding conceptualization in the data of lived experience helps to ensure that therapy is tailored to address and meet the needs of the individual client, thereby maximizing its effectiveness. Approaching treatment in this way helps the clinician avoid excessive reliance on theoretical preconceptions that may hinder accurate understanding of the constellation of life experiences and current difficulties that are unique to each client. At the same time, some type of structure is needed for translating the complexities of a conceptualization that attempts to encompass the multiple possible influences on PCA survivors' presenting difficulties into a coherently organized program of intervention. Plunging into the therapeutic process without the guidance of a well thought-out, planned approach creates the risk that treatment will meander indefinitely in an aimless and unproductive fashion. At the other extreme, adhering rigidly to a set therapeutic blueprint without regard for the idiosyncratic aspects of the client's personality, history and current life circumstances can foster the deployment of interventions that are irrelevant to or inappropriate for her or him, resulting in a similarly ineffective outcome.

☐ The Rationale for Prioritized Treatment Goals

In order to strike a balance between the need for a systematized plan of action and the need to remain open to adjusting the intervention plan based on the emerging specifics of a particular case, I propose a model of intervention structured around a set of prioritized treatment goals. The word "priorities" is intentionally and carefully chosen. There are several reasons for referring to the elements comprising this framework as priorities rather than as stages. The wide variety of difficulties experienced by many PCA survivors will require comprehensive treatment that encompasses a broad and diverse range of treatment objectives. The use of the term "priorities" recognizes the necessity of organizing treatment by systematizing the order in which these goals are addressed. Unlike stages, however, priorities do not form a fixed, invariant sequence. While certain priorities are sometimes prerequisites for others, this is not always the case. The objectives constituting a particular priority, therefore, are not expected to be achieved before beginning to tackle those connected with lesser priorities. At any given point in treatment, a specific priority may yield to one lower on the hierarchy in response to immediate needs of the client, the direction that the process of therapy takes as it unfolds, or the circumstances of the moment. Often elements of several priorities will be addressed within the span of a single session.

The model of treatment priorities originated with the clinical observation that encouraging survivors of PCA to confront the traumatic material comprising their abuse experiences too early in the treatment process resulted in dramatic exacerbation of distress and disruption of functioning rather than improvement. This eventually led to the conclusion that in this particular population exposure to traumatic material could only be constructively dealt with and resolved if it was instituted *after* prerequisite adaptive living skills had been developed. Trauma, after all, represents experience so overwhelming that it can compromise functioning even among individuals who appear to be managing the stressors of daily living fairly well prior to its occurrence. In the case of PCA survivors, many of whom had never developed effective living skills or established a stable life structure to begin with, it seemed, in retrospect, obvious that exposure to traumatic material would almost inevitably be destabilizing rather than constructive.

On the basis of this reasoning, it seemed that "remedial" training in daily living skills needed to be established as the first priority in treatment for PCA survivors. Once these abilities were firmly in place, it was presumed, that various forms of intervention related to exposure to traumatic material could be instituted productively. Based on the intervening years of clinical experience, a somewhat more intricate perspective has evolved. It is true that it is crucial to assess, at any given point in treatment, whether a client has sufficient abilities and supports to productively process traumatic experiences. However, it is not as if the development of these resources must be the sole focus of treatment and must reach a particular level of completion before any degree or type of trauma work can be initiated constructively.

Instead, a pattern of alternately concentraing on acquisition of remedial living skills, examination and progressive fortification of the therapeutic alliance, exploration of the influence of the family-of-origin environment on present-day functioning and beliefs, investigation and amelioration of the impact of abusive experiences on current adjustment, and analysis of the relationship between these various domains can be allowed to emerge. The sequence of fluctuating emphasis on these tasks will vary considerably from one client to another, and from one point in treatment to another. It will follow a logic that is determined by the needs and circumstances of each individual, and unfold primarily under her or his direction.

Although the processing of abuse trauma may occur relatively early in the course of therapy for some clients, the decision regarding when, whether, and how to address traumatic material is based on a careful assessment of readiness to do so without substantial risk of decompensation. This determination is predicated, in turn, on evaluation of whether progress in the other major foci of treatment—development of a strong collaborative alliance, construction of an understanding of the impact of family and social contest, and mastery of adaptive living skills—is sufficient to reasonably conclude that abuse trauma can be addressed without instigating appreciable destabilization.

In this manner, the processing and resolution of the sequelae of abusive experiences can occur in piecemeal, titrated fashion. This is an especially important consideration for PCA survivors, since the duration and frequency of incidents of maltreatment to which they were subjected are often extensive, frequently encompassing multiple types of abuse by several perpetrators. It is also critical to distinguish between two general approaches for addressing and resolving trauma—encouraging the production of detailed description of specific incidents of abuse (e.g., as in exposure methods), and investigation and processing of the distorted beliefs, disturbing emotions, and maladaptive behavioral consequences resulting from abuse in a way that entails more global and less explicit accounts of traumatic events (e.g., as in cognitive restructuring). While these two strategies are not mutually exclusive, it is possible to employ each of them more or less independently of the other. As a general rule, therefore, when it seems indicated to address abuse trauma relatively early in the therapeutic process, it is most likely to be appropriate to do so with those methods that do not require extensively dwelling on graphic particulars.

The general notion of balancing these different themes rather than making trauma work the main or only thrust of treatment usually makes a great deal of sense to clients with a PCA history. It is an approach to which they are consequently very willing to subscribe. Several years ago, before the recovered memory debate, when trauma-focused treatment for PCA survivors was not viewed as controversial, we did occasionally encounter clients who entered therapy convinced that the sooner they confronted their abusive experiences the more rapidly their problems would resolve (see, for an example of this, the case of Brad described in Chapter 15). In these instances, we would use the following analogy to help explain why we had not found this approach productive:

> A traumatic experience is an extraordinary event. It therefore constitutes an extraordinary challenge to your capacity for coping. You would not take on an extraordinary physical challenge, such as skydiving or repelling, on a whim. To safely and effectively jump out of a plane or scale a steep rock face, you would first make sure you mastered the necessary training, obtained the appropriate equipment, inspected your equipment to verify that it was in good working order, and confirmed that you knew how to use it properly. The same is true of confronting traumatic material. Before rushing ahead, it is essential to first obtain the necessary training and equipment. Then you can approach the traumatic experience in a way that will be productive, rather than recklessly proceeding in a way that is only likely to endanger you.

At a time in the evolution of the field of traumatology when it was taken for granted that resolution of traumatic effects required confrontation of traumatic material, this perspective helped to bring the distinction between means and ends into sharp relief. It helped to remind us that exposure to traumatic material, until then the sine qua non of therapy for the sequelae of PCA, was, after all, a means rather than an end in itself. Ultimately, the purpose of any psychotherapeutic treatment is to decrease emotional suffering and to bolster adaptive functioning. In order for confrontation of traumatic content to be beneficial rather than disruptive, PCA survivors would first need assistance in developing their capacities for productively managing distress and their abilities to cope and function effectively.

☐ The Component Skills

Having established this much, the next consideration was to identify the component skills required to productively address and come to terms with traumatic material. Gradually, it occurred to us that just as developing these skills was a prerequisite to addressing traumatic material in PCA survivors, the skills themselves could be viewed as hierarchical, forming a logical progression. Although skills earlier in the hierarchy were not always absolute prerequisites for those that followed them, they did, for one reason or another, carry a higher priority in the course of treatment. In some instances, while not entirely essential to the attainment of subsequent goals, they would make the achievement of later goals simpler or easier. In other instances, a goal may assume a higher priority than others due to its significance to the client. For example, reaching certain goals was seen as leading to more effective outcomes when placed earlier in the sequence because they increased clients' sense of hopefulness, confirmed that improvement was possible, or fueled motivation for further change. In most instances a particular goal appears in the order it does in the sequence for several of these reasons.

To be honest, both the particular elements comprising the model and their order have changed repeatedly over time as our knowledge and understanding of PCA survivors has expanded. There is no reason to assume that the goals comprising the model and the recommended sequence for addressing them will not continue to undergo refinement. In the final analysis, appreciating and understanding the rationale underlying the sequence is considerably more important than memorizing it or adhering to it in a rote manner. It is the conceptual framework that ultimately guides the treatment process, rather than any particular order of goal setting and attainment. What appears below, therefore, is the most current version of what should be considered an evolving paradigm.

Managing and Modulating Distress

The highest priority in the sequence of goals is helping the client to learn to tolerate, manage and reduce her or his level of distress. As long as clients are restricted by anxious avoidance, paralyzed by the hopelessness and despair of depression, or distracted by the torment of other forms of distress, their ability to concentrate on and work productively and consistently toward subsequent goals will be severely limited. Conversely, relief from emotional distress provides palpable evidence that change is possible and constitutes a potent incentive to persevere in treatment. In the face of the intense affect that traumatic material can arouse, it is essential to have the ability to modulate and channel emotional reactions. More generally, proficiency in the management of affect allows the development of the capacity for cognitive processing to benefit from the information provided by feelings, without allowing judgement and reasoning to be overpowered by the immediacy or intensity of emotion.

Fostering Experiential Presence and Continuity

Dissociative experiences are a common complaint of PCA survivors (Anderson, Yasenik, & Ross, 1993; Chu & Dill, 1990; Kluft, 1990). While there is a range of phenomena subsumed under the term "dissociation" (American Psychiatric Association, 1994; Phillips & Frederick, 1995)—such as amnesia, depersonalization and derealization (feeling that oneself and one's surroundings are unreal or dreamlike), and identity fragmentation (lack of a cohesive sense of self)—the common core of these experiences appears to be dissociative absorption (Ross, Ellason, & Anderson, 1995; Ross, Joshi, & Currie, 1991; Sanders & Green, 1994). Dissociative absorption consists of becoming so immersed in flashbacks or other inner experiences that awareness of one's immediate surroundings becomes tenuous or, in extreme instances, may be entirely lost for the moment. Dissociative absorption, as distinguished from focused concentration, becomes problematic (i.e., "pathological") when it is not entirely under volition or control. The person experiencing it is drawn into the experience without freely electing to focus on it, and to a significant extent cannot readily opt to shift her or his attention back to the here and now.

Dissociation is commonly construed as being triggered by and as a mechanism for avoiding the discomfort of anxiety (Cardeña, 1994). In effect, dissociative absorption and other dissociative experiences can occur automatically, in a way that can be conceptualized as conditioned responses to anxiety. Reports by dissociative clients suggest that these states, which originally may have been elicited by traumatic experiences or other extreme circumstances, can generalize over time, so that they gradually come to be triggered by progressively less extreme cues. It follows from this supposition that interventions that successfully reduce anxiety can be expected to concomitantly yield a diminution in the intensity and frequency of dissociative experiences. Therefore, when distress management is established as the first priority of therapy, gains can already be expected to have been made in moderating dissociation even before it is expressly addressed as a treatment goal in its own right. Conversely, in the absence of the capability to moderate anxious feelings, it is unlikely that much progress can be expected to occur toward gaining control over dissociative processes.

Once a client has developed a degree of proficiency in managing distress, she or he can learn to acquire greater levels of control over dissociative reactions. As the ability to modulate dissociative phenomena evolves, it becomes increasingly feasible to cultivate the capacities for recall of both recent and remote events, for perception of continuity of experience, and for a sense of cohesiveness of identity. With the acquisition of these faculties it becomes more and more feasible for the client to learn to direct and regulate attention and concentration.

Learning to Exercise Judgment and Critical Thinking

As a result of having grown up in a family context that was not equipped to provide them with adequate learning experiences, many PCA survivors manifest relatively fundamental cognitive difficulties. While it is frequently true that the content of their cognition is distorted and faulty, they also often have significant deficits in the underlying cognitive processes and strategies required for the exercise of sound reasoning. Once a degree of control over dissociative reactions is established, allowing for greater regulation of attention and concentration, it becomes much more feasible to work productively on other, more complex areas of cognitive functioning. This is the rationale for making the establishment of the ability to maintain focused concentration by learning to regulate dissociative processes a higher priority than that of developing the capacity for effective reasoning.

Growing up in a chaotic, controlling, ineffective family environment affects cognitive functioning in at least two major respects. The most obvious of the two is in the content of thought. While overt abuse experiences engenders faulty convictions about self, others, and the world (Janoff-Bulman, 1992), the constant distorted feedback created by growing up in an inadequte family environment may be an even more powerful contributor to these kinds of misperceptions. Erroneous negative beliefs acquired from such a family context, particularly perceptions of self, can be extremely resistent to correction, because they were often acquired through repeated exposure to the viewpoint in question from an early age.

The other major, much more fundamental way in which being reared in an ineffective family environment affects cognitive functioning is in its failure to provide adequate training in basic cognitive processes such as the exercise of effective judgement and critical reasoning skills. Although one or another factor may predominate in a particular case, the failure to develop these basic reasoning skills is often due to a combination of forces that characterize the family systems of PCA survivors: a controlling parental stance exemplified by injunctions to "do what I say . . . because I say so"; a detached parental style that does not actively teach the child basic reasoning skills; the inability of family members to actively transmit or implicitly model effective cognitive strategies because they do not possess them themselves; or some combination of these factors. Whatever the reason for the gaps in cognitive skills, it is unlikely that much progress can be expected to be made in rectifying the content of erroneous beliefs unless remedial training in these processes is made an explicit component of treatment. Within this general arena of cognitive intervention, remediating cognitive processing skills such as faulty judgement and deficient critical thinking are a higher priority than challenging specific distorted beliefs.

Breaking and Replacing Maladaptive Patterns

Some of the most salient and troublesome difficulties commonly experienced by PCA survivors consist of problematic behavior patterns that are generally classifiable as addictive or compulsive in nature. They include a wide spectrum of activities such as substance abuse, self-mutilation, eating disorders, sexually compulsive behavior, compulsive spending, or engaging in high-risk thrill-seeking ventures such as high speed driving or violent confrontations. Despite the diversity in appearance of these various maldaptive patterns, they can be construed as sharing a common function—coping with distress. They are often engaged in as an attempt to relieve painful emotional experiences by altering mood, serving as a distraction from disturbing preoccupations, supplying a (usually illusory) sense of control and prowess, or through some combination of these effects. Simultaneously, many of them represent an attempt to break through the emotional and sensory numbing symptomatic of dissociative reactions or posttraumatic stress disorder.

Many practitioners may be puzzled that these maladaptive patterns, many of which are potentially lethal or otherwise harmful, are not assigned a higher priority in the treatment model outlined here. Undoubtedly there are instances in which these behaviors must be the first priority of treatment. When a client presents with a substance abuse disorder, eating disorder, or self-injurious compulsion that is imminently life-threatening, helping her or him to break that maladaptive pattern must take precedence over any other therapeutic goal. Even if such a client were a survivor of PCA, those issues are inordinately less pressing than the dire matters of imminent endangerment raised by an addictive or compulsive process that has progressed to an extreme stage of severity. In the context of such a situation, it would be irrelevant to explore or even raise issues of PCA survivorship until considerable gains have been made toward stablization of control over the addictive or compulsive behavior. In fact, self-endangering behavior of immenently life-threatening proportions would be one of the chief contra-indicators for implementation of the treatment model presented here. For individuals whose addictive or compulsive difficulties are that prominent and extensive, those areas should be the exclusive focus of treatment. PCA survivors in this category most frequently come to the attention of mental health professionals precisely because of these severe maladaptive processes. In the early stages of their treatment for these potentially lethal behaviors, the therapy should be directed almost exclusively toward the management of these self-damaging patterns, with little or no emphasis on historical issues, including PCA.

Many PCA survivors who present for treatment manifest addictive and compulsive behavior patterns, but do not fit the above description. Instead, they typically fall into one of two other groups. One of these is comprised of individuals who have already been through extensive treatment for an addictive or compulsive problem, such as a substance use or eating disorder, and are well established in the recovery process. They are usually stable enough in recovery that they have not engaged in the problem behavior for quite a while, and they are justifiably confident that they are in little or no danger of relapsing into active addiction or compulsivity. However, as the struggle to avoid indulging in the maladaptive behavior subsides, they become increasingly cognizant of other problems in functioning. Previously, they may have thought of these other difficulties as secondary consequences of substance abuse or other addictive or compulsive activities. However, as their period of abstinence from engaging in addiction or compulsion lengthens, it becomes progressively clearer that their more pervasive difficulties in daily living have not substantially diminished. By the time they enter treatment for these latter problems, they are often at least dimly aware that these problems are related to the elements of abuse, chaos, and deprivation that characterize their personal history. Although their primary addiction or compulsion may be under control, often there are other maladaptive patterns that they continue to indulge in as a means of managing distress.

A second category of PCA survivors may never have relied extensively on any particular addictive or compulsive pattern. Rather, individuals in this group tend to invoke a variety of such behaviors, either simultaneously or serially, in an effort to manage and soothe the more or less constant distress that they experience. As a result of the diversity of malaptive strategies they use, no single one may have progressed to a sufficiently high level of intensity to prompt them to seek treatment for it. Individuals in this group are more apt to seek treatment for general problems in daily adjustment, such as difficulties in social interactions or with functioning at work, than for any of the addictive or compulsive behaviors on which they rely. Consequently, they are usually still engaging in these patterns when they enter treatment, and continue to do so to some extent through the early phases of therapy.

For individuals in these two groups, for whom maladaptive behavior patterns are not of sufficient proportions to pose an appreciable threat to physical well-being, reducing and eventually eliminating reliance on these activities is most likely to be successful once they have already made substantial progress toward managing distress, maintaining focused concentration and an experiential sense of continuity, and developing reasoning and critical thinking skills. Since the function of addictive and compulsive behaviors in PCA survivors is frequently to moderate distress, having other means of accomplishing this at their disposal makes it more feasible and palatable for them to consider relinquishing these maladaptive patterns. With the establishment of the capacity for concentration and continuity, these clients are better equipped to observe and report about the salient components of the cycles comprising their addictive and compulsive behavior patterns. Access to critical judgement and reasoning allows them to examine the elements of maladaptive behavior cycles, understand their function, and participate collaboratively with the therapist in arriving at strategies for diverting or disrupting these patterns.

Expanding Adaptive Living Skills

We now come to the crux of treatment for PCA survivors—enhancing the capacity for confronting the challenges of day-to-day living in an effective, responsible, fulfilling manner. Central to the conceptual framework underlying this treatment model is the contention that among individuals with a PCA history, difficulties in adult adjustment are largely attributable to the lacunae in learning and faulty learning of an inadequate family context, rather than solely to the disruptive impact of abuse trauma. It needs to be remembered that this is a system of priorities, rather than a sequence of stages. Thus, higher priorities in the model—managing distress, maintaining concentration and continuity, augmenting the capacity for critical reasoning, and breaking maladaptive patterns—are not prerequisites for an explicit focus on remediating gaps in adaptive living skills. To some extent, this will be a component of intervention from the outset of treatment, as challenges in functioning spontaneously come to the attention of client and practitioner.

However, intensive remediation of breaches in adaptive living skills is likely to be most effective once the previously discussed priorities are soundly in place. This is not primarily a question of necessity, but rather one of practicality, economy and efficiency. As long as distress, distractedness, clouded judgement and reasoning skills, and maladaptive behavior patterns are prominent features of the client's functioning, they are likely to interfere with her or his ability to adequately attend to, comprehend, and benefit from extensive training in daily-living skills. The degree to which these other capacities are in place, however, is that to which client and therapist are afforded the "luxury" of concentrating productively on remediating these areas.

The scope of abilities I have in mind when I refer to adaptive living skills is a diverse one, varying widely in content and specificity. The spectrum of capabilities ranges from concrete and practical issues such as how to balance a checkbook, obtain telephone service, or practice dental hygiene, to ones as broad and abstract as how to establish an intimate relationship, maintain stable work productivity and employment, or sustain a comfortable, effective, and gratifying balance among diverse components of one's life structure. In actuality, the more concrete instances of these life skills are more easily acquired than the relatively abstract ones, so that mastery of the latter group of abilities becomes increasingly viable as treatment progresses.

Resolving Trauma

Once substantial progress has been made toward the attainment of the previous five prioritized goals, the PCA survivor client can be considered to be adequately prepared to productively confront and come to terms with the traumatic material comprising her or his abusive experiences. A key assumption of this model is that it is precisely the capacities represented by these five therapeutic goals that differentiate the PCA survivor from the survivor of exposure to a single, circumscribed traumatic event in adulthood. Alternately stated, the lack of these five capacities can in large part be construed as encompassing the distinction between "simple" posttraumatic stress disorder and complex PTSD. My contention is that until appreciable gains have been secured in the goals constituting the first five priorities in this treatment model, trauma-focused interventions have a high probability of leading to decompensation rather than to resolution.

The placement of trauma resolution at the bottom of the inventory of priorities highlights the extent to which the contextual model of psychotherapy for PCA survivors presented here deviates from other forms of treatment for this population. Rather than being the centerpiece of treatment, confrontation of traumatic material is a relatively peripheral concern. In some cases it constitutes a footnote or afterthought. For many PCA survivors who have secured substantial progress toward the four highest priorities in the treatment model, direct exposure to traumatic material will simply be irrelevant and unnecessary. Not only will their posttraumatic symptomatology be considerably diminished once this point is reached, but daily life will no longer seem tainted and overshadowed by the past hardships that previously seemed so pervasive and insurmountable.

ACQUIRING TOOLS FOR DAILY LIVING: THE STRUCTURE OF THE THERAPEUTIC PROCESS

This section delineates the set of prioritized goals that serves to organize the treatment process in the family/social context approach to treating adult survivors of prolonged child abuse. Specific strategies for achieving the components of each of the prioritized goals are also delineated. The overriding objective of this form of treatment is teaching clients adaptive living skills for moderating distress and enhancing daily functioning. Extensive processing of past traumatic incidents is attempted only if there are clear indications that doing so will advance the primary aim of bolstering adjustment in the here and now. A primary focus on the mastery of strategies for effective adult functioning that were not adequately transmitted in the family of origin can foster profound improvements in the quality of daily living for survivors of prolonged child abuse.

10
CHAPTER

Security: Managing and Modulating Distress

The frame of a building delineates its structure. It comprises such an integral component of the whole that buildings are often referred to as "structures." The frame is so salient, essential, and defining that it is the major element represented in a building's blueprint or layout; it is the feature of that most readily lends itself to depiction. However, although it lends coherence and order to the finished product, the frame is by no means equivalent to the building as a whole.

The framework of prioritized treatment goals delineated in this section is analogous in this respect to the frame of a building. It lends structure to the therapy, organizing the numerous, diverse components of treatment and providing them with coherence and direction. Like the frame of a house, this structural element is a defining feature of contextual therapy. The objectives, skills, and particular intervention skills comprising the structure are the aspects of contextual therapy that are the easiest to depict and convey. They are, however, by no means the totality of the contextual approach.

Contextual therapy is conceptually driven, rather than protocol-driven. Construing the difficulties of PCA survivors as resulting not only from abuse trauma but also from a deficient family background illuminates the need to make remedial skills training a central element of intervention. However, the ineffective family environments that many PCA survivors were reared in, in addition to failing to transmit discrete skills, also frequently result in faulty interpersonal attachment and a pervasively detrimental system of beliefs. Consequently, the reader will be misled if she or he equates contextual treatment with the specifics covered in this section, allowing them to eclipse concern with the issues of fostering the therapeutic relationship and collaboratively developing a conceptual framework discussed in the previous section. The therapeutic relationship in contextual treatment is not merely the medium through which interventions occur, but in itself an important corrective for the attachment difficulties experienced by the survivor. Similarly, in this form of therapy, conceptualization refers not merely to the practitioner's formulation of the origins and causes that guide intervention, but just as importantly to the client's evolving understanding that rectifies the misconceptions about self and others that were created by growing up with abuse and in an ineffective family environment.

Consequently, the reader should keep in mind, while absorbing the particular strategies for teaching the adaptive living skills described in the ensuing chapters, that this represents only one of three intersecting components that comprise contextual therapy. These three interconnected aspects of the treatment model—the interpersonal context, the conceptual context, and the practical context—are depicted in Figure 3. The interpersonal context consists of the collaboration between client and therapist in the formation of a working relationship that gradually allows the client to transcend the opposing counter-productive pulls of mistrust and dependency. The conceptual context refers to the development by the

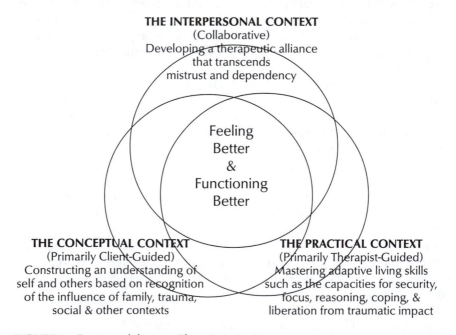

THE INTERPERSONAL CONTEXT
(Collaborative)
Developing a therapeutic alliance
that transcends
mistrust and dependency

Feeling
Better
&
Functioning
Better

THE CONCEPTUAL CONTEXT
(Primarily Client-Guided)
Constructing an understanding of
self and others based on recognition
of the influence of family, trauma,
social & other contexts

THE PRACTICAL CONTEXT
(Primarily Therapist-Guided)
Mastering adaptive living skills
such as the capacities for security,
focus, reasoning, coping, &
liberation from traumatic impact

FIGURE 3. Contextual therapy: Three intersecting components.

client, mainly under her or his own direction, of an understanding of self and others that is informed by a growing understanding of how the contexts of family, trauma, society, and other influences have contributed to and maintain problems in living. The practical context is composed of the acquisition of those adaptive living skills that were not adequately transmitted by the client's family of origin or other socializing agents. The client's acquisition of these capacities occurs largely under the guidance of the therapist via instruction in particular methods and strategies for exercising more effective functioning. The therapist's attempts to teach the skills that comprise the practical context will be rendered ineffective if they are divorced from the interpersonal and conceptual contexts. In order for efforts to transmit these daily living skills to be effective, there must be, in each session, a constant shifting and interplay between these three interacting contexts. In fact, if one of these realms is more central and essential than the other two, it is the interpersonal context.

☐ The Collaborative Alliance: A Higher Priority Than Treatment Goals

The concrete, pragmatic component of goal attainment can only be expected to lead to effective outcomes if it is balanced against and embedded in attentiveness to the interpersonal context of therapy. Just as the failure to acquire effective living skills in a client's formative years is attributable to inadequacies in the interpersonal context of the family and the larger society, the remediation of those deficits depends to a great extent on the development and maintenance of an emotional connection and collaborative alliance with the therapist. Growing up in a deficient family and social context often deprives PCA survivors not only of the opportunity to learn and master daily-living skills, but also to experience a sense of belonging and of affiliation with others. For many survivors, especially those with the most extreme histories of maltreatment and deprivation, the gnawing loneliness and sense of desolation bred by the absence of stable interpersonal attachments will make this a much more salient and compelling concern than their deficient instrumental skills.

Particularly at the outset therefore, but to some degree throughout the course of treatment, it is essential that the clinician pay explicit attention to monitoring and facilitating the development of the collaborative elements of the therapeutic alliance. Initially it is here, rather than on goal-directed priorities, that the primary focus must be placed. Whether by virtue of previous therapy, fortuitously salubrious interpersonal connections forged in everyday life, or a high degree of personal endowment and resiliency, some PCA survivors will be able, fairly early in treatment, to engage with the clinician in productive, goal-oriented efforts. In these cases, effective work on the first of the prioritized goals, managing distress, may be initiated within the first few sessions of treatment. In other instances, however, it may be as long as several months before this or any other of the prioritized treatment goals can be consistently and productively addressed. In working with the latter category of clients the practitioner will need to be particularly mindful of the nuances of the therapeutic relationship. The more strongly a PCA survivor's interpersonal style reflects the conflicting forces of mistrust and dependency, the more attentive the clinician will need to be in developing the type of cooperative alliance that is conducive to the constructive pursuit of treatment objectives. The more careful the practitioner is to nurture the establishment of a productive working relationship with the client in the earliest phases of therapy, the more effective and efficient the remaining course of treatment is likely to be.

If one does not immediately begin to work on prioritized treatment goals, then exactly how does one proceed? How does the clinician help the PCA survivor to develop the sufficient sense of trust and security in the therapeutic relationship needed to engage in and benefit from goal-directed intervention? One facilitates this process in a number of related ways, most notably:

- by providing a forum for the expression of what is important and meaningful to her or him;
- by listening and attending, thereby implicitly validating the value of what she or he has to say;
- by encouraging the identification and expression of feelings;
- by providing the opportunity to sort out, make sense of, and gain some perspective on his or her life experiences.

Throughout contextual treatment, however, interventions aimed at fostering attainment of the skills comprising prioritized treatment goals are interwoven and integrated with conceptualization of contextual issues and development of the collaborative alliance. Careful review will show that the transcript of Rick's therapy session presented in Chapter 3 embodies all three of these aspects of contextual treatment. Rick explores the ways in which the dual contexts of his family of origin environment and childhood molestation have influenced his current functioning, perceptions, and feelings. Doing so provides him with the opportunity to develop and practice his capacities for critical judgement and reasoning (skills acquisition). Furthermore, the formulation he arrives at provides him with a new understanding of his past history and its impact on his present functioning, allowing him in the process to correct some of his previously erroneous conclusions and forming the foundation of an alternative way of perceiving himself (conceptualization). In the process he begins to gradually come to understand that what he previously assumed constituted evidence of inherrent personal weakness may actually be attributable to the impact of external circumstances, most notably abuse trauma and an inadequate family environment. Finally, by doing this within the interpersonal framework of the support and validation of, and empathic connection with his therapist, Rick simultaneously is exposed to experiences that will foster the development of new capacities for relating and attachment (collaborative alliance).

Establishment of a strong therapeutic alliance, in addition to being a prerequisite of cooperative goal-directed treatment, is a powerful medium for correcting many of the PCA survivor's misconceptions about interpersonal relating. The dual influences of overt abuse and inadequate family environment often engender deeply entrenched conclusions that others will find one reprehensible, can be expected to be unresponsive and rejecting, and are motivated by self-serving and exploitive intentions. Convictions of this type, particularly because they are based on extensive, compelling, and extremely painful direct interpersonal experience, are unlikely to be decisively impacted by the force of logical verbal arguments, and may even persist in the face of observable countervailing evidence. Due to these convictions, coupled with the intense pain aroused by a sense of being alone and outcast, some individuals with a PCA history will initially be too consumed by the opposing pulls of mistrust of and dependency on the clinician to maintain a productive focus on attaining therapeutic goals. It is often only gradually, through consistent interaction marked by nonjudgmental acceptance, compassion, and integrity on the part of the clinician, that these deeply rooted beliefs begin to erode.

However, it is vital to acknowledge that the creation of a collaborative therapeutic alliance is a necessary but not sufficient condition for resolution of the PCA survivor's difficulties. It may, at times, appear that all or most of the survivor's problems will remit in response to the consistency of an empathic connection with the clinician. This is a grave misconception that can lead to serious errors in the way treatment for this population is conducted. Although a strong collaborative alliance is an indispensable precondition for effective intervention, it can not be relied on to operate as the major source of therapeutic change.

☐ The Relation Between the Therapeutic Alliance and Distress Reduction

The first of the priorities in the contextual treatment model for PCA survivors presented here, managing distress, is particularly well-suited for illustrating and clarifying the distinction between the need for a resilient therapeutic alliance as a prerequisite for productive intervention and the limitations of the therapeutic relationship as a mechanism of enduring change. Undeniably, the security fostered by a responsive practitioner frequently has a profound, immediate effect on the client's sense of well-being, appreciably reducing her or his level of distress. Due to the neglect, rejection, and abandonment experienced in her or his family-of-origin environment and frequently in subsequent relationships as well, the survivor client may react with an intense sense of relief and gratitude to simply being consistently attended to and empathically understood by the therapist. The profound pull of years of accumulated dependent yearning fueled by emotional deprivation may make it tempting for the PCA survivor to avoid the practitioner's efforts to promote self-sufficiency in order to linger in the comfort of a sense of connection. Many survivor clients believe that the establishment of the capacity for independent functioning will lead, once again, to being abandoned. Some of them will overtly voice a fear of achieving their treatment goals, due to the conviction that this will result in the loss of the therapeutic relationship.

Nevertheless, as potent as the relief provided by the therapeutic relationship may seem initially, it is inevitably tenuous and transitory. It does not reflect the client's attainment of an enduring ability to modulate distress independent of continued interaction with the clinician. From the beginning of treatment, therefore, the clinician needs to monitor the balance between the supportive and the instrumental components of the collaborative alliance. Without some degree of predictability and security in the therapeutic relationship, the PCA survivor client will remain too agitated to focus productively on goal attainment. Conversely, if the client becomes too reliant upon and complacent about the soothing qualities of the connection with the practitioner, she or he will experience little incentive to develop the capacities for self-sufficiency represented by attainment of the prioritized treatment goals.

Let us consider how maintaining an adequate equilibrium between the reassuring and motivating facets of the therapeutic alliance applies, for example, to helping the client to master the skills necessary for productively managing distress. To a greater or lesser extent, most PCA clients will enter therapy with appreciable levels of both depression and anxiety (Briere & Runtz, 1988a; Herman, 1992b), usually of a more or less chronic nature. Regardless of the degree to which anxiety or depression predominate in the clinical picture, however, it is not uncommon that, even in the absence of purposeful intervention, diminution of levels of both forms of distress will occur, seemingly spontaneously, in the early phases of treatment. Undoubtedly, this in itself is not a phenomenon exclusive to PCA survivors. Due to the hope, reassurance, and soothing engendered by forming a cooperative alliance with the practitioner, many types of therapy clients experience a reduction in distress fairly early in treatment.

What distinguishes some individuals with a PCA history from other clients is their reaction to the relief from distress that they experience in response to engagement with an accepting and understanding practitioner. While other individuals will often spontaneously build on the relief they experience by working toward becoming more emotionally and behaviorally independent of the therapist, survivor clients are often inclined to respond very differently. Particularly at the beginning of treatment, as they become less depressed and anxious, they may grow more emotionally attached to and behaviorally reliant upon the clinician. The most common and least intense example of this consists of seeking reassurance and soothing from the therapist in session, while refusing to or simply failing to carry out suggestions for self-soothing between sessions. Somewhat more overt examples include reports of frequently thinking and fantasizing about the therapist, voicing the wish that the therapist could be constantly present in their everyday life, and expressing discomfort about the span of time between sessions. In the most extreme instances, this sub-group of PCA clients may implore the practitioner to increase the length or frequency of sessions, or may repeatedly seek out contact between sessions. If these reactions are left unchecked, they may rapidly lead to an apparent precipitous decrease in level of functioning and the proliferation of crisis situations that purportedly demand the attention of the therapist.

These responses on the part of certain PCA survivors probably reflect their conviction of their own ineptitude. They often indicate an implicit assumption that any improvement must be largely or wholly attributable to the agency of the practitioner rather than to her or his own capability for change. Based on numerous unfortunate past interpersonal experiences, reactions such as these are often also linked to the association of the establishment of behavioral self-sufficiency with emotional and interpersonal desertion. The more ingrained these convictions remain, the more likely the survivor is to cling tenaciously to the therapeutic relationship, while avoiding taking the steps needed to develop the capacity for independent functioning.

☐ The Transition From Relationship Building to Goal-Oriented Collaboration

The clinician's failure to recognize these powerful influences will, obviously, result in therapy which is chaotic, counter-productive, and ultimately frustrating and emotionally depleting for both parties involved. Even with an awareness of the possible presence of these trends, the practitioner may be perplexed as to how to manage them in a way that will promote the development of a productive therapeutic alliance. The key to effectively containing, counteracting, and eventually eliminating these tendencies is to structure one's interactions with the client in a way that deliberately reinforces competency rather than unwittingly encouraging the client's sense of inadequacy and neediness. This approach, extrapolated from the work of Linehan (1993) on treating individuals with borderline personality disorder, consists of making continued or expanded contact with the practitioner contingent upon productive engagement in and use of therapy, instead of increasing its availability in response to decompensation and crises. Linehan cogently described the rationale behind this strategy:

> As soon as the relationship is established, the therapist begins to communicate to the patient that the rules have changed. Whereas the patient might have believed previously that if she got better she would lose the therapist, she is now told that if she does not improve she will lose the therapist more quickly. (p. 98)

Increasing the frequency of individual therapy sessions beyond once a week, for example, if it occurs at all, should be instituted not in reaction to feelings of desperation and disorganized behavior, but only in response to consistent and sustained indications of improvement, signaling readiness to accelerate progress. Similarly, it has been our experience at the Trauma Resolution Integration Program (TRIP) that crises are considerably less likely to occur when it is established that someone other than the primary therapist, and ideally someone outside the primary treating agency such as a hotline or hospital emergency room, is to be contacted to respond to them. I strongly suspect that this is because the soothing, reassuring, and distress-reducing effects of contact with the therapist constitute a subtle inducement for the client to "fall apart." I do believe that in most instances this is a conditioned and unintentional response on the part of the client (cf. the discussion of "manipulation" in Linehan, 1993). We have observed at TRIP that when clients know that someone other than their primary therapist is to be contacted to respond to between-session crises, such situations either dramatically decrease in frequency or cease entirely, and overall client functioning improves rather than deteriorates.

These principles point to two major complementary implications regarding management of the therapeutic alliance in the initiation and execution of the first of the prioritized treatment goals, distress reduction. The first of these two tenets is that explicit attempts to teach distress modulation skills should only be attempted once the practitioner is convinced that the client is ready. This means that she or he has established a sufficient sense of confidence in the stability and reliability of the therapeutic relationship to be able to productively engage in goal-oriented endeavors. The other tenet is to select and structure the introduction of the particular methods of distress management employed in a way that is appropriately matched to the degree of self-sufficiency the client is able to tolerate.

☐ Facilitating Self-Sufficient Problem Resolution

To illustrate the latter point, let us specifically consider the utilization of anxiety reduction techniques. A conceptual framework that takes into account the interplay between distress reduction and the therapeutic alliance underscores the idea that the primary objective is not to decrease the client's anxiety, but to teach the client how to decrease her or his own anxiety. In the face of the immediate urgency of a client's intense emotional pain it is easy for practitioners to lose sight of this distinction. However, in the long run, therapists do a grievous disservice when they rely excessively on trying to remove distress directly rather than facilitating development of the client's capacity to do this for her- or himself. Consequently, when working with PCA survivors it is particularly important to be familiar with a range of methods of anxiety management, and to be cognizant of the ways in which each of them entails reliance on the clinician or promotion of client self-sufficiency. Early in treatment, some clients with a PCA history may legitimately need relaxation techniques that involve some level of dependence on the therapist's direct, indirect, or symbolic assistance. For example, some survivors' concentration will be too impaired to allow them to successfully execute anxiety reduction methods that depend on focused or sustained attention to self-generated stimuli such as visual imagery. Others may be so certain that they are incapable of mastering new tasks that they may not even attempt to learn a relaxation technique. Similarly, some PCA clients may not believe that self-soothing is possible, and may therefore only be willing to put credence in the efficacy of approaches executed by the practitioner.

The clinician, therefore, needs to assess the extent to which it is feasible for a particular PCA survivor client to employ methods that are primarily carried out independently, or whether she or he will initially need techniques that are to some degree initiated or executed by the therapist. Moreover, the practitioner will want to approach the intervention in a way that anticipates increasingly shifting control over implementation of anxiety reduction to the client. From the outset, therefore, the client's reliance on the therapist is used as a conduit toward and reinforcer of client accountability, efficacy, and self-sufficiency. For instance, due to impaired concentration, lack of belief in their own efficacy, or skepticism about the feasibility of self-soothing, some PCA survivor clients may reasonably need an imagery-based relaxation method to be audiotaped by the practitioner for her or him listen to between sessions. Many clients in this category will also prefer this sort of method because access to the clinician's voice provides a sense of continuity with and connection to the therapeutic bond. The risk in this sort of approach is that it may foster both emotional and instrumental dependency on the practitioner, thereby restricting the impetus toward self-sufficiency.

In cases such as these, the most tenable solution is not to deprive the client of the soothing provided by audio-taped relaxation imagery. While selection of the particular type of relaxation technique used is a key consideration, the way in which it is implemented is at least equally important. The practitioner needs to structure the introduction and use of the anxiety-reduction method in a way that fosters the collaborative aspects of the therapeutic relationship while maximizing the client's level of involvement, ownership, and accountability in the construction and use of the tape. For example, when using a method involving taped imagery, the therapist should avoid presenting the client with a ready-made tape, taping a preexisting "script," or making a recording consisting of imagery which the therapist assumes the client will find soothing. Rather, the clinician should discuss the possiblity of using a relaxation tape and the client's interest in and willingness to employ such a method before proceeding. If it is agreed upon that a tape will be used, the particular imagery adopted should, to the greatest extent possible, come from the client. This requires detailed interviewing to identify cues in the form of people, objects, situations, and settings that the client associates with a personal sense of security and calmness. The client should then be encouraged, to whatever degree she or he is capable, to collaborate with the therapist in the development of the integration and sequencing of these elements into the scenario or "script" to be taped. It can be anticipated that at least one full session will be needed to adequately complete these phases before the actual taping. Similarly, at least one additional session should be set aside for the actual taping of the scenario, with a debriefing afterward in which the responses elicited by the imagery are processed with the client. In some cases, this feedback may lead to a mutual decision to modify and re-record the script in order to augment its effectiveness and to eliminate any cues or wording which the client found to be discordant or disturbing.

☐ The Importance of Practice and Accountability

Once the tape has been completed, its utility will hinge largely on explicit agreements about how it will be used. This topic presents an opportunity for the practitioner to employ the client's reliance on the therapeutic relationship as a motivator for adherence to a mutually agreed upon plan of action. Through the mechanism of accountability, the client's compliance with such a strategy can constitute an initial step toward greater autonomy and self-efficacy. Just about any sort of therapy derives some of its effectiveness from a sense of accountability to the clinician, as an outside party, and is not likely to exist if one has to answer only to oneself. It is for this reason that people are likely to think about and discuss matters with a therapist that they may not be moved to examine independently. An important step toward promoting self-sufficiency in anxiety management, therefore, is to make use of the leverage represented by this sense of accountability by having clients keep written records of their use of relaxation techniques to review with the therapist in session. One of the intrinsic advantages of this procedure is that it helps to make the expectation explicit that the technique be practiced and mastered, rather than used merely when needed. Another advantage is that record keeping of this type, while initially requested by the therapist, often becomes directly reinforcing to the client. The visible record of the accomplishment of consistent practice and of the resulting progress becomes a source of reinforcement in itself. As a consequence, what might have initially been engaged in out of a sense of accountability to the practitioner is often persisted in out of a growing sense of accountability toward oneself.

For this reason, at TRIP we routinely provide clients with a log sheet on which they are instructed to record their level of anxiety before and after each instance of practicing the relaxation technique (see Figure 4). This is done regardless of the specific anxiety reduction method being employed. Clients using an audiotape of relaxation imagery, for example, are told to record their distress level before and after listening to it, in the same way that they would be instructed if they were using a more autonomous, self-guided approach.

Anxiety levels are recorded using a Subjective Units of Distress (SUD; Wolpe, 1969) scale. Clients are instructed to rate their level of anxiety on a scale of either zero to ten or zero to 100, with zero indicating the complete absence of anxiety and ten (or 100), representing "the most anxious you have ever felt." The client records her or his SUD level, using the zero to ten scale, on the log sheet immediately before and following each instance of practice. Inspection of the log form will show that it is set up to accommodate up to three practice periods each day. In most instances we will instruct the client to consistently practice at least twice a day: upon awakening (while preparing for the day's activities), and in the evening (shortly before retiring). Frequently, especially when the client is not employed outside the home or otherwise engaged in a daily routine that

<u>Instructions</u>: Use the scale pictured below to show, from 0 (completely calm) to 10 (the most nervous you've ever felt) how you are feeling. In the "before" column, write down a number from 0 to 10 showing how you are feeling before you practice the exercise. Then do the exercise for several minutes, and write down in the "after" column where the number is when you are done.

◄──►

0   1   2   3   4   5   6   7   8   9   10

Calm   Anxious

DAY/DATE	AWAKENING (0-10) BEFORE	AFTER	MIDDAY (0-10) BEFORE	AFTER	BEDTIME (0-10) BEFORE	AFTER

FIGURE 4. Practice Record Sheet

occupies her or his waking hours, we will suggest a third practice session during the day.

We emphasize that practice is to be conducted at these preestablished times each day *regardless of whether a particular need to relax on any given occasion is experienced.* Usually, we will take some time to provide a detailed rationale for this directive, to maximize the likelihood that clients understand its purpose and importance. This provides the opportunity to make it explicit that the ultimate objective of this exercise is not merely to experience momentary relief from anxiety, but *to develop the capacity to modulate and reduce anxiety levels.* While clients are assured that they may make use of the anxiety reduction technique(s) they are learning when-ever they feel a need to, it is stressed that *in addition*, they are to practice these method(s) the agreed upon number of times a day at the prear-ranged periods. The metaphor we usually employ to explain this injunc-tion is that of a fire drill:

> The optimal time to conduct a fire drill is not once a fire breaks out. A fire drill is most effective when there is no fire, so that practice can occur with-out the distraction and urgency of an immediate emergency. Practice in addressing a stressful situation is most likely to be effective and to lead to mastery of the skill involved when it occurs in the absence of the circum-stances it is designed to address.

Introduction to the practice and recording procedure also presents an opportunity to describe the anticipated sequence of increased self-reli-ance in executing relaxation procedures:

> Of course, as with any skill, there will come a time when practice is no longer necessary. This may be difficult to imagine right now, but eventu-ally you will be able to achieve the same effect without having to system-atically execute the relaxation technique [e.g., listen to the tape; call up that image; do that deep breathing exercise]. There will come a time when that response will be so second nature that you will be able to draw upon it without using the procedure you just learned. The key to reaching that point, however, is to consistently practice the technique at regularly sched-uled times.

In this way the technique initially provided, even though it may entail some degree of dependence (upon the practitioner, upon certain instru-mentation such as a tape and tape player, or upon a specific procedure) is framed from the outset as merely comprising a rudimentary stepping-stone toward autonomous self-soothing. As a result, incremental gains in the ability to modulate and reduce anxiety are experienced by the client not only as a welcome relief from the oppressive and constricting conse-quences of distress, but also as implicit evidence of self-efficacy. Therapy conducted in this manner subtly but profoundly contradicts the client's previously held convictions of incompetency and of the hopelessness of her or his situation.

The data provided by the rating form yield several useful types of infor-mation. The most obvious of these is the effectiveness of the relaxation technique being used, assessed by comparing the "before" and "after" rat-ings of each instance of practice. One can examine whether the "after" ratings are consistently lower than the "before" ratings, and if so, what the magnitude of the difference between ratings is and how consistently this magnitude is achieved. In addition, by comparing the "before" rat-ings down the column, one can evaluate whether the client's baseline level of distress is decreasing and if so, at what rate. Similarly, comparing the "after" ratings down the column can help one determine whether relaxation attained with ongoing practice is increasing (as reflected in progressively lower "after" ratings). Finally, comparison of "before" column ratings for different practice times can help to clarify whether a client's baseline level of distress consistently differs at these different times of day. If a consistent pattern is found, the client and therapist should explore further what may account for these differences, in order to identify and address the factors that contribute to higher levels of anxiety at certain times of day. The same logging form and procedure is used regardless of the particular method of distress reduction being practiced.

Once those clients who started out with an audio-taped relaxation technique master it well enough to become less reliant on an external stimulus, they should be introduced to a more autonomously executed method. Although initially such clients may need to depend primarily on the therapist to create the relaxation imagery, a transitional step toward more independent control over relaxation can eventually be implemented. For example, a new tape can be constructed using imagery that is collaboratively composed with greater input from the client.

For the large number of PCA survivor clients entering therapy whose capacity for concentration is adequate enough that the external guidance of an audio-tape is not necessary, a "safe place" imagery technique is frequently a highly effective means of relaxation. One tremendous advantage of this approach, for those clients who are capable of productively using it, is that it produces a much higher sense of self-efficacy and empowerment than does reliance on audio-taped relaxation imagery. This is because the initial formation of the imagery itself is largely under the direction of the client, and because during practice the imagery is independently evoked by the client without reliance on an audio-tape.

The safe-place imagery method we employ at TRIP is a modification of a procedure described by Shapiro (1995). (In contrast to Shapiro's version, and other variations, we do not include the use of eye-movements.) We begin by describing the zero to ten SUD scale to the client, if it has not been used previously in treatment, and asking, "where on that scale are you right now?" Having obtained an initial SUD level, we then request that the client think of the place where she or he would feel the most relaxed (or "safe," "secure," "calm," "at peace," "at ease," or "tension-free," depending on the terminology that the client uses spontaneously). We usually assure the client that the place she or he chooses can be one "where you have always wanted to visit but to which you have never been," and that "it can even be an imaginary place." This stipulation is included because some PCA survivors with particularly severe, violent, and pervasive histories of trauma have difficulty imagining that they could feel safe or at ease in any real-world locale. Some clients in this category, however, have been able to benefit from this technique by initially imagining themselves in a fantasized setting such as deep space, far from any other living creature or in a specially constructed, bullet- and explosive-proof building.

Once the client has identified a safe place, we ask her or him to "look around and describe what you see." We encourage the client to identify as many visual cues as possible, usually immediately repeating each back to her or him. The repetition acts to subtly prompt additional responses from the client, while helping the therapist to remember each of the visual elements generated by the client. Once it is clear that the client can not think of any additional visual clues, we ask, "and while you are there in that place, what do you hear?" Once again, we encourage the client to produce as many auditory cues as possible, repeating each response out loud. The same procedure is replicated to generate any olfactory ("what scents or aromas do you notice while you are there?") and tactile ("what sensations do you notice on your skin?") cues. Throughout this phase of the process, the practitioner needs to make an effort to remember as many of the cues from all of the sensory modalities covered as possible.

Once the visual, auditory, olfactory, and tactile cues have been generated, we sometimes ask the client, especially if she or he appears visibly more relaxed at this point, "where are you on that scale now?" This demonstrates that without any effort or even the intention of accomplishing anything, a noticeable drop in tension level has occurred merely by describing and thinking about the chosen safe place. Whether or not we ask for a SUD rating at this juncture, we proceed by saying, "Now, I'd like you to make that place as vivid as you possibly can. Look at the . . . " We then enumerate in turn as many of the visual, auditory, olfactory, and tactile cues as we can recall. Once this is done, we clarify by saying, "in other words, I'd like you to create as realistic a three dimensional, technicolor, surround-sound, virtual reality reproduction of that place as you can . . . Let me know when you have it as clear as you can make it." It is usually only a few seconds before the client indicates that she or he has accomplished this. We then ask for a SUD rating. If the client has made it to this part of the procedure, she or he will almost invariably report a drop in SUD level, frequently of several points. We explain to the client the importance of regularly practicing the safe place technique between sessions and introduce the Practice Record Sheet and how to use it. The ultimate aim is, with practice, to be able to evoke the response simply by thinking of the name of the chosen "safe place," without having to conjure up and focus on the related imagery.

☐ Reducing Anxiety: The Need for the Therapist to Be Familiar With a Range of Techniques

I have covered the audio-taped imagery and safe place imagery approaches in detail because these are methods that we have found at TRIP to be most effective for the majority of PCA survivor clients. However, practitioners working with this population should become familiar with and adept at a number of diverse relaxation techniques. Some people, for example, are simply unable to summon up sufficiently vivid images to generate a substantial level of relaxation. Imagery techniques belong to a large class of methods that evoke a response through the use of cognitive or mental stimulation. Certain individuals find it easier and more effective to use physical approaches that more directly target the physiological component of the relaxation response, such as breathing techniques or muscle relaxation. The therapist may be able to detect clues in the client's vocabulary or self-reports about the type of approach that is most likely to be effective for her or him. Nevertheless, it is essential to anticipate that in some instances the clinician will attempt to teach a particular relaxation technique to a client only to find that it does not yield an appreciable response for that individual. In instances such as this, in order to avoid feelings of hopelessness or failure on the part of the client, the practitioner needs to communicate calmly and confidently that there are many ways to achieve the same end, and that no one method is effective for everyone. The underlying message is that it is not a matter of whether the client can learn to self-soothe, but which particular method will work for her or him. Clearly, this will only be convincingly conveyed if the therapist has a range of relaxation techniques at her or his disposal that can readily be drawn upon.

Adequate preparation, therefore, necessitates familiarity with a range of techniques that span a variety of categories. This would include, for instance, imagery-based techniques such as autogenic training (Linden, 1990; Schultz & Luthe, 1969) and certain methods of hypnotic induction (Hammond, 1990); breathing techniques such as diaphragmatic breathing (Davis, Eshelman, & McKay, 1995); and physical techniques such as progressive muscle relaxation (PMR; Jacobson, 1938; Lehrer & Carr, 1997). An excellent comprehensive and detailed overview of all of these types of techniques can be found in Davis et al. (1995).

As diverse as these techniques are, what distinguishes them from those used in many trauma-centered approaches is that they are relaxation and deconditioning procedures rather than exposure-based methods. I have already discussed in some detail why we avoid a heavy reliance on exposure-related techniques for clients with a PCA history, particularly early in treatment; in the absence of adequate adaptive coping abilities or external supports, exposure to traumatic material will most often result in increases in distress and interference with daily functioning. Although exposure techniques are widely recognized as having been empirically demonstrated to be effective for PTSD, anxiety management techniques have similarly been shown to be effective in diminishing PTSD symptoms (Foa & Meadows, 1997). Our clinical experience at TRIP has been that distress reduction approaches are, in general, preferable to exposure methods in treating PCA survivors. Particularly early in treatment, the employment of exposure carries a high risk of resulting in destabilization and decompensation rather than leading to improvement (Gold & Brown, 1997). We believe that this is because many PCA survivors never learned the distress management and other adaptive living skills that were mastered by many survivors of single catastrophic events before the occurrence of the trauma. It has been our impression, moreover, that for many PCA survivors generalized arousal is extremely prominent both in the clinical picture and in day-to-day experience. This means that, in comparison to clients without a PCA background, many survivors have lived for many years with an extremely elevated level of anxiety. One of the implications of this observation is that their heightened arousal levels dramatically lower their thresholds for experiencing a wide range of other symptoms. These symptoms include, for instance, flashbacks of traumatic events, panic attacks, dissociative reactions, various types of self-harm, addictive patterns, and compulsive behaviors that either commonly occur in response to distress or are attempts to dampen it. Therefore, regular practice of relaxation techniques, by gradually lowering baseline arousal levels, can also help to reduce the frequency and severity of this wide range of related difficulties. In this respect, the capacity to modulate arousal is a precursor to and provides a foundation for the achievement of many other therapeutic goals later in treatment, such as modulating dissociation and decreasing reliance on addictive and compulsive behaviors.

☐ Identifying and Mobilizing Existing Skills and Resources

Formal instruction in relaxation procedures, however, is not the only means for helping PCA survivor clients to learn to manage distress. In their eagerness to be helpful, therapists can lose sight of the fact that even clients who grew up with inadequate opportunities for learning daily-living skills can be expected to have some adaptive behaviors in their repertoire that are effective means of self-soothing. We identify these strategies by asking clients to describe the activities that they enjoy and that provide them with relief when they feel stressed or tense. Some of the more common examples of such activities are: talking to a friend or relative on the telephone; taking a walk; watching television; reading a book; working on a computer; taking a drive; doing artwork or crafts; working out; doing household chores; or listening to music. The advantage of behaviors such as these is that they do not have to be learned or practiced, and the client already has firsthand experience confirming that they can be effective in relieving distress and distracting her or him from immediate concerns at least some of the time. It simply may not have occured to the client that these activities can be appropriated for this purpose. Even though they represent the capacity to self-soothe, many PCA survivors have never learned (or somehow felt that it was not allowed) to routinely or systematically apply them to this end. Moreover, many clients with a PCA history may commonly experience some level of dissociation under stress that makes it difficult for them to remember to make use of these behaviors to help calm themselves.

Consequently, once these behaviors have been identified, it is extremely useful to have the client, in session, write them down on the back of a business card, on an index card, or on a small piece of paper. This list can then be carried in the client's purse or wallet as a concrete reminder of the availability of these sources of relief. Although in the midst of anxiety or stress the client may not be able to readily recall the entries on the list, she or he can easily get into the habit of pulling out the list, scanning it, and selecting one of the activities to engage in as a means of self-soothing.

☐ Reducing Depression: Concrete Behavioral Strategies

These approaches can be effective regardless of the type of distress experienced. Posttraumatic stress disorder (PTSD), which is classified in the DSM-IV (American Psychiatric Association, 1994) as an anxiety disorder, is the diagnosis most commonly associated with PCA survivors in the minds of many professionals. Depression, however, is undoubtedly at least as prevalent a form of distress in this population as anxiety. A number of empirical studies, for instance, identify depression as a more common long-term consequence of childhood sexual abuse than PTSD (Browne & Finkelhor, 1986; Finkelhor, 1990). Moreover, several of the diagnostic criteria for PTSD, including insomnia, difficulty concentrating, irritability, and diminished interest in usual activities, overlap with those for Major Depression (American Psychiatric Association, 1994). Some experts have argued, in fact, that comorbidity patterns (Bleich, Koslowsky, Dolev, & Lerer, 1997; Deering, Glover, Ready, Eddleman, & Alarcon, 1996; Green,

Lindy, Grace, & Leonard, 1992) seem to suggest that PTSD may have more in common with depression than with anxiety (P. Resnick, personal communication, March 26, 1999). At TRIP, Major Depression is the second most common primary diagnosis after PTSD; moreover, most of our clients meet criteria for more than one diagnosis, and the most common combination of diagnoses among them is PTSD with either Major Depression or Dysthymic Disorder (Kuchinsky, 1996).

The commonly observed comorbidity of major depression and post-traumatic stress symptoms among abuse survivors, and the overlap in diagnostic criteria for these two syndromes, illustrates that often the distress of these clients is not neatly parceled into depressive and anxious components. It is not surprising, therefore, that many PCA survivors grapple with appreciable levels of both anxiety and depression. In fact, in actual clinical practice it is not unusual to observe that there is considerable coexistence and overlap of depressive and anxious symptomatology, so that the two are not clearly differentiated. This means that early in therapy, when the major focus is on the priority of helping the client learn to modulate distress, there is often a need to target both forms of dysphoria more or less simultaneously. We usually lead with relaxation techniques, in the manner previously outlined. An advantage of this strategy is that the immediate reduction in distress experienced while learning these procedures provides persuasive evidence that relief is available. This experience, in turn, helps to engender hopefulness and optimism that further changes are possible. Presenting these methods in a manner that emphasizes that the effect is under the client's control, and therefore that efficacy is contingent upon her or his active efforts, diligence, and persistence, sets an importance precedent for interventions designed to address depression.

Our initial tactics for teaching PCA survivor clients to reduce depression are primarily behavioral, rather than cognitive, in nature. As opportunities to do so present themselves in session, we certainly do employ Socratic questioning in order to encourage the examination and confrontation of erroneous beliefs. However, the combination of elevated levels of distress and deficits in judgement and reasoning skills that often exists at the outset of treatment can appreciably restrict the effectiveness of cognitive interventions. Consequently, these are approaches that we tend to employ more extensively once clients have achieved some mastery over the disruptive effects of distress and dissociation.

Early on, we rely more heavily on interventions aimed at helping the client to recognize how her or his lifestyle choices and general activity level may be creating or compounding their depressive mood and symptomatology. We examine daily patterns of behavior and habits pertaining to sleep, eating, exercise, work, socializing, and recreation. This provides an excellent opportunity to derive a detailed picture of the client's daily life. The immediate aim of this exercise is to assess the ways in which her or his lifestyle may provoke and sustain depressed mood. Simultaneously, however, it will yield more comprehensive information about the types of deficits and defects in daily-living skills that are present and will need to be targeted for remediation. In addition to its indispensable role in developing interventions, this evaluation produces valuable baseline information to be compared against subsequent changes in behavior.

We conduct this assessment by having the client verbally "walk through" a typical day, starting with awakening and her or his morning ritual. In order to be useful, the information obtained must be relatively concrete and detailed. Executing the evaluation therefore requires that the therapist be skilled at eliciting detailed responses while maintaining a sufficient degree of interpersonal connectedness with the client, to avoid sacrificing the level of rapport that has been established with her or him. This, of course, includes offering a clear rationale for the level of specificity that will be needed before beginning the inquiry. The clinician might preface the questioning, for instance, with an explanation such as the following:

> In much the same way as you are developing the ability to gain control over anxiety by practicing the relaxation technique you have learned and keeping a record of your progress, you can learn new habits to decrease depression. Without our even realizing it, when we feel depressed we often act in ways that feed the depression and keep it going. This is because depression saps motivation. When we feel depressed, we don't have much enthusiasm for doing things. It is tempting to stay at home, vegetating in front of the television, lounging in bed, or even sleeping for much of the day. That is the nature of depression. However, if you stop and think about it, if you were forced to stay in the house and forbidden to be productive, you would quickly begin to feel depressed. In other words, if we give in to it, depression is self-perpetuating. The most rapid way to combat and overcome a bout of depression is to refuse to give in to the pull to stay inactive. Even though we don't feel like doing much of anything when we're in the middle of a depression, if we get moving and get active regardless of how we feel, it won't be long before we begin feeling better. The trick is to do things whether we feel like it or not. In order to help you develop new habits that will counter-act the occurrence and continuation of depression, we need to explore in detail the current patterns of behavior that you engage in day-to-day. This will help us to identify the things you are doing now that you probably don't realize are increasing the likelihood that you will feel depressed. So, take me through your typical day [or, alternatively, "let's take yesterday as an example"]. What time do you usually wake up?

From here the therapist proceeds by asking in as much detail as possible, in chronological order, how the client spends her or his time. How does the client wake up? Does she or he use an alarm clock, routinely wake up within a given time period without the aid of an alarm, linger in bed for extended periods of time after awakening without getting out of bed? What is the first thing she or he does after getting out of bed—smoke a cigarette, make and drink one or several cups of coffee, immediately shower and dress, have breakfast? Does she or he usually eat breakfast? If not, why not? If so, what constitutes a typical breakfast meal for her or him?

As the interview continues, the clinician will want to be alert for indications of: (a) a lack of routine, structure, and planning in the day-to-day life of the client; and (b) habits or routines that foster depression, such as lingering in bed, drifting back to sleep, skipping meals, lounging around the house without showering and dressing, and avoiding contact with other people. When evidence for either of these patterns is encountered, the therapist should make a mental note of this without interrupting the interview to discuss it then and there with the client. The inquiry alone, if conducted at an adequate level of detail, can easily consume an entire therapy session. Examination of the client's daily-living patterns will be most fruitful if it is approached not as a rote checklist of items to be covered, but as a collaborative exploration between therapist and client. In the session after the inquiry is completed, the clinician can review with the client each of the areas identified in which there is either the lack of a structured routine or a pattern that is deemed to be conducive to the development or maintenance of depression. Each of these items is then considered with the client, and alternative behavior patterns are jointly negotiated. Finally, a chart is constructed: the Daily Activity Log, on which execution of these new behaviors can be recorded. One such log is presented in Figure 5. The specific behaviors comprising the sheet will differ for each client, so the row headings will differ for each individual. The number of behaviors listed to be worked on at any one time should not exceed 10 to 12. The sample Daily Activity Log in Figure 5 consists of fairly basic behaviors that might need to be established by a PCA survivor with relatively severe deficits in daily-living skills, who is in the early stages of treatment. The client indicates those activities that have been done each day by placing a check mark in the appropriate box on the chart. As certain behaviors on the log become firmly entrenched, they are deleted from the list and replaced by additional ones. In this way, progressively more advanced and complex components of daily living can be addressed as the course of treatment advances.

As with the Practice Record Sheet, this log is to be brought to each session to facilitate conjoint review of the client's progress in instituting and maintaining these new patterns. The Practice Record Sheet and Daily Activity Log provide a bridge between accountability to the therapist and

Day/Date: _____

Activity

Activity						
up by 8a.m.						
walk 30 min.						
shower/dress						
eat breakfast						
take a.m. Rx						
clean house						
eat lunch						
job search						
take p.m. Rx						
eat dinner						
mail, bills						
bed by 10						

Notes: _____

FIGURE 5. Activity record sheet

the internalization of habits. Adherence to the components of the Daily Activity Log form a foundation from which the client can develop the skills to structure daily living that were not adequately transmitted in his or her family of origin.

Once the Practice Record Sheet and Daily Activity Log are consistently being used, client and therapist can turn their attention to the next of the priorities: modulating dissociation and promoting experiential presence and continuity. This shift in focus does not mean that attention to the reduction and modulation of distress is complete and therefore ceases. As with all of the priorities, work on this goal will continue as needed. However, as we will see presently, learning to decrease reliance on dissociative reactions is contingent on the ability to modulate distress.

CHAPTER 11

Focus: Fostering Experiential Presence and Continuity

The term "dissociation" refers to a seemingly disparate set of experiences that have come to be associated with each other conceptually (American Psychiatric Association, 1994; Phillips & Frederick, 1995; Putnam, 1989). Extensive evidence suggests that they are more frequently found among clients with a PCA history than among any other population (Briere & Runtz, 1988b; Chu & Dill, 1990; Chu, Frey, Ganzel, & Matthews, 1999; Kirby, Chu, & Dill, 1993; Zlotnick et al., 1996). These experiences include:

- Absorption–diminution of awareness of one's immediate surroundings, often colloquially referred to with terms such as "spacing out," "zoning out," or "blanking out";
- Depersonalization–sensations of not feeling real, of not feeling "like myself," of being detached from and observing one's own experience, so that one experiences oneself as an object rather than subjectively;
- Dissociative Amnesia–inability to recall discrete events, including very recent ones, or extensive aspects of one's personal history, in the absence of the evidence of organicity, and of sufficient proportions that it is not attributable to normal, commonplace forgetfulness;
- Identity Fragmentation–a compelling sense of being divided into parts, selves or aspects of self that feel separate from each other.

These experiences are construed by some theorists as forming a continuum (Phillips & Frederick, 1995) ranging from milder, more mundane and com-

154

monplace forms, such as dissociative absorption, to more radical and unusual varieties, such as identity fragmentation. The dissociative phenomena just described comprise some of the salient points along this continuum, listed in order from most to least commonplace.

☐ A Family Context Model of Dissociation

A conception informed by family and social context leads to different conclusions and forms of intervention for treating dissociative symptoms than does an exclusively trauma-based perspective. The majority of specialists on dissociative symptoms and disorders construe dissociation as either primarily or exclusively being a direct consequence of exposure to traumatic events (see, e.g., Cardeña, 1994; Kluft, 1996; van der Hart, Steele, Boon, & Brown, 1993; Putnam, 1989; Ross, 1997). The trauma model of dissociation suggests that these experiences constitute a defense against being overwhelmed by the emotions aroused by traumatic incidents or triggered by their recollection (Cardeña, 1994). A corollary of this perspective is that confrontation and resolution of traumatic material will lead to the elimination of dissociative reactions.

In contrast, there are several authors who have proposed a position closer to the one advanced here. These theorists contend that disordered attachment relationships in the family of origin play a pivotal role in the development of pathological dissociation (see, e.g., Alexander, 1992; Anderson & Alexander, 1996; Barach, 1991). This model proposes that ongoing emotional detachment and unresponsiveness on the part of the parents induces a complementary tendency for interpersonal disengagement in the child (Barach, 1991). As in the family context model, the disordered attachment model acknowledges that traumatic experiences make a substantial contribution to the evolution of dissociation and other symptoms. Barach (1991), for instance, postulated that the proclivity for interpersonal and emotional disengagement that emerges in reaction to the parents' detached stance provides a foundation for the establishment of frankly dissociative defenses in response to abuse trauma. In this respect, both the family context and disordered attachment perspectives construe trauma as exacerbating preexisting difficulties and deficits attributable primarily to defective patterns of family interaction (Alexander, 1992; Barach, 1991; chapter 4, this volume), rather than as being the sole or principal source of a dissociation. Neither model considers the confrontation and processing of traumatic material to be an effective central strategy for resolving the symptomatology manifested by PCA survivors. Instead, both of these conceptual frameworks point to the therapeutic relationship as the logical medium through which to reverse the interpersonal and adaptive restrictions created by a predilection for detachment and dissociation.

The family context model differs from the disordered attachment model mainly in its overt recognition of the crucial role other aspects of family functioning beyond attachment play in the creation and maintenance of the long-term difficulties endured by PCA survivors. While the family context perspective recognizes the contribution of disordered attachment in the formation of dissociative tendencies, it also emphasizes the family's and larger society's role in fostering persisting problems in adjustment by failing to provide adequate training in adaptive living skills. Consequently, in contrast to the disordered attachment model, and in a manner analogous to the goal of learning to modulate distress, the development of a secure, collaborative therapeutic relationship is seen as being a necessary prerequisite, but not a sufficient condition, for the attainment of the goal of moderating dissociation. Once some measure of security in the therapeutic alliance is established, survivors need to acquire specific strategies in order to learn how to modulate dissociative experiences.

One way of conceptually linking the seemingly disparate experiences grouped under the term "dissociation" is to construe them as a variety of modes of experientially distancing or disconnecting oneself from distress-provoking stimuli. As Cardeña (1994) noted, in some instances dissociative experiences may arise spontaneously and unbidden, and in others they may be invoked intentionally. In either case, dissociation appears to constitute and to be triggered by the avoidance of emotional discomfort. From a family context perspective, therefore, addressing dissociative reactions logically builds upon the skills acquired in learning to manage distress. Both arenas are construed as reflecting inadequate mastery of the capacities needed to effectively cope with unpleasant feelings. This concept, that dissociation is a response to distress, is a crucial guide to the construction and execution of interventions designed to moderate it. Attempts to modify dissociative responses in ways that do not take into account the existence of underlying distress are unlikely to be limited in their effectiveness. It is for this reason that learning to moderate distress is assigned a higher priority than modulating dissociation; to a substantial degree the latter capacity is predicated on the former. The less frequently and intensely elevations in distress occur, the less likely dissociative reactions are to be automatically triggered, and the less impetus there will be to deliberately employ them. In addition, when the ability to contain distress is available, dissociative responses, when they do occur, are much less likely to reach extreme proportions. This renders them much easier to interrupt, attenuate, or manage.

A fundamental tenet of the family context model is that the overarching aim of psychological treatment is to remediate adaptive capacities that the family of origin failed to adequately convey and that abuse trauma derailed. In its broadest terms, therefore, the goal of this form of therapy is to assist the PCA survivor in acquiring these capacities, which can be grouped into two broad categories: how to feel better (i.e., reduce distress); and how to function better (i.e., effectively manage the challenges of daily living). Particular objectives are considered to be legitimate treatment goals only to the extent that they fulfill one or both of these two criteria. The only justification for targeting a response for modification or elimination, therefore, is that it propagates distress or interferes with adaptive living—not merely because it is exotic or unconventional. Alternately stated, adaptive functioning is primarily defined in terms of effectiveness, rather than in terms of conformity to prevailing social norms. Accordingly, the moderation or elimination of dissociative reactions is not deemed to be a defensible goal in and of itself. It is only tenable to make dissociation the object of intervention when or if it creates distress or demonstrably hampers daily living. Alternately put, the function of psychotherapy is to expand, rather than curtail, the client's range of choices (Lankton & Lankton, 1983). Contextual therapy aims to provide the client with the option to control dissociative experiences when they arouse emotional upset or interfere with effective functioning, rather than imposing on her or him the goal of eradicating these experiences.

☐ DID: Risks of Excessive Emphasis on Extreme Forms of Dissociation

A related concern is the potential for the therapist to place undue focus on dissociative manifestations, exploring and attending to them extensively without adequately considering the therapeutic value of doing so. The sensationalistic quality of some dissociative phenomena can be so "fascinating" (a word commonly used by clinicians upon first encountering them) that it is easy to lapse into exploring them as an end in itself. In such instances, there is a high probability that the practitioner (and frequently as a result, the client as well) will lose sight of whether this enterprise is likely to lead to substantive gains in the overarching goals of reducing distress and augmenting adaptive capacities. If left unchecked, this venture can consume protracted expanses of time without yielding any substantive therapeutic gains.

Of course, while dissociative experiences are commonly found among PCA survivors, not all clients with this type of history can routinely be assumed to dissociate. My impression is that, particularly within this population, forms of dissociation at the extreme end of the dissociative spectrum, such as Dissociative Identity Disorder (DID; formerly designated as

Multiple Personality Disorder) are over-diagnosed, while more subtle varieties of dissociative experience may go undetected. Too often, the presence of phenomena at the more extreme and dramatic end of the dissociative spectrum, such as those constituting DID, is deduced on the basis of the detection of less extreme dissociative experiences, such as absorption or episodes of amnesia. It is as if some clinicians assume, for example, that if periods of amnesia exist, this in and of itself is evidence of the emergence of identity fragments, commonly referred to as "alters," during those amnestic episodes. The logic applied here is that if there is evidence that the individual engaged in activities in the midst of an amnestic episode, then "another part" of her or him must have executed those activities. This, however, is not a reasonable assumption. If it were, then anyone who continued to function in the midst of an alcoholic blackout would have to be presumed to be manifesting the activation of an identity fragment. In the course of discussing with the therapist, (T), how she previously engaged in self-mutilation during amnestic episodes, a client, (C), seen in treatment at TRIP implicitly recognizes that it is unnecessary to presume the existence of alters. In addition, the matter of seeing dissociation as a legitimate choice, rather than as something to be denigrated and eradicated, is touched upon.

C: What I do know, about myself and my own activities . . . it's funny because some of them are behind a veil, where I simply have to conclude based on logic, you know . . . if I was alone in the house and there was no one else there for a period of time, let's say through the night, and in the morning I have a burn, then I must conclude that I, that that occurred, and there was no one else to do that but me. You know? So I, I kind of can look at it that way, without forcing myself to, to scrupulously remember what happened. But I can do that too, and it's exactly like a videotape for me.

T: You're saying that it's a choice.

C: It is! Exactly! It is! And that statement does not bring up feelings of shame in me at this time. . . . Exactly, it is a choice that used to make me feel so bad about myself as a person. Because I could choose to remember or not remember. And the choose [sic] to not remember would be like, um, an abandonment of responsibility, and um, um, a desire to hide from the truth. But at this point in my life I really recognize that I don't have to face every single truth there is, and I don't have to prove anything to anybody anymore. That's not what's going to heal me.

It seems that people equate phenomena at much lesser points in the dissociative spectrum with DID due to a tendency among professionals, including those who specialize in this area, to slip into using these terms interchangeably. The same woman quoted above, who freely acknowledged having had frequent and intense episodes of amnesia, but who neither reported nor manifested evidence of identity fragmentation or other signs of DID, expressively described her previous encounters with mental health professionals who insisted that she was "a multiple":

C: There are so many people [psychotherapists] out there, I think the greatest number of people out there, are out there with this whole, you know, comedy routine: "How many . . . alters do you have?" You know? "What!" You know, "What? Wait, let me check the census!" You know? I have no idea where these people are coming from, and I was ready for this [her course of treatment at TRIP] to be another thing of that. So I avoided it [being coerced into accepting a diagnosis of DID in previous treatment programs] with my intelligence and with my own acuity. I went home and sat there and said to myself, "Oh shit, this is not ok." Ok? "This is not me, and this is not ok." And, um, that's what saved me. You know, just, just an absolute refusal to buy somebody else's rubric that they impressed on me.

One risk in the type of scenario this client describes is that of the practitioner pressing her or his convictions about the client's experience with an adamance that contradicts and invalidates, or even attempts to forcibly override, the client's reality and perceptions. This state of affairs sets up a coercive interpersonal interaction with the therapist that can be disturbingly and destructively reminiscent of the abusive situation to which the client was subjected in childhood (Gold & Brown, 1997). One client, for example, reported having been reprimanded by a previous therapist for engaging in denial about her DID status because she used the pronoun "I" instead of "we." In the face of this type of duress, individuals who are not as trusting of their own perceptions and judgement as the woman quoted above can be intimidated into accepting the clinician's conviction that they have DID, even when this is not the case.

Some authors have asserted that clients with an abuse history are particularly susceptible to conforming to others' viewpoints because they are suggestible (Ofshe & Watters, 1994; Yapko, 1994). It is noteworthy that this formulation is implicitly disparaging to survivors, implying that they are weak-minded and gullible. However, at least one research study indicates that clients reporting recovered memories of child abuse were found to be *less* susceptible to suggestion than other clients (Leavitt, 1997). There are, nevertheless, several other factors that could account for a client accepting an inaccurate diagnosis of DID. When one considers the power differential inherent in the therapeutic relationship, the vulnerability of the client, the status inherent in the practitioner role, the extensive history of invalidation that render PCA survivors susceptible to doubting their own experiences and being convinced by others that their perceptions are inaccurate, and the intense emotional dependency that many survivors may feel toward their clinicians, it is not difficult to imagine how these factors could culminate in acquiescence to an unfounded diagnosis of DID.

☐ Absorption: Risks of Overlooking Subtle Forms of Dissociation

Conversely, I suspect that the presence of dissociative reactions at the lower end of the continuum often go undetected. The most notable examples of dissociative difficulties such as these are involuntarily triggered episodes of absorption of sufficient intensity to profoundly interfere with awareness of the immediate present. PCA survivors sometimes learn to appear responsive to others (e.g., via head-nodding and the maintenance of eye contact) while fully immersed in such states. Obviously, the corresponding truncating of awareness this can engender will create difficulties both in session and outside of therapy by restricting the client's access to vital information. Often this dissociative pattern can also arouse considerable anxiety for the survivor that others will become angry, and possibly rejecting, if they detect that she or he is "not paying attention." The incentive to prevent others from noticing episodes of intense absorption can therefore be substantial. In addition, the pervasive low self-esteem of many PCA survivors often leads them to make a host of negative self-attributions on the basis of the "inattentiveness" and its adverse effects. The following account by a man in his early twenties, whose childhood was marked by extensive emotional neglect and long-standing sexual abuse, touches on both of these issues: the toll dissociation can take on self-image and the evolution of the capacity to dissociate without being discovered.

C: I was really disappointed with how my life turned out.

T: In what way?

C: Well, I quit school, and, um, and I'm not as smart, you know, I'm kind of stupid. I'm not as smart as I would have liked to have been. And...

T: How did you come to that conclusion?

C: What?

T: That you're not as smart as you'd like to be.

C: Oh um, 'cause I don't know anything. I mean don't know how to, I don't know how to divide, I don't know how to multiply. I don't know . . . I can read. But, you know that kind of stuff, I don't know anything about science, or social studies or that kind of shit.

T: How do you explain that?

C: I never paid attention in school. I was always, I . . . always floating around in my head somewhere. I never paid attention, ever. . . . It's like zoning out, but only like, on like, I mean, a hard core level. You know, it's not like daydreaming.

T: Right.

C: It's like I'm in there real deep somewhere.

T: Uh huh. And you don't know what's going on around you?

C: No. There could be like a holocaust going on and I wouldn't know it.

T: So if somebody would come up and talk to you, you won't hear them?

C: [Nodding] Mm hmm.

T: Do you have that now?

C: No, not as bad. Now I'm like, I'll be doing it, but someone will talk to me, it's like, I don't know, I've gotten used to it to where I can zone out and have a conversation at the same time.

The construct of a continuum of dissociation, in conjunction with clinical observations, suggests to me that absorption is at the root of other, more exotic or complex dissociative phenomena, in much the same way as I see the intrusive, numbing, and avoidance components of PTSD as being in many respects secondary reactions to or consequences of anxious arousal. Beginning with absorption, the progression of experiences along the dissociative continuum can be viewed as the products of increasingly extreme degrees of diverting attention from and, in their more intense and elaborated forms, completely obliterating awareness of, disturbing situations. At the more severe end of the dissociative spectrum, extensive chronic lapses in attention, and in the sense of continuity of experience, recollection, and awareness are incompatible with the formation of a cohesive sense of identity and maintain fragmentation of self-experience. When applied to treatment, this conception is helpful because it guides intervention in the direction of building the ability to maintain attention and expand awareness, rather than toward dismantling and demolishing existing dissociative capacities.

To summarize, these conceptual considerations suggest the adoption of a number of guiding principles for addressing dissociative phenomena therapeutically. PCA survivors may have exerted considerable effort to develop the ability to mask their dissociative reactions, in order to prevent having others notice that they are oblivious to or amnestic for what is going on around them. Careful observation may therefore be needed to detect the presence of dissociative reactions. While a certain degree of vigilance may be required to recognize dissociative episodes, it is equally important to refrain from allowing conjecture to over-rule observation. Stick as close as possible to the observable evidence, rather than making unwarranted assumptions. For example there is no justification for presuming that a client experiences phenomena at the extreme end of the dissociative spectrum on the basis of having witnessed her or him manifesting more commonplace types. In order to guard against making such groundless generalizations, and to minimize the likelihood of conveying these types of conjectures to the client, it is safest to abstain from asking leading or suggestive questions. Instead, it is best to conduct interviewing about dissociative experiences in an open-ended, non-directive fashion, asking the client to describe them rather than inquiring about the presence of particular phenomena. Remember that neither exploring nor eliminating dissociative experiences is a legitimate therapeutic objective in and of itself. These practices are only tenable to the extent that it can be reasonably justified that they will contribute to reductions in distress or enhancement of adaptive functioning. Dissociation often serves a protective and adaptive function. Rather than presume that dissociative responses need to be eliminated, focus on expanding the client's options by providing alternative strategies and means of increasing safety and security. To the degree that the client becomes adept at reducing and tolerating rather than avoiding emotional discomfort, particular dissociative responses are likely to no longer be needed. Once this occurs, even though the ability to access them may remain, habitual reliance on them will often spontaneously subside.

☐ Training in Grounding Techniques

There is rarely a need to proactively and directly inquire whether a client dissociates. Sensitive observation will usually suffice in extemporaneously revealing dissociative responding during the course of therapy. Proceeding in this fashion reduces the risk of engaging in unintentionally leading questioning about dissociative experiences. When this approach is adopted, training in modulating dissociation will most likely be initiated in response to unanticipated dissociative reactions, as they emerge spontaneously in session. The therapist may come to suspect the presence of dissociation, for example, upon noting that the client seems preoccupied to the extent of being only tenuously aware of the immediate present, is unable to recall an interchange that transpired just moments before, or appears to have shifted her or his style of self-presentation in an incongruous and unsettling manner. In instances such as these, the practitioner might respond by gently inquiring, "What are you experiencing right now?" If the client is able to reply fairly readily and with some measure of comfort to verbal questioning, then the interviewing can proceed in a casual, low-key tone to client-directed exploration of the experience.

However, if she or he appears too apprehensive to formulate a response, or too removed to have even registered the question, then it can be pointless or even counterproductive to continue this line of inquiry. It is crucial to remember that dissociation is most commonly triggered by anxiety. Consequently, the evocation of a dissociative reaction in session is, at times, an indication that something has occurred in the interchange with the therapist that the client perceives as threatening. For example, the topic being discussed or a seemingly innocuous remark by the clinician may have triggered a flashback of a traumatic experience or elicited a particularly vivid and frightening transference reaction. Where it appears that probing has aroused wariness and trepidation, it is usually best to desist and instead to help reduce the client's anxiety by calmly redirecting the interchange to another, less threatening topic. If particularly extreme levels of discomfort appear to have been provoked, the therapist may want to consider offering to help guide the client through a relaxation exercise. Where the level of dissociation seems to be so intense that contact with the immediate surroundings is tenuous, anxiety-reducing interventions will probably need to be supplemented by methods to help reestablish the client's connection with the here and now. These procedures are commonly referred to as grounding techniques (Simonds, 1994).

Consider two related but somewhat different types of dissociative responses that are among the most common to occur in session. Both may involve a level of reverie so intense that they may create disorientation for person, time, place, or some combination of the three. The more fundamental of the two types of reactions is dissociative absorption, in which to a greater or lesser degree the individual loses awareness of her or his surroundings. Experientially, there may be engrossment in imagery, thought, or some other content of consciousness competing with awareness of the here and now, or, alternatively, only awareness of being blank. From an observer's viewpoint, indications of absorption might include a dazed look in the eyes, a vacant facial expression, a marked degree of immobility, or an apparent obliviousness to external stimuli. If the clinician happens to be talking when she or he first notices signs that absorption may be occurring, a useful initial response is to simply immediately fall silent. If the client is dissociating, but to a relatively mild degree, this subtle cue may be sufficient to recapture her or his attention. Where this is the case, the therapist can then gently probe by nonchalantly asking, "What just happened?", or "What were you experiencing just now?" Recognizing that the client may expect the practitioner to be irritated that she or he was "not paying attention," it is important for the clinician to that take some pains to ensure that the tone of the question conveys an attitude of acceptance and mild curiosity, and an invitation to join in investigating what just occurred. In instances where silence alone does not rouse the client, one might proceed to call her or his name, taking care not to shout (which could be heard as "scolding"). If this still does not elicit a response, the practitioner can calmly repeat the client's name and ask, "Can you hear me?" or "Can you see me?" It is important to take care in the wording employed, in order to avoid unwittingly increasing the client's anxiety. For example, it is best to make a point to avoid employing wording such as "Look at me!", or "Listen to me!", since many clients may have heard phrases such as this angrily shouted at them by an abuser when they were berated, beaten, or molested.

Unless the client appears to be in distress, if attempts to stir her or him are unsuccessful, it may be best to watch and wait until reorientation occurs on its own. It helps to remember that all episodes of dissociative absorption eventually will end, even when active attempts are not made to arrest them. Whether in response to intervention or on its own, once absorption does cease, the therapist can then inquire about what just transpired, being mindful that the client may feel guilty or fearful about having been "inattentive." If interviewing her or him about the experience confirms that it was in fact dissociative in nature, this provides an opportunity to normalize the phenomenon by explaining that these experiences are seen sometimes among PCA survivors and by elaborating briefly on why this is the case.

Up until this point, the practitioner will have been actively directing the reorientation process. However, as soon as the client is sufficiently reoriented to remain in communication with the therapist, the focus can be shifted to teaching her or him how to assume control over this process, which is often referred to as "grounding" (Blake-White & Kline, 1985; Simonds, 1994). As with procedures for distress management, the introduction of grounding methods should be guided by the intention of placing them under the client's direction as much as possible and as soon as is feasible. This is in keeping with the philosophy that the end-goal is to equip the client with the capacity to modulate dissociation independently of intervention by the practitioner.

In general, grounding techniques are methods of resisting the pull to drift into a dissociated state by intentionally experientially anchoring one's attention in the here and now. It is generally best to start by invoking grounding procedures that draw the client's attention to tactile sensations. Simonds (1994) points out that the pull to withdraw from the immediate present (represented by dissociation) is often accompanied by a tendency to physically recoil from one's surroundings in a way that inadvertently supports and augments the dissociative process. For example, in the midst of a dissociative episode a client may spontaneously pull her or his legs up off the floor and curl them up on the chair, draw her or his arms in toward the torso, and look downward, away from the gaze of others.

A useful way to begin to familiarize the client with grounding skills is to identify, immediately following an episode of absorption, the behavioral concomitants of dissociation she or he is displaying, and explain how these responses help to sever awareness of the surrounding environment. This establishes the rationale for purposefully reversing these behaviors as a means of modulating the dissociative experience. Placing feet on the floor, lowering arms to one's sides, and attending to the tactile sensations of being supported by the floor and the furniture help to experientially reconnect with one's surroundings. If these steps do not sufficiently diminish the dissociative stupor, then standing up, moving around, and walking around the room while focusing on the tactile sensations these actions evoke will substantially amplify the grounding process. If moving and walking around seems indicated in session, it is often useful for the therapist to offer to join the client in doing so, while being careful to maintain a respectful distance. Once tactile contact has been firmly established, it is useful to supplement it by visually attending to elements of the surroundings, carefully noting their appearance and qualities (e.g., shape, color), and perhaps even silently labeling them (e.g., "chair . . . picture . . . carpet . . . light switch"). In session, making eye contact with the therapist ("Can you see me?") may be helpful. Finally, noting sounds in the immediate environment (e.g., "voices . . . traffic sounds . . . ventilation system") can further reinforce orientation to the here and now. After being guided to invoke these procedures in session in order to dispel an incident of absorption, the practitioner and client can discuss how the same methods can be employed by the client elsewhere.

In addition to forming an experiential connection to the physical environment through tactile, visual, and auditory channels, the client can then employ a strategy designed to help orient her or him to the present time. Orientation to time is secured by employing cues of the present and of one's current age, status, and interpersonal affiliations. Examining one's wedding rings, car keys, recent pictures of one's offspring and other loved ones, business cards, and other objects associated with adulthood, parenthood, and career, if necessary accompanied by silent self-talk (e.g., "These are my car keys; I am an adult and I drive.", "This is my spouse. I am grown up and married." "These are my children. I am a parent.") acts as a tangible conduit to the present day.

A somewhat more complex manifestation of dissociation is a traumatic flashback. As in simple absorption, a flashback involves some degree of unawareness of and unresponsiveness to external stimuli. However, in this case it is specifically accompanied by the recall of a traumatic event, retrieved so powerfully that it is reexperienced rather than merely cognitively recalled, which obscures contact with the immediate present. In its most extreme forms, flashbacks of trauma may almost entirely eclipse orientation to the present. In the throes of a particularly realistic flashback, the trauma is revivified so intensely that the person consumed by it may compellingly experience actually being back in the time and place, and regressed to the age, at which the event originally took place. Frequently, therefore, observable signs of being disconnected from the here and now associated with dissociative absorption will be accompanied by indicators of immersion in vivid and intensely distressing reverie. In the midst of a flashback, the client may flinch, cower, or curl up in a fetal position. Instead of displaying a dazed or vacant expression, he or she may grimace or wince in terror or pain. Where the revivified trauma is one of interpersonal victimization, such as sexual molestation or physical abuse, the client may talk as if the perpetrator is present (e.g., "No! Stop! Please, don't hurt me! Leave me alone!").

In actuality, when therapy is conducted within a contextual framework, it is much less likely that flashbacks will arise in session than if a trauma-focused approach is used. Alternately stated, the risk of evoking flashbacks is much higher when intervention centers on the review and processing of frankly traumatic material. In most cases in which a family context model is used, therefore, episodes of dissociative absorption are much more likely to be encountered than are intense flashbacks. However, in those rare instances when flashbacks do occur in session, it is imperative that the practitioner be prepared to help the client attenuate and manage them.

It can be appreciably more challenging to reorient a client engulfed in a flashback to than one engrossed in dissociative absorption. In instances in which the client spontaneously verbalizes, furnishing the practitioner with some notion of the nature of the event being experienced (e.g., "No! Don't! He's going to get me!"), these cues can be a valuable tool in the reorienting process. The more compelling the flashback, the less likely immediately speaking to the client from a current-day perspective is to successfully penetrate the dissociative state, although there is usually no harm in attempting this. If, however, this approach is unsuccessful, it may be necessary to "enter into" the event by speaking as if one is "there" with the client. The following dialogue approximates the type of interchange that might ensue between therapist (T) and client (C).

C: No! Don't! He's going to get me!

T: [Matching the sense of urgency in the client's voice, but with a tone of reassurance.] Don't worry! We can get away! Come with me! [It may seem a minor point, but it is generally best to try to emphasize joining with the client rather than taking an explicitly protective stance, using language such as "We can get away" rather than "I'll save you!" and "Come with me!" instead of "Follow me!"]

C: No! He'll get you too!

T: [Purposely remaining vague about particulars such as whether the locale is indoors or outside, to avoid incongruence with the client's experience.] It's okay! Come with me! See over there? Look! We can get away! Can you see? Let's go!

C: [Fearfully.] Are you sure?

T: Yes! Come on! It's okay! Let's go! Are you with me?

C: [Hesitantly.] Yes . . . okay.

T: [Emphatically.] Come on! Here we go! Stay with me now!

C: Okay.

T: Keep up with me! Are you with me?

C: Yes . . .

T: We're almost home free! Can you see?

C: Yes!

T: Come on, come on . . . are you with me?

C: Yes.

T: See? We're safe now.

C: [With a tone of relief.] Yes! Yes!

Throughout this interchange, the therapist should be vigilant for signs of reduction in the client's arousal level, adjusting her or his tone and statements to optimize the probability that the client will feel reassured and perceive her- or himself to be out of danger. At that point, the protocol that has been described for reorientation from dissociative absorption can be initiated. This protocol culminates in transmitting strategies to the client for her or him to use to disrupt dissociative experiences as they arise outside of therapy.

☐ Learning to Modulate Absorption

In addition to managing dissociative episodes by recognizing triggers and prodromal signs and thereby interrupting them before they develop, many clients can learn to directly modulate their level of absorption and blocking. This is accomplished by requesting that the client apply a SUD rating to her or his degree of dissociative absorption. (In practice, it may be useful to describe dissociative absorption to the client as the level of connection with and awareness of her or his surroundings. This frames the ensuing exercise as the acquisition of a skill, rather than as an attempt to discard a "symptom.") A rating of 10 is used to represent the greatest intensity of absorption the client has ever experienced, with zero indicating full experiential contact with the here and now. The technique itself is adapted from procedures described by Erickson and Rossi (1980), which are based on the principle that responses experienced as being outside of one's control can often be voluntarily intensified fairly readily when one attempts to diminish them. Once the capacity to increase the response has been accessed, it becomes much easier to reverse direction and reduce it.

Having established a SUD rating for the current level of dissociation, the client is then asked to picture a visual analogue for the SUD scale, such as a calibrated dial or meter with a pointer. She or he is then asked to envision the indicator on the dial slowly moving upward. The idea is that as the number on the dial increases, the level of absorption will be magnified correspondingly. This effect often occurs spontaneously, without explicitly alerting the client to expect its occurrence. (Erickson would maintain that direct instructions of this sort would either appreciably lessen the likelihood that the intended effect would occur or considerably attenuate the intensity of the effect.) After the client has successfully "moved the dial" upward several degrees, it can then be suggested that she or he adjust it back downward to its original position, then back upward again, and finally downward, continuing to a notch or two below the starting point. Some time should be spent guiding the client through this procedure of shifting the dial indicator up and down until she or he has attained a reasonable level of proficiency at this task. This exercise can then be practiced on a daily basis between sessions, logging the starting SUD level, the highest number attained, and the lowest rating reached. One of the advantages of this approach is that it readily lends itself to the idea that the objective is not to eliminate dissociative responding, but to develop the ability to modulate its intensity.

☐ Learning to Disrupt Dissociative Episodes

In order to optimize their value to the client, grounding techniques and the capacity to modulate absorption directly need to be combined with the development of the ability to recognize "early warning signs" of the emergence of a dissociative reaction. These indicators of the onset of a dissociative episode fall into two main categories: (a) triggers–stimuli (whether environmental, such as loud voices, or experiential, such a anxiety) that consistently precipitate dissociation; and (b) prodromal signs–sensations and perceptions that accompany the incipient stages of a dissociative experience. In session, the therapist and client collaboratively identify both triggers and prodromal signs of dissociation. This is accomplished by exploring a particular instance of dissociation in detail, either by examining a dissociative episode immediately following its occurrence in session, or by having the client choose a dissociative experience that recently took place outside of session. The key to the success of this procedure is to scrutinize, in as much detail as possible, the associated circumstances and the corresponding subjective experience preceding the inception of the dissociative state. The practitioner introduces this process by asking the client to recount the last thing she or he can remember before dissociating. From there, the therapist and client work backward in time, identifying the events and experiences leading up to the onset of dissociation. Once several instances of a particular variety of dissociation (e.g., absorption, flashbacks, or amnesia) are explored in this way, it becomes possible to deduce what triggers the experience and what the subjective signs are that the experience is about to occur. As the client becomes adept at recognizing these signals as they arise, disruption of the sequence that previously culminated in dissociative episodes becomes an increasingly viable option by invoking relaxation techniques, utilizing grounding strategies, directly modulating dissociative absorption, or drawing upon some combination of these skills. With practice, she or he can refine the ability to intervene and short-circuit the dissociative process so that this technique can be enlisted progressively earlier in the sequence.

Once the triggers and prodromal signs are identified, it is often useful to expand investigation of dissociative episodes to the circumstances and experiences that are commonly associated with their cessation. This can be conducted by once again examining particular instances of dissociation, and isolating the first thing the client can remember upon emerging from the dissociated state. In this way, secondary reactions to the dissociative experience—such as feeling fearful that others have noticed what was happening and will be angry, self-denigrating thoughts about having "drifted off," attempts at dissembling and confabulating to cover up the episode—can be articulated, more clearly recognized, examined, and questioned. The entire enterprise of closely scrutinizing the typical antecedents and consequences of the client's dissociative experiences renders them more predictable, less mysterious, and accordingly less shameful and anxiety-provoking. In the process, a conception of the meaning, purpose, and mechanisms behind the onset, exacerbation, and diminution of dissociative reactions emerges that makes them more comprehensible, less threatening, and, somewhat paradoxically, more acceptable to the client. She or he comes to appreciate that dissociation in and of itself is not a problem, and that it has constituted and can continue to serve as a means of coping. Dissociation has created difficulties when it has been poorly understood, feared, and consequently inconsistently and inadequately regulated by the client.

☐ Addressing Dissociative Amnesia

The usefulness of this approach is not limited to dissociative absorption and flashbacks. The same general procedure can effectively be applied to other dissociative phenomena, such as episodes of amnesia or depersonalization. The following excerpt from a therapy session conducted at TRIP illustrates the application of this intervention strategy to amnesia, a process which had already been introduced to the client in previous sessions. The "orange ball technique" referred to in the transcript is an imagery-based method of relaxation in which the client pictures all the arousal and tension in her body gradually flowing into and inflating an orange ball floating in front of her, and then visualizes the ball deflating until it vanishes.

T: Could you give me an example where you could guide me through the last thing that you remembered and then what happens and when you suddenly remembered that you lost some time. Could you guide me through one of those events?

C: . . . While I was driving, there was construction. And the next thing I know there was no construction. And I have very often an awful vision, like, um, in this case I had a vision that my daughter June had died, and... immediately I know that I am awake and I am not sleeping. It's not real but it's like, there's like a whole series of thoughts that wants to, that want to, that like . . . like, I don't deserve to drive the car and be relaxed on a Sunday afternoon, so something terrible is going to happen. So then I have this thought that June died, and, um, I, I realize that this is what I am doing now. And I am thinking that this a negative energy and that I have to . . . get this out of me, and I can do that. And then I, I think about pushing it out of my mind into the orange ball. And then, trying to read road signs, trying to drive the car, and realize that this negative energy will go away, and I can breath and that soon it will all be dissipated into the universe, and whatever the actual reality is will come back to me, and it does.

After a digression, therapist and client continue to the topic of dissecting and disrupting the amnestic process.

T: Let me ask you a question. Uh, you were talking how just after you come out [of an amnestic episode], when you "wake up" and you use the orange ball technique, there are also times when just before you would lose time you would use the orange ball technique. Isn't that what you told me before?

C: Yes, and I am doing that more and more often.

T: And is that helping you to . . . to prevent losing time?

C: Yep. It is absolutely the best thing that has ever happened to me, because it is not so much that it prevents me from losing time. It prevents me, or it reduces . . . the terrific onslaught of fear thing—that thing, that terror thing that snaps is so vicious that is so . . . and so threatening and so overpowering, that I am realizing that it is literally harmful to my life in and of itself. And it is absurd. From a tiny bird jumping on a dry leaf, I can be literally to a point of needing an emergency room and being revived. And you know, it is kind of silly. It's kind of sad in a way to abuse my body. It's like I am punishing myself after all these years. And I am safe and I am alone and nobody out there is trying to hurt me, but saying that to yourself doesn't work. What does work is recognizing that it [i.e., the terror and distress] is a negative energy. And getting the negative energy out [via the orange ball relaxation technique] leaves kind of a reduced [dissociative] effect of that. I still have the effect of that, but it is nowhere near the level that I have had in the past.

T: So now we are doing what is called orange ball therapy.

C: Yeah.

T: And it is working.

C: Yeah.

With less articulate clients the practitioner will have to engage in much more active questioning than was required here. Otherwise, the information obtained about external circumstances, thoughts, feelings, sensations, and behaviors that arise sequentially as the dissociative episode is triggered and unfolds will not be sufficiently detailed to develop a plan to disrupt it. What is very typical about the previous excerpt, however, is the clinician's focus on promoting and maintaining a collegial, collaborative, and encouraging therapeutic alliance.

☐ Addressing Identity Fragmentation

Dissociative phenomena that fall within the realm of identity fragmentation, while they share the characteristic of discontinuity of awareness with other dissociative experiences, are qualitatively different in several important respects. Although disconnection from external stimuli, absorption in inner experience and imagery, and the capacity to diminish awareness and recollection may support compartmentalized self-experience, they do not necessarily indicate the presence of identity fragmentation. (This point is eloquently conveyed by the client quoted earlier in this chapter who would find herself burned after episodes of amnesia.)

A family context conception of identity fragmentation and DID differs in certain crucial respects from other perspectives. The most widely accepted models attribute this form of dissociation to the disintegrating impact of abuse trauma on self-experience and identity (see, e.g., Putnam, 1989; Watkins & Watkins, 1997). In general, trauma-oriented theories tend to presume that a cohesive identity existed before the child was subjected to overt incidents of abuse. In contrast, the framework of family context alerts us to the observation that often long before explicit physical or sexual assault occurred, the PCA survivor was submerged in an interpersonal environment that was chaotic and unpredictable. The behavior of her or his caretakers may have shifted radically from one encounter to the next, determined more by their momentary moods and whims than by a consistent philosophy on child rearing, a stable style of interaction, or the conduct of the client. In a family atmosphere such as this, where similar behavior under similar circumstances may have been alternately reviled, lauded, or ignored on different occasions, where personal boundaries were routinely violated or disregarded, and where subjective experience was frequently invalidated, a cohesive sense of self may have never been forged in the first place. In this type of interpersonal context, where the attributions and appraisals of a child made by the people closest to her or him vary wildly, more or less independently of the behavior displayed, it is easy to imagine that the experience and perception of self would be similarly confused, mercurial, and disjointed.

One of the benefits of a conception such as this is that it demystifies the seemingly extraordinary and uncanny phenomena observed in connection with discontinuity in self-experience and erratic self-presentation. In point of fact, it is critical to maintain a clear conceptual distinction between these two components of fragmented identity—subjective experience and objectively observable behavior. Just as other forms of dissociation do not automatically signal the existence of identity fragmentation in general, the complimentary components of discontinuity of self—disjointed inner experience and inconsistent outward appearance and conduct—cannot always be presumed to coexist. I have seen clients manifest dramatic shifts in their apparent age, demeanor, posture, and voice tone, apparently corresponding to a transition in ego state (Bloch, 1991; Watkins & Watkins, 1997), who report neither amnesia nor a subjective sense of discontinuity in connection with these alterations. Conversely, I have worked with clients who convincingly recount an inner world inhabited by a diverse collection of alters, yet who rarely or never exhibit external signs of switching. To me these observations serve as a reminder that DID is primarily a subjective configuration of self-experience. It is not and was never intended to serve as an outward manifestation. In fact, many clients report going to considerable lengths to prevent their fragmented inner world from being detectable to others. Consequently, I avoid treatment approaches that encourage overt switching and external presentation of alters.

As with other difficulties experienced by PCA survivors, the family context model views identity fragmentation as being a consequence of growing up in a chaotic and inadequate family environment, which is subsequently exacerbated by exposure to abuse trauma. Thinking of identity fragmentation as originating from a lack of development of a cohesive sense of self, rather than as solely constituting a reaction to and consequence of abuse trauma, carries with it pervasive implications for conceptualization and intervention. A trauma-oriented perspective highlights the disintegrating impact of abuse. This conceptualization encourages the practitioner to think of the client as shattered pieces that emerged as a response to and means of coping with trauma, and that need to be explored, deciphered, and reassembled into a cohesive whole. To the extent that we think of a discontinuous self as reflecting the failure of an inconsistent, unpredictable, and invalidating family environment to foster integration of self experience, however, our attention is drawn to the global phenomenon of identity fragmentation, rather than to investigating its manifestations in the form of particular alters.

This conception underscores the need to view the client as a whole person whose inner experiences of disintegration mirror the chaotic environment in which she or he was reared. Rather than valuing the therapist's ability to detect subtle nuances in client presentation that may constitute evidence of the appearance of an alter, this approach encourages the practitioner to recognize the importance of being able to maintain a cohesive perception of the survivor despite the client's own subjective experience of being fractured. The challenge to the clinician in responding therapeutically to identity fragmentation is to be able to acknowledge and validate component alters as being subjectively real without lapsing in her or his own mind into reifying them as individual, independently existing entities. If one successfully avoids slipping into the latter mind set, it will be possible to discern an underlying organization, coherence, and coordination beyond the apparent divisions and discord among alters. This is analogous to the way in which, from a family systems perspective, the overt conflicts among members of an interpersonal organization can be viewed from a larger context as the coordinated workings of an underlying unitary system (Bryant, Kessler, & Shirar, 1992).

From the vantage point of the family context model the integration of alters into a more cohesive sense of self is only of value to the degree that it leads to an enhanced sense of well-being and to the augmentation of adaptive capacities. The key issue is not whether the experience of the self as being comprised of component alters persists. The issue is, instead whether this experience either creates distress or perpetuates internal conflict or disorganization that interferes with effective daily functioning.

Recognizing the impact of external circumstances on inner experience helps the clinician to remain mindful of the necessity of maintaining an optimal level of consistency and predictability in the therapeutic alliance in order to foster the development of a sense of integrity for the client. Collaboratively exploring the origins of a disjointed sense of self in the contexts of family environment and abuse history has the effect of making identity fragmentation comprehensible and less distressing through demonstrating that it is a consequence of what the survivor has experienced, rather than being a sign of inherent weakness or badness. The emphasis here is not on tracing the roots of each discrete identity fragment, but on developing a comprehensive understanding of the discontinuous quality of the survivor's self-experience. While the role of particular part-identities is acknowledged and incorporated into this inquiry, this is always embedded in the larger context of considering their position in relation to the larger self-system.

The therapist, by maintaining a holistic view of the client from the outset, and encouraging the client to be able to recognize the alters as components of a greater whole, attempts to avoid unwittingly compounding the survivors' sense of inner compartmentalization. For this reason, if it is acceptable to the client, I prefer to use the designation "parts" rather than terminology such as "alters" or "personalities," because this implicitly conveys the notion of a component of a larger unity rather than of autonomous existence. Within a family context model, part identities are understood as being adaptations to chaotic (family) and threatening (traumatic) conditions that no longer exist. This helps to foster the understanding that even though they may appear to be separate and in conflict, "parts" are components of a coordinated internal effort to maintain safety and equilibrium. They are not independent entities designed to reveal themselves or to overtly interact with other people.

When parts spontaneously communicate directly to the therapist, this is accepted. However, parts are not actively encouraged to manifest externally in order to converse with the practitioner. It is generally preferable, where communication from alters seems desirable, to establish a precedent early on that their messages be transmitted in the form of writings composed between sessions, which are then discussed by client and therapist in session. This circumvents the need for identity fragments to manifest externally, which can unintentionally intensify the client's perception of them as being autonomous entities with an independent existence.

Wherever feasible, negotiation to resolve contention between parts is encouraged. While it may be appropriate and even desirable for the clinician to mediate these disputes, wherever possible she or he should avoid becoming embroiled in them directly or aligning with one part or con-glomeration of parts against others. The goal here is not integration or fusion of parts, but a cooperative engagement that benefits both the system as a whole and the individual components of the self. Therapists can offer clients reluctant to subscribe to this viewpoint an analogy of people riding together on a bus.

> Imagine a group of people all riding on the same bus, each of whom wants to travel to a different destination, or whom insists on taking a different route to the same destination. They end up bickering with each other, and eventually they actually fight for control of the driver's seat, all trying to grab the steering wheel at the same time. It isn't difficult to picture what the path of the bus would look like to someone watching from outside the bus. It would be one of complete chaos, haphazardly veering this way and that. Most importantly, no one on the bus would ever get where she or he wished to go.

This metaphor graphically illustrates the futility of struggles for control amongst parts in the larger self system. Simultaneously, it implicitly communicates that it is cooperation, rather than merging into a single entity, that is essential to more productive functioning. Clinical observation suggests that the establishment of collaborative relationships among parts often eventually leads to their spontaneous integration.

In one particular case, for example, a woman who was diagnosed with DID during a hospitalization immediately preceeding her admission to TRIP reported relatively rapid changes in her experience of self in response to this approach. Initially she complained of panic attacks and switching between alters that was so disruptive she had to quit work. She indicated that she suffered from daily panic attacks and that about three or four times a week she switched parts with sufficient intensity to elicit blackouts lasting several hours. Moreover, approximately one month after beginning therapy she was in a serious automobile accident which she contended was due to her switch to a child alter while driving.

A few weeks later, she told her clinician that she was extremely distressed because she had blacked out for two days and that she related this to intense feelings that were arising in response to treatment. An alter emerged in session, and assumed responsibility for the blackout, claiming to have taken over awareness because the client was unable to handle these powerful emotions. The therapist encouraged more communication between part identities, offering the explanation that this type of appropriation of awareness without warning was almost as unsettling to the client as the feelings from which it was intended to protect her. The client was able to report that she had previously not experienced emotions with appreciable intensity, and that she recognized that the blackouts and switching seemed to be a response to her difficulty in managing strong affect. She likened the experience to a box that had opened, inundating her with feelings from which she had previously been detached.

Building on her metaphor of a box, her therapist suggested that perhaps she could find a way to put a lock on the box, so that she would not be flooded with emotions at times when they would be likely to create difficulties for her. In the next session, the client reported that an agreement had been developed among parts stating that the box could be open at certain times, such as during therapy sessions, but that it would be locked in situations where strong feelings were likely to create problems, such as at work. She said that in response to this agreement, she had already begun to notice a detectable difference in the quality of switching, with an increased sense of communication, cooperation, and permeability between parts. This was followed by further changes in the same direction. Switching was no longer experienced as other parts taking over executive control, but rather as hearing the parts talk to her, offering suggestions and advice. She was able to return to work and function well without having further panic attacks. Gradually the quality of switching transformed again, so that parts were less and less distinct, and more experientially recognizable to the client as aspects of herself. This was reflected in her use of language. She went from making statements such as, "Eloise did this," to "This is the sort of thing Eloise would do," to "I was acting the way that Eloise used to."

For about three months the client indicated being free of both switching and panic attacks, and treatment was centered on other problem areas. However, the client switched once each of the last two weeks before her clinician was scheduled to leave TRIP, and had two panic attacks the last week before termination. When she expressed concern that she was backsliding, her therapist reassured her that it was not surprising that she would have these familiar types of responses to the stress of ending their work together, and that with continued practice of the new forms of coping she had learned these recurrences would undoubtedly become increasing rare. Consequently, she ended treatment with him expressing confidence that although she didn't welcome termination, she could cope adequately for the next few weeks until a new practitioner would be available to work with her.

The type of "spontaneous" integration depicted in this case vignette in response to skilled-based treatment is an outcome that we at TRIP have found to be very common among our clients with identity fragmentation. This effect appears to be attributable to the fact that once parts are cooperatively engaged with each other, their separateness is rendered obsolete. One of the more striking aspects of this phenomenon is that it occurs without extensive or prolonged exploration of the parts comprising the client's self system. As can be seen in this account, although the existence and characteristics of the parts are implicitly acknowledged, this is not the major focus of investigation and intervention. Instead, material regarding parts is tacitly incorporated into the more fundamental process of examining the issues, conflicts, and processes represented by the parts and by their interconnection. This approach has the advantage of circumventing protracted detours into explicitly probing and interacting with alter identities in a way that can unintentionally make the alters and the conflicts between them seem more substantial, differentiated, and insurmountable to the client. However, in those cases where integration does not occur, there is really no need for the practitioner to get caught up in purposefully seeking or lobbying for this outcome. As long as the client's intentions and behavior are coordinated, functioning will be effective, even when the subjective experience of inner division remains. If the client is comfortable with this state of affairs, it is difficult to see a legitimate reason for the therapist to impose the agenda of integration on her or him.

12
CHAPTER

Reasoning: Learning to Exercise Critical Thinking and Judgment

One of the most pervasive sources of distress and dysfunction among adult survivors of prolonged child abuse (PCA) is a tenaciously negative constellation of beliefs and expectations. PCA survivors commonly hold extremely derogatory views of themselves, while simultaneously anticipating being attacked or rebuffed by others. Their mood and behavior are therefore powerfully dominated by apprehension that they cannot confidently rely on either their own resources or the support and good will of others. There are three major factors that support and perpetuate these unproductive and debilitating convictions:

- Adverse Experiences–Extensive first hand experiences encountered by the client, both in the past and currently, that appear to provide evidence of her or his own wretchedness and incompetence, or of the untrustworthiness of others.
- Pernicious "Programming"–A series of detrimental beliefs that were inculcated into the client's world view through exhortation and repetition throughout her or his formative years by members of the family of origin and which continue to insidiously taint her or his perceptions and reasoning.
- Deficient Transmission of Reasoning Skills–Inadequate opportunities to learn effective reasoning, in conjunction with extensive modeling of faulty logic and capricious behavior by the family of origin that leaves the client with insufficiently developed capacities for critical judgement.

☐ Adverse Experiences

In general, trauma-based models attribute faulty reasoning and beliefs among PCA survivors primarily, although not necessarily exclusively, to the effects of abusive experiences themselves (see, e.g., Janoff-Bulman, 1992; McCann & Pearlman, 1990). In the treatment of abuse survivors, therefore, interventions generated by these models tend to target adverse experiences in the form of discrete incidents of abuse as the main cause of distorted thinking. Within the framework of trauma-based models, pernicious programming in the form of critical and demoralizing statements made by perpetrators and unsympathetic others may be acknowledged as a secondary source of erroneous beliefs (Courtois, 1988; Dolan, 1991; Waites, 1993).

A family context conceptualization acknowledges the impact of adverse experiences, including abuse, on cognition. However, it additionally draws our attention to the ubiquitous impact that interpersonal interactions with family members throughout the survivor's formative years have on her or his seemingly intransigent negative worldview. Familial relationships characterized by neglect and emotional detachment, domination and criticism, and erratic and unpredictable behavior powerfully instill convictions in the survivor that she or he is unworthy and inept, and that others are malicious and unreliable.

In the course of tracing their origins to interactions with the family during childhood and adolescence, it is easy to lose sight of the fact that these beliefs frequently seem to continue to receive confirmation in subsequent interpersonal experiences both within and outside the family. Interpersonal experiences that appear to provide evidence for these beliefs, therefore, not only occurred in the distant past, but frequently persist into the present day. The dual influences of growing up in a deficient family context and being subjected to discrete incidents of overt abuse lead many survivors to develop an interpersonal style that greatly increases their vulnerability to further maltreatment, rejection, and condemnation. Just as the unassertiveness and emotional dependency engendered by the family context renders a child more susceptible to abuse, the exacerbation of these characteristics by explicit abuse magnifies survivors' risk of being abandoned, taken advantage of, and re-victimized.

Often survivors will persevere continuously or periodically throughout adulthood in seeking out the validation and acceptance from their family of origin that they never received as children. In most cases these efforts will lead to replaying of the same patterns of interaction that occurred in their growing-up years, culminating in the same outcomes as before: criticism, rejection, and in some instances, even frank re-victimization in the form of physical battering or sexual assault. In some cases, reexperiencing these scenarios as an adult allows for the evolvement of a more informed perspective that makes it easier to recognize how senseless and irrational these exchanges are, and how unjustified the maltreatment they have received has been. Sadly, much more often the intense emotional pull to preserve the hope that close family can be trusted (Freyd, 1996) ultimately prevails over objective judgement. Many survivors conclude, once again, that they are somehow flawed or at fault.

Experiencing the repetition of similar interpersonal patterns with individuals outside the family and with society at large also contributes to what may seem to the survivor as incontrovertible evidence that she or he is defective and deserving of maltreatment. The same factors that can make it challenging to establish a constructive alliance with the survivor in therapy (e.g., mistrust, dependency, deficient social skills, allowing feelings to overwhelm reasoning) routinely lead to volatile and contentious relationships outside of treatment. For some clients, having ubiquitously encountered hurtful and conflictual interchanges with others both within and outside their family of origin, it may seem impossible to escape the conclusion that, "It can't possibly be that the whole world is crazy; it must be me."

The larger society context compounds this perception by stressing individual autonomy and responsibility without clearly recognizing or acknowledging the learning and practical resources required to develop and maintain these capacities. Even well-meaning, ill-informed exhortations to "forget the past," "just get over it and move on," and "forgive and forget," imply that survivors are willfully clinging to past injuries and could simply let go of them and move forward if only they were committed to doing so. In effect, the prevalence of this outlook leads to the same type of invalidating and demeaning exchange that occurred routinely in the family of origin, this time recapitulated on a much broader social scale. The survivor ends up being blamed for what is actually the failure of the family and society to adequately equip her or him with the resources required for effective functioning as an adult. It is as if someone has tied the laces of a child's two shoes together, and then, when she or he inevitably trips and falls, berates her or him for being so clumsy.

☐ Pernicious Programming

In these various ways, therefore, a family and social context model points to a range of adverse experiences beyond explicit abuse that instill and foster erroneous beliefs among PCA survivors. Similarly, by emphasizing the impact of familial interactions during childhood and adolescence on the content of the PCA survivor's thinking, this conceptual framework highlights the the inculcation of pernicious programming, not only by perpetrators of overt abuse, but also by family members who may not have engaged in overt battering or molestation. Often, when asked about the source of a particular irrational belief about themselves (e.g., "I don't deserve to exist.") or others (e.g., "When people seem to treat me well, they don't really like me. They are just being polite because they feel sorry for me."), PCA survivors are able to immediately identify that these are ideas regularly repeated to them, in almost precisely the same words, by a member of their family of origin. Once this has been established, it becomes possible for the survivor to move toward the recognition that these are not, in effect, her or his own beliefs; they were not arrived at based on her or his own observations and conclusions. Rather, they were acquired in response to hearing them reiterated over long periods of time by parents or other relatives. Being exposed to these assertions repeatedly, at a young age, from caretakers or another loved one, made it difficult if not impossible to dispute them. As a result, they were tacitly accepted and incorporated into her or his own thinking. The value of these observations and of the perspective they engender is that they can constitute a tremendous aid in expediting active questioning of the validity of the survivor's convictions.

The term applied to this mode of acquiring groundless but extremely detrimental beliefs, pernicious programming, is not meant to imply that family members' *intention* was to "brainwash" the client. Rather, the purpose of the expression is to clearly convey that whether or not indoctrination was the objective of incessantly reiterating these assertions, it is nevertheless the *effect* repetition has had on the client. In fact, it can be useful in many cases to stress, if the client's report is consistent with this notion, that the programming or brainwashing effect was not at all calculated or deliberate. The aim of offering this conceptual framework is to avoid encouraging bitterness toward family members, while helping the client question the legitimacy of ideas that have been assimilated in this way. It is hoped that it will eventually, if not immediately, be obvious that simple recapitulation of a thought does not constitute reliable evidence that it is true. The purpose of this line of reasoning is to demonstrate that beliefs acquired in this manner take on a life of their own, so that they automatically arise and persist not *because* they are valid, but in response to a mechanism *completely unrelated* to whether they are accurate.

☐ Deficient Transmission of Reasoning Skills

Programming or brainwashing through simple repetition, since it may have been engaged in either by perpetrators of abuse or by non-offending family members, is an etiological explanation for erroneous beliefs that are compatible with both trauma-based and family context models. Where the family context perspective more notably diverges from trauma-oriented conceptualizations is in how it accounts for gaps and warps in the reasoning *process*, as opposed to the content of thought. The empirical literature on the family-of-origin environments of PCA survivors, combined with clinical material exemplified by the therapy transcript in Chapter 3 of this volume, points to how unlikely it is that these clients' families modeled sound judgement and reasoning skills. Additional evidence for this is furnished by the often irrational, odd, or capricious reasoning reflected in the beliefs of PCA survivors that appear to have been indoctrinated in them by parents and other family members. When one also considers the poor judgement indicated by impulsive, erratic, and chaotic behaviors and interactions in the survivor's family of origin, it becomes evident how improbable it is that sound reasoning abilities would be developed in such a setting.

One of the most important treatment implications of the family context model, therefore, is that addressing the *content* of erroneous cognitions is not a sufficiently comprehensive goal when working with PCA survivors. In many cases considerable intervention will also need to be directed at cognitive *processing*. Gaps in judgement and reasoning abilities need to be systematically remediated. Once assimilated, these capacities can be applied toward collaboratively reevaluating particular faulty cognitive schemas and beliefs in session. Just as importantly, these same reasoning skills can be appropriated by the client to make more sophisticated and effective decisions in day-to-day living.

☐ Cognitive Processes: Developing Critical Reasoning Skills

One of the major obstacles PCA survivors face in their attempts to overcome the difficulties they experience is a strong tendency to become immobilized by the sense of hopelessness generated by a deep and abiding conviction that they are irredeemably incompetent. A central implication of the family context model is that it offers an alternate, more productive explanation for what many survivors see as their own inherent failings. In many instances, survivors' efforts at adaptation are unsuccessful because they were never taught the skills required for effective functioning and problem resolution. The practical value of this conception is that it helps survivors to transcend the self-denigration that keeps them mired in despair and inaction. Simply put, survivors will need to be reminded periodically throughout treatment that "You can't be expected to know what you've never been taught." This tautology is the foundation of the rationale for making therapy for PCA survivors skills-centered rather than trauma-centered. When applied to cognitive intervention, it fosters the understanding that, to a considerably greater degree than for most other client populations, treatment for survivors needs to target not only the content of thought, but the process of thinking itself. Survivors need to learn effective reasoning skills.

One of the pitfalls of which the practitioner must be vigilant when working with a PCA survivor is the potential for imposing her or his own beliefs on the client. Remembering that the main objective of this prioritized goal is to assist in the development of critical reasoning skills operates as a safeguard against this possibility. Helping the survivor to revise distorted beliefs is unquestionably an essential secondary component of this goal. In general, however, correcting these misconceptions must not be permitted to justify the use of overly forceful or patronizing methods. Such an approach would only serve to subvert the goal of assisting the client to cultivate independent critical judgement. Little more would be accomplished than substituting one set of "programming" for another. Not trusting her or his own judgement, and having a long history of having appropriated the beliefs of others, the PCA survivor is particularly susceptible to replacing her or his existing convictions with those of the clinician.

Training in the principles of constructive reasoning skills for survivors needs to be structured and systematic. However, if they are presented in an overly abstract and didactic fashion, it is unlikely that clients will be able to apply these principles to actual situations encountered in daily living. The reader needs to be cognizant, therefore, that the mode in which this material is conveyed here differs appreciably from that which would be used to impart it in therapy. In actual clinical practice, these principles are transmitted by applying them, in conjunction with the client, to the analysis and resolution of specific problematic situations as they arise. Once they have been introduced in this way, and the client has had the opportunity to understand them in the context of their pertinence to particular situations, it may then be useful, as a mnemonic device, to review them in the more structured, codified form in which they appear here. After the concepts underlying these principles have been grasped, many clients find that key words from them (e.g., "effectiveness," "balance") serve as useful cues for evoking and employing these principles.

Principle 1: The Purpose of Thinking is to Increase Future *Effectiveness*

An integral component of early family life for many PCA survivors was being criticized and berated for having made poor decisions about a situation. This often occurred despite the fact that no one offered them guidance on how to handle the situation in advance or provided constructive advice about how it could have been better managed in retrospect. Consequently, survivors are disposed to engaging in protracted, unproductive second-guessing and self-denigration for missteps in hindsight, without being oriented toward learning from and preventing similar outcomes thereafter. In effect, they carry out an inner dialogue that recapitulates the type of destructive, debilitating condemnation that they frequently heard from family members during their formative years. Cognitive processing is routinely used to engage in destructive self-criticism, rather than to promote effective functioning. Therefore, survivors need to be directed toward developing the habit of stopping and thinking through situations more extensively before the fact and of restricting the unproductive habit of replaying them in their minds after the fact. They need to come to see post-hoc analysis as being justifiable only if it is conducted in the spirit of constructively learning from past errors in order to avoid similar future outcomes. They must learn that, in contrast, rage-filled self-denigration, because its content is destructive and its tone is emotionally debilitating, perpetuates poor judgement and thereby impedes effective functioning.

Prinicple 2: Identify, Acknowledge, and Find a *Balance* Between Emotional Pulls and Logical Considerations

One of the unproductive habits frequently modeled in the families of origin of PCA survivors is a proclivity for acting on the intensity of momentary feelings and impulses, untempered by logical reasoning. A particularly conspicuous example of this is the tendency of parents in a chaotic household to strike out in rage at each other, at the children, and less commonly, at individuals outside the family circle. In effect, the tension reduction afforded by venting emotions is indulged with little or no consideration for the consequences beyond the heat of the moment. Feelings are habitually allowed to overshadow and supplant logical reasoning aimed at establishing more effective, enduring solutions to problems and interpersonal conflicts. Children growing up in an atmosphere such as this have little opportunity to learn to modulate feelings, to think difficulties through in order to generate productive response options, or to resist urges to carry out impulsive behaviors to alleviate the distress of the moment.

Many survivors grew up in an interpersonal atmosphere in which situations, people, problems, and solutions were framed in terms of polar extremes, with minimal recognition or acknowledgment of nuances, extenuating circumstances, or exceptions. Extensive exposure to this type of thinking makes it difficult for many survivors to conceive of either inner or interpersonal conflicts in ways that transcend a cognitive framework of irreconcilable opposites. A tendency toward dichotomous thinking interferes with the potential to view categories such as thought and feeling, for example, as representing anything other than mutually exclusive and inherently contradictory categories. This perspective disposes many survivors to see rationality as good and emotionality as bad (i.e., unacceptable and destructive), periodically motivating them to make desperate but futile efforts to obliterate feelings.

Particularly in the early phases of addressing the prioritized goal of developing the capacity for critical reasoning, therefore, the therapist will need to make a special effort to help the survivor discern conceptual possibilities that transcend diametrically opposed frameworks such as this. In relation to thinking and feeling, this will entail, for example, explaining that attempting to suppress feelings entirely in an effort to act on logic alone is not a viable or even a desirable solution. Feelings are neither superfluous nor a nuisance. They have a purpose. Far from being antithetical to productive reasoning, emotions are an essential component of this process. They convey information essential to decision making about what we want and don't want, what we find desirable and unpleasant.

In order to make this point more comprehensible, I often find it useful to draw an analogy between emotions and physical pain.

> On the surface physical discomfort seems to be nothing more than a bothersome sensation that is best to avoid. Consider, however, what would happen if we did not have the capacity to experience pain. Think of those times when you noticed that you had a minor cut and were bleeding, but realized that it must have occurred early that day without you being aware of it. What if you received a larger, more serious physical injury, but did not notice it because there was no physical pain? You might literally bleed to death, because without pain you would be without a signal to alert you that something was wrong and needed attention.

Pain is unpleasant, but it has a purpose. It carries important information. In the same way, emotions, whether enjoyable or disturbing, have a function. In any given situation, they are one element to take into account in choosing which course of action to follow. When combined with objective information and logical analysis, they enhance, rather than detract from, the decision-making process. Effectiveness is maximized by drawing upon both emotions and reason in planning a course of action, rather than relying on either to the exclusion of the other.

Principle 3: Weigh the Relative *Costs and Benefits* of Immediate Relief and Long Term Gains

Generally speaking, feelings are most likely to create difficulties when they are the *exclusive* basis for behavior, or when they are permitted to override other, cognitively-based considerations. Problems are created, in other words, not by feelings themselves, but when feelings are allowed to obscure rationality. Once again, the experience of physical pain provides an apt analogy.

> By making us aware of a situation that needs to be attended to, physical pain fulfills an invaluable function. However, if we were to make decisions solely on the basis of what does or does not feel good physically, pain would lead us in the *opposite* direction. Instead of mobilizing us to seek out medical attention, concern that surgery or other procedures may intensify the pain, if left unchecked, could actually entice us to avoid seeing a doctor. It is when we combine the pain's message that something is wrong with the intellectual understanding that things could get worse without medical treatment that we are best equipped to make a wise decision.

The physical pain analogy graphically illustrates the mechanism via which feeling-based decisions, untempered by cognitive reasoning, tend to compound rather than resolve problems. Actions grounded solely on emotions often are effective when viewed in a limited time frame: in the short run, they are likely to successfully provide relief from or avoidance of discomfort. However, from a long-term perspective there is usually a heavy price to pay for immediate relief. The original source of the problem that created the emotional distress remains intact, and is allowed to fester and magnify. Succinctly put, difficulties are usually compounded when choices are based on the pursuit of short-term comfort at the expense of long-range solutions. Maladaptive coping strategies fitting this description—such as heated verbal altercations, domestic violence, alcohol and substance abuse, sexual acting out, procrastination, and avoidance—are precisely those responses to distress that were modeled for PCA survivors in the interpersonal landscape in which they were reared. Conversely, survivors are much less likely to have been exposed to tactics for resisting impulsively acting on intense feelings in order to examine a problem situation with sufficient dispassionate rationality to construct viable and enduring solutions.

Principle 4: Develop an Expanded Perspective in Order to Find the *"Middle Ground"* Between Extremes

A pervasive difficulty for many PCA survivors is being able to look beyond the extremes and perceive the broad "middle ground" territory that lies between polar opposites. This means, for example, recognizing that decisions can be made on the basis of the combined appraisal of *both* thoughts and feelings, immediate relief and long-term outcomes, self-interest and concern for others, and so on, instead of restricting oneself to an either/or model of cognitive processing. For instance, if one focuses entirely on assuaging momentary distress, this will obviously interfere with constructive problem resolution. However, development of a response to a problematic situation that will yield progress toward the achievement of long-term solutions does not necessarily entail the complete renunciation of the alleviation of immediate discomfort. It is not necessary to choose between these two objectives. Both can be obtained. Seeking a long-term solution does not require sacrificing efforts to relieve distress, as long as comfort is not pursued at the expense of attending to the problem at hand.

Principle 5: Identify a *Range of Choices* Including Several That Fall Within the "Middle Ground"

Difficulty recognizing the existence of the middle ground creates numerous obstacles to effective daily functioning by concealing a vast range of alternatives and choices available when one is able to discern the possibilities that lie beyond "either/or"dichotomies. The environment in survivors' families of origin was often characterized by conditions that limited, obscured, or negated the choices available to them. An excessively controlling, authoritarian, or capricious family atmosphere typically focuses on communicating what is *not permissible,* and the limitations created by an oppressive family system often actually *restrict* the options available to the survivor throughout her or his growing up years. Child rearing in such families often concentrates primarily on blocking access to options rather than on revealing the presence of and facilitating access to opportunities. Particularly when combined with a cognitive set that is disposed to perceiving situations in terms of incompatible opposites, this experiential background can severely hamper survivors' ability to be aware of the choices potentially available to them. Consequently, it is often not sufficient for the practitioner to simply help the client to locate the middle ground. Frequently, the survivor will then need further assistance in recognizing that the territory constituting the middle ground is much broader than a single intermediate option.

Principle 6: *Weigh* the Alternative Choices and *Select* a Course of Action

Once a spectrum of alternative responses to a situation has been generated, a strategy must be employed to determine which choice to select for implementation. This process will often consist of some variation of the proverbial method of generating and evaluating a list of costs and benefits potentially associated with each option that has been identified. However, the procedure is somewhat more complex in several respects. For one thing, the alternatives to be assessed will consist of more than two mutually exclusive courses of action. Moreover, the client is encouraged to evaluate the advantages and disadvantages of each choice being considered to help generate further intermediate, compromise, or compound solutions that may not have occurred to her or him earlier. In addition, the client is alerted to be mindful that choices are not necessarily irrevocable. Once decided, one can often continue to assess the effectiveness and desirability of his or her choice and revise one's course of action accordingly.

☐ Cognitive Content: Re-examining and Revising Erroneous Convictions

The conceptual framework provided by the family context model alerts us to the unusual degree to which many PCA survivors' reasoning processes are likely to be characterized by gaps and deficiencies. Moreover, the critical and controlling atmosphere in which many survivors grew up often leaves them prone to doubting their own perceptions and beliefs and vulnerable to accepting convictions imposed on them by others. This proclivity has often been further reinforced by instances of overt abuse, statements and threats by abuse perpetrators that were aimed at contradicting and defining the survivor's perception and experience of these events, secrecy surrounding the abuse, and unwillingness of authority figures to believe the survivor when she or he tried to reveal the abuse. Consequently, therapists have to exert special care not to inflict their personal views on survivor clients. This can be an especially formidable task when attempting to help survivors question and revise cognitive distortions. How can the practitioner accomplish this essential goal without offering alternative beliefs derived from her or his own perspective?

One of the most effective ways to accomplish this objective is to rely primarily on a client-directed approach based on Socratic methods of questioning. This tactic allows the clinician to encourage the survivor to clarify her or his viewpoint without either directly challenging it or proffering alternate conclusions. It also circumvents the likelihood that the interchange between therapist and client will degenerate into an impasse or adversarial conflict over contradictory beliefs. Instead, the client is encouraged to defend and support her or his convictions, and in the process to identify and examine the reasoning and evidence underlying them. If her or his conclusions are not sustainable when investigated under the light of logic and concrete evidence, this creates an opening for the formulation and appraisal of alternatives. An additional advantage of this format is that besides facilitating revision of the content of distorted beliefs, it implicitly instructs the client in the process of logical reasoning; after repeated interchanges of this type in session the client gradually learns to generate a similar line of inquiry in her or his own train of thought.

Although primarily oriented to the treatment of the effects of single event trauma, Meichenbaum's narrative constructivist approach to treating PTSD (Hoyt, 1996; Meichenbaum & Fong, 1993) is very similar to the method for facilitating the correction of distorted beliefs advocated here. The major difference is in the material that is selected to be processed. Meichenbaum's central concept is that experience and behavior are strongly influenced by the stories (i.e., narratives) we construct about ourselves and the events we encounter (Meichenbaum & Fong, 1993). Meichenbaum's emphasis, because he applies his model to ameliorating the impact of circumscribed traumas, is on the traumatic event itself (see, e.g., Meichenbaum, 1995). With PCA survivors, similar interventions are directed toward examining clients' narratives about themselves, their family backgrounds and other salient interpersonal experiences, and their current circumstances and potential. This application is not at all discrepant with Meichenbaum's perspective; he explicitly acknowledges that "narrative reconstructive efforts are not limited to only major stressful events" (Meichenbaum & Fitzpatrick, 1993, p. 714). In fact, his conception is philosophically compatible with a family context model in many respects, and the mode of intervention he advocates is highly consistent with the client-directed focus of a contextual approach to treatment. In Meichenbaum's own words:

> I go beyond understanding, to nurturing the client's discovery process by using Socratic questioning.... I encourage clinicians to use strategically their bemusement, their befuddlement; I want them to be collaborators. (Hoyt, 1996, p. 128)

The use of the terms "bemusement" and "befuddlement" is noteworthy. It is indicative of a manner of listening to clients, and particularly to PCA survivors, which is critical to effectively intervening to facilitate the identification and revision of distorted beliefs. This mode of interaction differs significantly from that appropriated in everyday conversation. In casual social interactions, we generally take it for granted that we know what the other person means. Without even realizing it, we spontaneously fill in subtle gaps and inconsistencies in what the other person is saying to us. There is a practical reason for communicating in this way. We are implicitly aware that to incessantly and meticulously ask for clarification of the numerous ambiguities that commonly appear throughout a casual exchange would be disruptive. The other person would soon become irritated and withdraw. Even more fundamentally, we usually see no need for this type of questioning, because we assume that our core convictions coincide with those of the person with whom we are interacting.

A family context model of prolonged child abuse alerts us that it is precisely the latter assumption that is likely to be unwarranted. Not only are PCA survivors' beliefs distorted by the destabilizing influence of abuse, but they were also probably originally formulated in the context of a family that did not share or transmit the assumptions subscribed to by mainstream society. When we listen and respond to PCA survivors in session, therefore, we need to do so with this in mind. We need to collaboratively join with survivor clients in order to facilitate the process of helping them to identify and articulate their implicit assumptions. Then, by asking them to explain how they arrived at these conclusions, we can assist them in considering whether their core beliefs are consistent with logic and evidence.

This approach requires listening to the client with a very different orientation than the one we would assume in everyday conversation. Rather than automatically "explaining away" gaps and ambiguities in her or his own mind, or never noticing them in the first place, the practitioner must be constantly vigilant for their appearance, and prepared to ask for clarification. Accomplishing this entails continually asking oneself, "Do I really understand what is being said?" The objective is not to attack the client's beliefs or to raise doubts about them, but to display a constructive curiosity about them. What are the assumptions the client is operating under? How did they originate? Are they consistent with other aspects of the client's current understanding and knowledge? If not, how can they be modified to be more compatible with her or his present experience and perspective? By asking questions such as these, the practitioner powerfully and implicitly communicates that it is not her or his role to furnish answers to these queries, but the client's. The survivor is the final arbiter of her or his own truth.

One of the tremendous advantages of this approach is that it acts to substantially limit the degree to which the therapist's preconceptions are likely to influence and shape the material reported by the client. Open-ended Socratic questioning about the source of particular maladaptive beliefs is less prone than more pointed inquiry to elicit specific types of responses consistent with the practitioner's theoretical biases. The clinician may have formulated hypotheses in her or his own mind about whether a certain belief originated in an abusive experience, in the family-of-origin environment, or is traceable to some other factor or combination of factors. However, the determinant of whether the clinician's conjectures will be retained or discarded is the data generated more or less exclusively by the survivor.

Equally importantly, this procedure places the pacing of exploration primarily under the survivor's control. As a general rule, it has been my experience that clients will not venture into territory that they are not yet equipped to effectively cope with when the pacing of investigation is in their hands. They usually consciously avoid addressing material, such as potentially destabilizing abusive or otherwise traumatic incidents, that they are not ready to handle. In fact, the relevancy of such material is not likely to even occur to them if confronting it would be premature. An open-ended Socratic method of inquiry, therefore, is grounded in the assumption that the client's innate judgement is usually the best guide to the rate and direction in which exploration should proceed.

☐ Cognitive Content: Common Core Distortions

The enterprise of teaching the survivor to exercise critical reasoning and revise faulty assumptions is a particularly good example of how a treatment plan based on prioritized goals differs from one structured as an invariant sequence of interventions. In the presence of an appreciable level of distress or dissociation, the capacity to focus sufficiently to engage in extensive constructive cognitive intervention will be substantially limited. It is for this reason that modulating distress and bolstering the capacity for attention and concentration are assigned higher priorities in the treatment plan than revising erroneous beliefs.

This does not by any means necessitate, however, that cognitive intervention only begins once the two goals with higher priorities have been fully attained. Examination of the origins of erroneous beliefs, and questioning their validity, will in most cases occur from the earliest sessions of treatment as this material spontaneously emerges in session. However, to the extent that distress or dissociative experiences are salient, helping the client learn to moderate them will need to take precedence over protracted cognitive exploration and reframing. It is usually only once substantive progress has been made toward reducing distress and increasing focal awareness that extensive training in critical reasoning skills will be plausible. Since sustained, systematic work on core distortions is highly dependent on the application of critical judgement and reasoning, this aspect of cognitive intervention needs to be postponed until emotional discomfort and dissociative preoccupation no longer appreciably interfere with continuity of attention.

Just as exploration of faulty beliefs will be a component of treatment from its inception, this endeavor can be expected to continue throughout the course of therapy, long after formal training in critical reasoning skills has ceased to be a central focus of intervention. Not only will new distortions periodically emerge as treatment progresses, but erroneous beliefs that have previously been identified and processed can be expected to resurface repeatedly. Many of these convictions have been so deeply ingrained through repeatedly hearing them voiced by family members since childhood, and through their apparent confirmation in the form of abuse and other adverse experiences, that they only gradually fade in response to repeated examination. A less obvious reason why these negative expectations tend to be so unyielding is that they occupy an extremely pivotal position in the survivor's worldview. The more fundamental a belief is, the more corollary inferences in the individual's cognitive framework have been predicated on it (Beck, 1979; Kelly, 1955). Consequently, even convictions that appear negative in content are difficult to relinquish, because to do so entails changing vast portions of the worldview that made events seem predictable and comprehensible. Being cognizant of these factors can help the practitioner to expect, understand, and tolerate the possibility that distortions that may have seemed to have previously been addressed and corrected may well resurface at several subsequent points in treatment.

The specific cognitive distortions manifested by an individual PCA survivor can obviously vary considerably, depending on the particulars of her or his history of abuse, exposure to other adverse experiences, indoctrination in faulty beliefs by family members and abuse perpetrators, and warps in judgement and reasoning. This is one of the reasons why client-directed exploration is the preferred strategy for addressing cognitive distortions with PCA survivors. As clinicians we need to be educated by individual survivors' histories and resulting worldviews, rather than presuming to inform them, based on our own preconceptions, of what their erroneous beliefs are. This may seem self-evident, but in practice it can be a challenge for the practitioner to patiently allow the survivor's belief system to unfold. Consider, for example, the session transcript in Chapter 3, in which Rick struggles to articulate the impetus underlying his materialistic preoccupations. It can require considerable restraint for the therapist to trust the client's ability to accurately define her or his own experience. He or she must resist the temptation to offer a perspective that provides a sense of closure, and which may be extremely plausible, but which nevertheless is likely to be inaccurate. Ultimately only the client can know, express, and make sense of her or his own experience and the impact of that experience.

When PCA survivors are allowed the time and latitude to explore their own experience and articulate their own belief system, among the vast array of material that arises, there is one core cognitive distortion expressed with such frequency, that carries so much conceptual significance, that it warrants being considered here in some detail. This is the conviction of being *fundamentally flawed,* that is, *inherently and irrevocably incompetent, undeserving, and unlovable.* This triad of contemptuously pejorative self-attributions will emerge repeatedly in various guises, contexts, and permutations at various points in therapy. The scope, intensity, tenacity and pervasiveness of these convictions can vary appreciably from one individual to the next. Among survivors from the most chaotic and disturbed family backgrounds and with the most chronic and severe abuse histories, all three components of this conception are unambiguously present.

Painfully aware of the gaps in their daily living skills, the restrictions created by the distress with which they are plagued, and the avoidance with which they respond to it, it is difficult for many survivors not to conclude that they are hopelessly incompetent. Having been deprived of a family-of-origin environment in which they could master adaptive living skills and handicapped by the intrusive and debilitating impact of explicit abuse, it is almost inevitable for them to conclude that they are "stupid," "clumsy," "awkward," and irreparably inept. Gradually, by being provided with the opportunity to learn the skills that they have never been taught, and by exploring the origins of their functional limitations and coming to recognize the ways in which they have been deprived and undermined, the conviction of ineptitude erodes.

The certainty of being undeserving can usually be traced to the demoralizing influence of "programming" in the form of incessant exposure to criticism and condemnation throughout their growing-up years. Coupled with the impact of ongoing, crushing assaults in the form of overt abuse, it becomes comprehensible how the survivor developed the conviction that she or he is somehow intrinsically bad and deserves mistreatment. The value of a Socratic approach to cognitive intervention, inviting the client to provide evidence for and to justify her or his contention of being inherently unworthy rather than attempting to logically dispute it, is obvious here. This type of conclusion, particularly because it usually has so little rational basis to it, is especially difficult to rebut, but at the same time almost impossible to defend. As it becomes increasingly clearer to the survivor that the negative things she or he was repeatedly told about her or himself have no basis in fact, their credibility eventually fades.

Of the three major classes of derogatory self-perceptions frequently manifested by PCA survivors, probably the most central and poignant is that of being innately unlovable. Almost invariably, this conviction grows out of the profoundly affecting experience of being unloved, ignored, despised, scapegoated, and rejected by parents and other relations. It is as if the child reared in such a situation concludes, "who could possibly be expected to care about me, to find me worthy of their affection, if my own family, who knows me best, to whom I am closest, and who are entrusted with my well-being, treats me this way? Certainly, if my own family doesn't love or validate me, no one will." Overt abuse by family members or by perpetrators outside the family only serves to substantiate the survivor's perception of being contemptible. How can the clinician help the survivor to question this conviction? Often the evidence that the client was in fact unloved appears incontrovertible. The fallacy here, however, is the assumption that if one is despised and mistreated by one's own family, it is a forgone conclusion that she or he will be similarly received by everyone. Careful exploration of family members' treatment of individuals other than the client will frequently reveal that affectionate and caring interactions were rarely, if ever, apparent in their relationships with anyone. Often, therefore, the evidence strongly suggests that the client may have been deprived of affection, not because she or he was unlovable, but because the family had little capacity for loving behavior. Moreover, as the client's history unfolds, even though it may be riddled with experiences of rejection and maltreatment, there are also likely to be instances of relationships in which she or he was treated with respect, kindness, and tenderness.

There are a number of cognitive distortions commonly encountered in working with PCA survivors that seem to be derived from and to constitute reactions to this core triad of perceiving themselves as being incompetent, undeserving, and unlovable. One of the more commonly occurring amongst these is the idea *"only love will heal me"*—the belief that emotional security and reparation of the effects of past mistreatment are only attainable through obtaining the affection and care that was not available in childhood. It is as if the survivor hopes that somehow someone will come along who will demonstrate that she or he is, after all, worthy of love and attention. Nevertheless, believing her- or himself to be fundamentally undeserving of love and kindness, and consequently believing that such behavior cannot be trusted or will only be tenuously and fleetingly present, the survivor is prone to respond with either desperate clinging, retreating into self-protective isolation, or impulsively wavering between these two reactions. However, as long as this derogatory self-attribution of being unlovable remains intact, benevolent gestures are only apt to be discounted or explained away as signs of being placated, or assumed to be destined to abrupt withdrawal when the other person comes to realize how vile and unworthy she or he really is. Unless the fallacy of being unlovable is directly questioned and dismantled, therefore, no amount of nurturing by someone else is likely to dispel it.

A related conviction adhered to by many PCA survivors is that they must display unconditional kindness and deference in order to maintain an interpersonal relationship, and that this stance will eventually elicit reciprocity. For many of these individuals, "programming" in the form of repeatedly being told how unworthy, self-centered, and demanding they are, a controlling family environment that does not encourage or model adaptive assertiveness, and explicitly abusive treatment that cultivates submissiveness, combine to foster an interpersonal style of passive appeasement. Forces such as these imbue many survivors with the misguided belief that if they are only giving enough, agreeable enough, and accommodating enough, others will treat them with kindness and consideration. The flaw in this conviction is that it is maintained indiscriminately, that is, *regardless of how others treat them.* This not only exposes survivors to repeated victimization and maltreatment by people with malicious intent, but disturbingly, it also fosters being exploited even by those who are generally well-meaning and benevolent in their dealings with others. It is as if by being noncontingently conciliatory, they are unwittingly conditioning others to take advantage of their "good nature." Often without being aware of it, others slip into the habit of asking these survivors for favors, relying on them when they find it expedient, or assuming they will take on responsibilities, simply because they know implicitly that they can expect docile compliance. Survivors therefore need help understanding that reciprocity comes from asking for what you want rather than from indiscriminately giving, and that this is not only legitimate but an indispensable element in effective interpersonal relating.

Due to the tendency to think in terms of dichotomies, it is not unusual for PCA survivors to waver between the belief that "only love will heal me" and the opposing conviction that *"security is only found in isolation and self-sufficiency."* For most survivors, the latter belief is rooted in numerous interpersonal experiences of abuse, mistreatment, exploitation, miscommunication, disappointment, and hurt. Usually these instances date back to childhood and early family life, leading to the development of social interaction patterns that serve only to perpetuate further incidents of maltreatment, rejection, and anguish. Survivors, therefore, have often accumulated extensive evidence that seems to indicate that others cannot be trusted and that attempts at affiliation are only doomed to lead to further abandonment and misery. Some individuals act on this conclusion by behaving in ways purposely designed to keep others at a distance. Others simply avoid social contact.

However, the attentive practitioner will almost invariably find, even among those clients with histories marked by the most extreme and pervasive forms of mistreatment, abuse, and interpersonal discord, some examples of relationships that were characterized by warmth, support, and positive regard. These encounters are crucial sources of contradictory evidence for the survivor's belief that others will invariably be rejecting or abusive, or that constructive and gratifying interpersonal connections are unattainable due to her or his own irreparable defects. She or he will need assistance in gradually coming to understand how the warps and deficiencies in social adaptation created by a chaotic early family life and by abuse trauma have interfered with the establishment of more effective and rewarding interpersonal relationships. As these gaps in interpersonal functioning are identified and remediated in therapy, the palpably improved quality of the client's social life will constitute a powerful source of disconfirmation for previous assumptions that others are untrustworthy and malicious or that she or he is worthless and detestable.

One particular variation on the belief that "security is only found in isolation and self-sufficiency" that I have seen manifested among some PCA survivors, most commonly men, is to equate security with financial independence. This conviction usually manifests in the form of impulsively conceived and executed schemes to "get rich quick" via business ventures, investments, speculation, or gambling. Underlying this behavior is the certainty that only by becoming independently wealthy can one protect oneself from being controlled and exploited by others. Economic self-sufficiency is single-mindedly pursued because it is viewed as the only route to autonomy, and consequently to emotional security. Paradoxically, the urgency and impetuosity that fuel this goal cloud rational judgement, almost inevitably leading to financial reversals and an even greater sense of bitterness, desperation, and oppression. The clinician gently and nonjudgementally invites collaborative exploration of these ventures and the reasoning behind them from the point of their conception, through execution, and outcome. It is critical that the practitioner patiently anticipate several passages through this cycle before the client slowly comes to appreciate the degree to which an acute sense of desperation is allowed to subvert sober reasoning in the planning and execution of these endeavors. By investigating the thinking that drives these undertakings, and coming to recognize their origins in past coercive treatment, the survivor is eventually able to disrupt the sequence of maladaptive thinking, escalated agitation, and impulsive action. The same procedure, delineated in extensive detail in the next chapter, serves as the strategy for dismantling a wide range of maladaptive behaviors and supplanting them with more effective alternatives.

I have explicitly considered here how cognitive intervention is aimed at assisting the survivor in developing judgment and reasoning skills that were not taught or modeled in her or his family of origin. However, although cognitive restructuring has been addressed primarily as a separate treatment goal, this form of intervention, more than any other, permeates all of the goals and phases of the PCA survivor's therapy. Underpinning all aspects of treatment is the abiding effort to help her or him see that the bleak, unremitting pessimism that has seemed to characterize life until this point is not the only, or even the most accurate vision of reality, either now or in the future. With the growing capacity to handle life in more effective ways, the dawning apperception that things can in fact be different slowly materializes as a concrete actuality.

Coping: Breaking and Replacing Maladaptive Patterns

A wide range of maladaptive behavior patterns have been found to be associated with the presence of a PCA history. These difficulties include: alcoholism and drug abuse (Bennett & Kemper, 1994; Browne & Finkelhor, 1986; Spak, Spak, & Allebeck, 1997; Wilsnack, Vogeltanz, Klassen, & Harris, 1997); self-mutilation, most often in the form of cutting and burning (Lipschitz et al., 1999; Nijman et al., 1999); suicidal attempts and gestures (Briere & Runtz, 1986; Bryer, Nelson, Miller, & Krol,1987; Lipschitz et al., 1999; Mullen et al., 1996); eating disorders, (de Groot & Rodin, 1999; Fallon & Wonderlich, 1997); and compulsive sexual activity (Anderson & Coleman, 1991; Tedesco & Bola, 1997). As diverse as these behaviors may seem, they have been grouped together conceptually in at least two different ways. They have all been considered to fall under the general heading of addictive or compulsive behaviors. Most of them also have been construed as examples of self-injurious activities. To the extent that each of these designations is descriptive, rather than explanatory, neither of them account for why these types of difficulties are especially prevalent among PCA survivors.

☐ Conceptualizing Maladaptive Behavior Patterns

One of the particular difficulties with the term "self-injurious" is that it is often taken to indicate that not just the effect, but the *intention* of these behaviors is to be self-destructive. As Linehan (1993) notes, however, one can not legitimately deduce the intent of a behavior from its effect. There is no question that the activities listed above are dangerous and can be damaging. However, this does not establish that they are carried out for the purpose of being self-destructive.

Conceiving of these patterns as addictive or compulsive yields a slightly different understanding of why they are engaged in despite their detrimental effects. Instead of presuming that these activities are *intended* to be hazardous and destructive, this model focuses on explaining how individuals who engage in them *avoid recognizing* their harmful consequences. In other words, when these same behaviors are thought of as addictive or compulsive rather than self-injurious, they are seen as being maintained not by the *intent* to be self-punitive but as a result of *denial* of their damaging effects.

A family context conceptual model seeks to make sense of these patterns of activity by attempting to illuminate their possible origins. This perspective construes this same constellation of behaviors not as self-destructive, but as desperate efforts to grapple with and contain emotional anguish. Many PCA survivors grew up in families that did not provide them with productive strategies for coping with unpleasant affect. The combination of having deficient opportunities to learn constructive methods of emotional modulation, growing up in a family atmosphere in which impulsive and destructive forms of coping were routinely modeled, and protracted exposure to the extreme stressor of abuse trauma renders the development of maladaptive coping patterns practically unavoidable. In some instances these behaviors may be motivated to some degree by the intent to be self-injurious. When this is the case, it is because the twin forces of a rejecting and controlling family environment and of coercive abuse experiences have aroused intense rage in the survivor. As children, allowing their anger at others to show often would lead to further emotional abandonment and maltreatment. These experiences instilled the conviction that directing anger outward is unacceptable and can be extremely dangerous, provoking painful consequences. Many survivors also seem to internalize the hostile and denigrating attitudes displayed toward them by family members and abuse perpetrators. It is far from surprising, therefore, that the combination of self-loathing and the inhibition of external expressions of anger coalesce to result in frankly self-injurious behavior. Survivors sometimes report that the function of this punishment is to enforce the restriction on externally discernable displays of emotion, in order to avoid rejection and mistreatment by others. The ultimate purpose of these behaviors, therefore, is not self-punishment, but self-protection. Given the PCA survivor's past experiences and resulting convictions, self-harm may seem like the only, or the safest, avenue for venting rageful feelings.

This also holds true for other compulsive or addictive behavior patterns. They may have detrimental *effects*, but this is not their *purpose*. In general, these behaviors have the function of providing relief from painful, at times overwhelming, affect. Having never been provided with the resources that would have enabled them to master more adaptive ways to manage distress, PCA survivors come to rely on addictive and compulsive behaviors as a primary means of modulating disturbing affect. Explicitly self-punitive behavior is just one particular variation of this principle, in which the affect of intolerable rage finds expression in hostility directed toward the self. Other compulsive behavior patterns, however, may be appropriated to relieve a wide range of distressing emotions.

This conception of maladaptive coping patterns among survivors helps to inform the sequence of prioritized goals in the contextual treatment model. The model proposes that addictive and compulsive behaviors are relied upon because more adaptive methods of regulating emotional discomfort are not available. In order to successfully break and replace the deleterious behaviors that they utilize to soothe emotional agitation, survivors first need to have attained some degree of proficiency at: (a) invoking more effective strategies for reducing distress; (b) modulating dissociation; and (c) exercising critical judgment. Once an at least rudimentary ability to employ these three skills has been established, they can be applied to the investigation, evaluation, understanding, disruption, and, ultimately, elimination of self-damaging patterns of behavior.

☐ Precautions Regarding Maladaptive Behavior Patterns and PCA Survivor Treatment

One avenue of response to PCA survivors with addictive, compulsive, self-injurious patterns is to refer them out for specialized intervention for these problem behaviors. There are certainly both outpatient and inpatient therapy programs and well-delineated treatment protocols available that exclusively target each of the specific difficulties grouped here under the general rubric of "maladaptive behavior patterns." Unquestionably there are conditions under which such a course of action may be warranted, such as when these behaviors exacerbate to the point of precluding the pursuit of other treatment goals. In some such situations, it may be feasible to maintain contextual treatment while specialized intervention for a particular maladaptive behavior pattern is carried out simultaneously as an adjunct form of therapy with another practitioner or agency. In particularly dire circumstances, contexutal treatment may need to be interrupted or abandoned entirely for an extended period of time in favor of therapy that focuses more or less exclusively on an addictive, compulsive, or self-injurious behavior that has come to pose an acute threat to a client's safety.

This scenario, however, should be an exception. Ideally, contextual therapy for PCA survivors will not have been implemented to begin with in cases in which an addictive, compulsive, or self-injurious behavior is so salient, of such extensive proportions, or has progressed so far that attention to it to the exclusion of all other treatment goals is required. In instances such as these, a course of intervention designed to specifically address the maladaptive behavior pattern should be carried through to the point of stabilization before the initiation of contextual therapy is considered. In instances where it is judged that contextual therapy is appropriate, interruptions in the larger course of treatment in order to implement specialized intensive intervention for acute exacerbations of addictive, compulsive, or self-injurious behaviors can often be prevented. Careful adherence to the principle of refraining from premature or excessive confrontation of potentially destabilizing traumatic material, and instead placing greater emphasis on development of the capacities for distress reduction and adaptive coping, is essential in this regard.

☐ Disrupting Maladaptive Behavior Patterns

To summarize, when conceptualized from the perspective of a family context model, maladaptive behavior patterns in the form of addictive, compulsive, and self-injurious acts, although varied in overt appearance, have the following in common:

- They represent responses to and attempts to allay discomforting emotions.
- They are learned via interpersonal modeling or evolve in response to having not be taught more functional methods of modulating disturbing emotions.
- They may have damaging consequences, but are usually adopted in spite of, rather than because of this.
- They persist due to lack of awareness of more constructive strategies for managing discomfort, and because, despite their negative effects and adverse long term repercussions, they are for the most part successful in reducing immediate distress.
- They become habitual, and are therefore often carried out in a more or less automatic, impulsive fashion, accompanied by minimal cognitive examination.

These assumptions about the nature of the addictive, compulsive, and self-injurious behaviors exhibited by PCA survivors comprise the conceptual foundation for the general intervention approach to disrupting these habitual behaviors and replacing them with more effective alternatives. Particularly pivotal to this method is the observation that these types of behavior patterns are carried out with little cognitive appraisal either before, during, or after they occur. Almost without exception, activities of this kind are associated with some degree of secrecy. The presence, frequency, and extent of performance of addictive, compulsive, and self-injurious behaviors is usually minimized, not only to others, but often to the self.

A second crucial point is the role of affect in fueling repetition of compulsive behaviors. Shame about engaging in these activities, reluctance to relinquish them because of the relief that they provide from emotional discomfort, and the consequent disinclination to recognize their adverse effects, all act to inhibit a concerted examination of them. Since, according to the conception proposed here, compulsive patterns serve the function of relieving emotional distress, it follows that the shame of engaging in these behaviors only serves to increase the probability that they will be reiterated. Humiliation and self-contempt in response to having indulged the compulsive urge creates additional distress that contributes to the eventual recurrence of the compulsive activity in an effort to relieve the shame (see Figure 6).

The primary tactic in addressing these patterns is to build upon the two complementary conjectures about how they are activated and perpetuated. They are construed as maladaptive responses to distress, maintained by the disturbing affect that is aroused by self-condemnation and self-loathing for engaging in the compulsion, and by the consequent avoidance of thinking about the behavior and the circumstances surrounding it. Pressing for elimination of the behavior is only likely to arouse further shame about engaging in it and anticipatory anxiety about forfeiting a source of tension reduction. Therefore this is not the primary focus of intervention. Instead of urging abstinence from the compulsion, the therapist proceeds by inviting the client to join her or him in collaboratively exploring it. The general aim is to arouse curiosity about the behavior and to encourage the client to participate in investigating it and the circumstances and experiences associated with it.

The specific procedure used for collaboratively investigating the elements comprising and surrounding the compulsive or addictive pattern is functional behavioral analysis (Bellack & Hersen, 1988; Kanfer & Phillips, 1970; Nelson & Hayes, 1986). Usually, the practitioner will initiate this process by nonchalantly inquiring about a compulsion that the client has just revealed, after having established that she or he is willing to discuss it. Relevant areas for questioning would include when the compulsion first started, the circumstances surrounding its first occurrence, some spe-

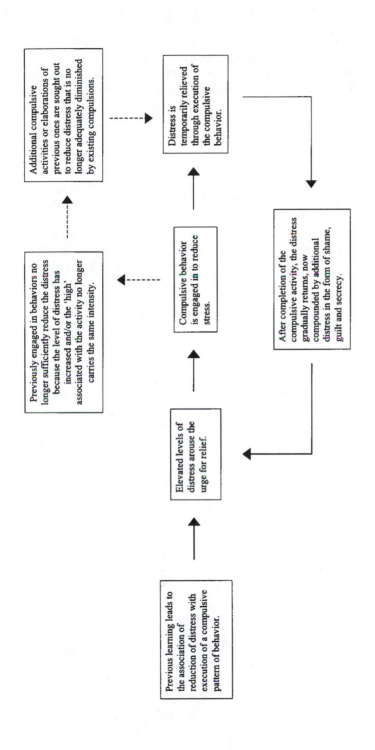

FIGURE 6. The Cycle and Progression of Compulsive Behavior Patterns. Note. From "Sexual Addiction: Many Conceptions, Minimal Data," by S. N. Gold and C. L. Heffner, 1998, *Clinical Psychology Review, 18,* pp. 367–381. Copyright 1998 by Elsevier Science Ltd. Adapted with permission.

cifics on what the behavior consists of, how often it is engaged in, and how it may have changed over time. Responses to questions such as these will obviously be of value in helping the therapist to understand the client's perception of and attitude toward the compulsion, and in developing a preliminary formulation of its nature and function. However, gathering information is of secondary importance at this point. The main objective is to provide the client with the experience of talking about the compulsive pattern in a calm, dispassionate way without either being judged harshly for engaging in the behaviors comprising it or being pressured to suppress or eliminate it. In this way, the practitioner implicitly and powerfully communicates to the client that it is safe to talk about the compulsion, and in doing so begins to help diffuse the shame and self-criticism connected with it. Continued interchanges of this type gradually erode the survivor's firmly entrenched expectation that acknowledging and discussing the behavior will elicit either badgering to relinquish it, or condemnation and abandonment.

As the client begins to exhibit signs of being able to talk about the compulsion without being overly guarded, apprehensive, or flustered, the therapist can proceed to the next step of the intervention procedure. This point may be reached only after several sessions, dispersed over a period of weeks or months, in which the pattern was explored in a more general fashion. Once the client seems to be able to talk about the compulsion without undue discomfort, the practitioner can proceed by enlisting her or his cooperation in identifying a particular instance when the behavior was executed. The incident chosen may be the most recent one during which the behavior was performed, the first time it ever occurred, the most extreme instance of its occurrence, or one which the client believes exemplifies the pattern especially well.

It is important, however, that a specific occasion is selected for examination, rather than relying on the client's global impression of what "usually" happens. Adhering to this procedure substantially increases the precision of the information reported to the therapist. An even more vital consideration is that this approach helps to ensure that the client develops a more accurate understanding of the compulsive pattern by attending to factual details rather than general presumptions about it. This is essential because as the investigative process unfolds, she or he will frequently discover many elements of the compulsive cycle and experience that were previously obscured. A key purpose of exploring the specific elements comprising the compulsive pattern is to dispel the client's misconceptions about it by bringing to her or his attention those circumstances, thoughts, feelings, and sensations connected with it that have previously gone unnoticed. As this information becomes accessible, the client's understanding of the nature, function, and significance of the behavior often changes radically, diminishing the strength of the forces that propel and perpetuate it.

Take for example, sexually addictive behaviors, which clinical observation and some empirical findings suggest to be especially prevalent among survivors of childhood sexual abuse (Carnes, 1991; Gold & Heffner, 1998; Timms & Conners, 1992; Tsai et al., 1979). Individuals who fit this pattern of being unable to adequately control their sexual activity, generally assuming that this difficulty indicates an unusually high sex drive, claim to find sexual activity to be extremely pleasurable. "I am obviously sex-obsessed because I enjoy it so much. Why else would I be constantly thinking about it and doing it?"

As long as inquiry is limited to information at the level of generalizations, this may seem to be a reasonable deduction. However, a very different picture emerges when questioning is conducted in a way that elicits a greater level of detail. Regardless of the particular type of compulsion being examined, the method of inquiry is basically the same. Once it has been agreed upon which specific instance of the behavior will be investigated, the practitioner asks the client to provide a step-by-step account of that incident. To start, the clinician might explain as follows:

> Ok, let's look at the last time you had sex with a stranger in a public place. You say that was two days ago. Could you walk me through that entire episode, moment by moment? Let's start from the very beginning. When did it first occur to you to seek someone out for sex? Where were you at the time?

When the client responds, the therapist continues by trying to help establish what set the entire process in motion. What was going on just before the idea of making an anonymous sexual contact first arose? Was there a feeling present that led to the thought? If so, what was the feeling, and what provoked it? If it was an incident, what was it, and did it immediately precede the onset of the feeling? If the incident occurred earlier in the day, what was it that got the client thinking about it at that particular point in time? In this way, therapist and client collaboratively reconstruct the series of events, thoughts, and feelings that culminated in the initial impulse to carry out the compulsion.

Having established this much, therapist and client then turn their attention to elucidating how the process evolved from there. Once the initial thought arose, what happened next? Did the client linger on the thought? If so, did it change in any way? Were there any feelings that accompanied it? If not, did the client begin to act on the thought? What did she or he do first?

The inquiry continues in this manner, tracing the sequence of thoughts, feelings, actions, sensations, and events, from the inception of the episode through its aftermath. In the process, the client becomes aware of aspects of the pattern and implications of these features that previously either went unnoticed, were ignored, or were explained away. The aim is not to reach definitive conclusions after having examined a single incident, but to give the client the opportunity to begin to become desensitized to talking in detail about the compulsion, to start to recognize some characteristics of it that were overlooked until then, and to entertain the possibility that it may have a different significance than she or he previously assumed it did.

In the case of compulsive sexual activity, for instance, the conviction of being oversexed and of enjoying the addictive sexual activity often begins to weaken in the light of closer examination. It is not unusual, by investigating the progression of specific sexual encounters in detail, to find that the client acknowledges that her or his sex life is characterized by several of the following features: (a) avoidance of sexual contact with her or his primary partner; (b) difficulty achieving arousal or orgasm either with the primary partner, or more commonly, in sexually compulsive situations, or both; (c) scrupulous avoidance of certain aspects of sexual interaction, such as penetration; (d) the absence of pleasurable sensations during sex; (e) a clearly discernible level of numbness during sex; (f) indications of dissociation during sex, such as clouding of consciousness and difficulty remembering the content of a sexual encounter that occurred as recently as earlier the same day; (g) characteristics of the sexually compulsive scenario that the client comes to realize parallel her or his childhood sexual abuse experiences, such as needing to choose a sexual partner who resembles the molester, or engaging in the same activities that comprised the sexual assault; (h) anxiety, somatic symptoms (e.g., upset stomach, headache), or other indicators of distress just before, during, or immediately after sexual encounters. Especially when a number of these attributes are identified as routinely accompanying sexual activity, the client's presumption that the behavior is sought out because she or he has an unusually high sex drive, or because it is intensely pleasurable, begins to deteriorate in the face of accumulating evidence. Similarly, repeated analysis of specific incidents of sexually compulsive behavior usually reveal that the impetus for engaging in the activity is a certain disturbing affect. The particular emotion involved varies from one person to the next. It may be anxiety, anger, low self-esteem, or loneliness. Usually, however, for each individual, the same affect or those closely related will consistently trigger sexually addictive episodes. Eventually, the survivor will come to the conclusion that the sexually compulsive behavior is not primarily motivated by sexual desire and interest, but rather by an effort to relieve distress. The mechanism via which the emotional disturbance is alleviated will vary. The sexual act may function as a distraction from preoccupying concerns, provide reassurance by establishing that someone else finds the client desirable, offer soothing by acting as a substitute for physical affection, or may serve some other objective. In any event, the client comes to realize that the compulsive behavior is being executed for a purpose other than the one it appeared to be initially. From there, it is a short step to the conclusion that more effective means, having fewer risks and costs, can be developed to achieve the same end.

Similar principles apply to other forms of maladaptive behavior. Self-mutilation, for example, may be stimulated by and act to assuage overwhelming rage, self-loathing, or anxiety. Instead of being motivated by a desire to be self-destructive, it may act as an expression of anger towards others, a way of attempting to show others how severe one's suffering is, a form of penance in response to perceived transgressions, or some combination of these or other functions (Chu, 1998; Linehan, 1993; Suyemoto, 1998). Binge eating, rather than occurring in reaction to hunger, may represent a means of regulating emotions or responding to interpersonal difficulties (Wiser & Telch, 1999), such as an attempt to diminish anxiety, a replacement for affection from others, or a mechanism for avoiding being approached sexually in the hope that weight gain will render one unattractive to others.

Regardless of the particular compulsive pattern targeted for intervention, the same general procedure can be applied. Once the first few episodes of carrying out the behavior have been jointly explored in session, the therapist asks the client to continue to report and discuss any subsequent incidents of its repetition. This pact has several consequences. It means that each time the client invokes the behavior, it will later be discussed in session. This helps to make the choice to engage in the compulsion less impulsive and automatic, thereby moving it more unambiguously into the realm of a conscious, cognitive decision. Description and examination of the meaning of the compulsive incidents also has the effect of reducing the secrecy and denial attached to them, associating them with a cognitive narrative, and consequently diminishing the disconnected, dissociative, dreamy aura that often surrounds these experiences. In being more open and candid with the practitioner about the compulsion, the client becomes more able to be honest in her or his own acknowledgment and appraisal of the behavior *as it is actually occurring*. This awareness creates an objective, observant stance that is antithetical to the affect-laden, driven quality that perpetuates the compulsion. Processing the incidents in therapy creates a more delineated cognitive structure pertaining to them that is activated during subsequent instances of "acting out." As in-session examination of the episodes is carried out collaboratively and the client finds that the practitioner responds in a respectful, accepting, non-judgmental fashion, the anxiety and shame elicited by indulging in the compulsion is defused. By correcting misunderstandings, misinterpretations, and misattributions about the compulsion, she or he comes to realize that the actual intention behind the behavior is reasonable and comprehensible, rather than depraved or bizarre. Identification of the real rather than apparent function of the activity is reassuring to the client and usually prompts her or him to seek out or develop more effective strategies for achieving the same objective.

As the joint investigative process continues, and the client becomes more committed to it, she or he can gradually be encouraged to assume an increasing level of responsibility for this process. Rather than simply report on compulsive episodes retroactively, she or he can begin to monitor them with a written log. The log can then be employed in session to produce an even more accurate and detailed account of the incidents than would recollection alone. The structure of this log can be tailored to suit the individual situation being examined, but will generally include entries regarding antecedants of the compulsion, specifics about the behavior itself as well as any thoughts and feelings that accompany it, and reactions following the episode. If a particular emotion or sensation has previously been identified as triggering the onset of the compulsion, it might be useful for the client to log her or his SUD level for that feeling before, during, and after its execution.

Once the logging procedure becomes established, the client will often begin to search independently for patterns among and explanations for compulsive episodes, rather than waiting for the therapist's assistance in doing this in session. Eventually, as the method of observation and analysis is assimilated, the client will begin to employ it outside of session. At first she or he may carry out the analysis in hindsight. Later it may be executed during compulsive incidents and used to interrupt them. Ultimately, the client will find her- or himself recognizing the triggers of the compulsive sequence before it is initiated, and will be able to stop it before it starts. With continued practice of this procedure, the stimuli that previously elicited the maladaptive pattern will no longer do so.

☐ From Maladaptive Patterns to Adaptive Functioning

Defusing a compulsive pattern will sometimes free the client to discover new resources and experiences that were previously unavailable or blocked. Frequently, she or he will need some assistance from the practitioner in accessing, developing, or strengthening and maintaining these new resources. To a surprising degree, however, much of the process will often unfold naturally and spontaneously. For example, anger, that was previously discharged through self-mutilation or overeating is directed towards and expressed to the individuals who provoked it. Numbness maintained by sexually addictive activities subsides and gives way to the capacity to tolerate, enjoy, and respond to sexual feelings. Efforts to boost self-esteem through reckless business deals are slowly displaced by more sober, deliberate, substantive achievements.

These new, more adaptive patterns can be expected to be fragile and tentative at first. During periods of exceptional stress they may well falter and relapse into episodes of previous compulsive behaviors. However, by this time the firmly established practice of divulging and examining these incidents in therapy will usually prevail. When this occurs, it is helpful for the practitioner to respond with a matter-of-fact acceptance based on having anticipated the possibility of recurrences of the compulsion, rather than engaging in pedantic lecturing. This approach will reassure the client that the gains attained until that point are not negated by sporadic instances of reverting to old, habitual reactions to distress. Calmly processing these occasional incidents assists the client in thinking of them not as setbacks, but as opportunities to better understand the compulsion. This stance considerably reduces the probabality that the client will revert to the tendency to become overly self-critical, which would only arouse negative affect and increase the risk for further acting out. Examining instances of "relapse" from this perspective allows the client to recognize how much less intense they are and how much less relief they provide than they did previously. Realizations such as these often taint further repetitions of the pattern, appreciably diminishing the incentive to maintain it.

As these maladaptive patterns disintegrate, survivors begin to foresee the implications of a life unencumbered by excessive distress, by the interference of unbidden dissociation, by distorted and limiting cognitions, and by the restrictions and complications created by compulsive and self-damaging methods of managing painful emotions. They can start to envision that life really can be different, that what has seemed to come so easily to others but always seemed to elude their own grasp is now somehow within reach. For some survivors, it is no less than astounding how much they can accomplish once they have made substantial progress toward being freed from the hindrances that formerly seemed ubiquitous and immutable. A few may find that at this point, therapy primarily serves the purpose of consolidating these gains by providing the opportunity to discuss their realization that daily life now has the potential to be radically different than it was before, and to receive validation and support for their new and broadened viewpoints, ways of thinking, and choices. Individuals such as these may also decide that it is time to terminate ongoing treatment, at least for the time being, and explore their recently acquired outlook and skills autonomously.

Most, however, will need more assistance and guidance in exploring the implications of utilizing the capacities they have developed in therapy to construct a more stable, constructive lifestyle. This may be the first time that they have experienced success in tackling some of the major areas of adult life: evolving parenting methods that are based on forethought and consistency; securing and maintaining stable employment; entering into and navigating an emotionally intimate relationship; establishing and cultivating friendships and familial relationships based on mutual respect and support; becoming an active participant in and contributor to a social network or community; managing finances thoughtfully and effectively; expanding the capacities for comfortable and gratifying sexual experiences. As they employ their nascent skills and ways of thinking to develop more adaptive approaches to these sectors of daily living, they may find there are unanticipated challenges, false starts, missteps, and instances of backsliding into previous maladaptive viewpoints and patterns.

The clinician's major role at this point is to assist the survivor in adopting a productive problem-solving perspective when confronting obstacles such as these. The primary strategy for accomplishing this is application of the principles of constructive reasoning skills (delineated in Chapter 12). The client is assisted in employing these principles as challenging situations arise in order to find constructive solutions to them.

For example, a man whose father was extremely critical and physically abusive toward him throughout his childhood had a history in his working life of seeking the mentorship and backing of employers who compensated him inadequately. They would promise to assist him in reaching his career goals or to provide him with commensurate financial compensation if he proved himself by producing for them. However, repeatedly they would end up exploiting him by failing to live up to their end of the "bargain." Despite this outcome, he would accept their excuses for why they did not follow through, believe their assurances that next time the outcome would be different, and continue working for them. Gradually during the course of treatment he was able to break this cycle. Nevertheless, periodically, when he became discouraged about his career or experienced a financial reversal, he would be enticed to return to these men and seek out their assistance. He was aware enough of the drawbacks of this course of action to discuss it with his therapist before implementing it. However, the temptation to proceed with his plans would lead him to present rationalizations in session that for one reason or another, in this instance the outcome would be different than it had been previously.

Through repeatedly applying the principles of constructive reasoning to these incidents as they arose, the pull to repeat this pattern weakened and eventually died out. He came to recognize that the decision to accept these offers was propelled by his doubt about his own abilities and a corresponding longing that someone else would watch over, protect, and take care of him. His track record of substantive accomplishments indicated that his low self-confidence was unwarranted. However, the negative appraisals of himself that he had internalized from his father's constant biting criticisms of him had prevented him from recognizing and feeling secure in his own abilities.

In reviewing previous instances in which he had made similar choices, it became clear to him that he had sacrificed opportunities for long-term career achievements in exchange for the immediate sense of emotional security that came with believing that he had a benefactor upon whom he could rely. In retrospect, however, it was evident that allowing his desire to feel protected had held him back enormously in terms of financial and career advancement. As he came to better understand how these factors had influenced him and developed a more realistic assessment of his intelligence and capacity for occupational success, the pull of this old pattern diminished. Simultaneously, he began to establish new patterns of interaction at work. Instead of viewing professional interactions as being characterized by polarized positions of dominance and submission, he began to discern an entirely new range of "middle ground" possibilities of mutually advantageous give and take at the office. Increasingly, his career decisions were grounded in unruffled planning rather than impulsivity borne of a sense of fear and desperation. As a result, his work productivity, financial stability, and level of professional attainment improved markedly.

For most survivors the consolidation of these types of attainments will be occurring simultaneously in several key areas of functioning. In the case just described, for instance, analogous gains were concurrently being made in the personal and interpersonal sectors of this man's life. He moderated a long-standing tendency to become overinvolved in work to the exclusion of other aspects of life. His relationship with his wife became much less conflictual and inordinately more fulfilling as they established new patterns and channels of communication. The two of them established much more productive ways of interacting with their adult children, whose movement toward autonomous functioning had previously been hampered by their apprehensive and overly involved parenting style. He pursued interests that he had harbored for a long time but which had been neglected in favor of career pursuits, becoming much more active in his church, the larger community, and in exploring various recreational interests.

At TRIP we have commonly observed wide-ranging gains such as these in response to contextual therapy for survivors. This type of outcome appears to be attributable to the broad scope of areas of functioning to which skills such as distress modulation and constructive reasoning can be applied. Nonetheless, there is one area that up until this point in the discussion of treatment may have appeared conspicuous in its absence, particularly because it is the central focus of other forms of therapy for PCA survivors: trauma. It is to this topic and its place in a contextual treatment approach that we now turn our attention.

14

CHAPTER

Liberation: Resolving the Trauma of Abuse

Almost all of the various forms of psychotherapy developed to ameliorate the effects of single event trauma advocate concentrating on the content of the traumatic experience (see, e.g., French & Harris, 1999; Foa & Rothbaum, 1998; Meadows & Foa, 1999; Resick et al., 1988; Shapiro, 1995). This is a reasonable procedure for those survivors whose general functioning may have been compromised by the trauma, but was not significantly impaired before the circumscribed traumatic event occurred. The effectiveness of this method with individuals who have been exposed to a single traumatic incident is well documented in the empirical literature (Foa & Rothbaum, 1998; Meadows & Foa, 1999; Resick et al., 1988).

☐ The Dangers of Trauma-Focused Treatment for PCA Survivors

This same strategy of intervention, however, does not appear to be well suited to adult survivors of prolonged childhood abuse (PCA). It is this observation that was the primary impetus for the development of a contextual approach to psychotherapy for PCA survivors. This population seems to be especially susceptible to deterioration rather than enhancement of functioning in response to trauma-focused treatment models (Gold, 1998b; Gold & Brown, 1997). I have repeatedly encountered evidence in the clinical arena—in the cases I have treated myself, in those of doctoral trainees I have supervised, and in the reports of clients who have been in therapy elsewhere—that goading PCA survivors into producing detailed accounts of their experiences of childhood abuse is destabilizing and counterproductive, and that persisting in this approach only serves to compound this adverse outcome. A major difference between survivors of a circumscribed traumatic event and survivors of PCA is that unlike many members of the former group, individuals in the latter group have typically never developed effective daily-living skills. It is predictable, from the family context perspective, that many PCA survivors will respond with a marked deterioration in functioning when confronted with the extraordinary stressor of memories of abuse trauma, since many of them were never taught to adequately cope with the commonplace pressures of everyday life.

Periodically, one encounters the acknowledgment among therapists that PCA survivors' symptoms frequently worsen in response to exposure to recollections of abuse (see, e.g., Herman, 1992a). However, this admission is often accompanied by the insistence that with continued confrontation of this traumatic material, improvement will eventually occur (see, e.g., Bass & Davis, 1988; Blume, 1990). This conviction, that trauma-focused therapy is not only an effective approach to helping PCA survivors, but is the *only* means of resolving their difficulties, persists with remarkable tenacity. My impression is that this belief has become such an ingrained part of the conventional wisdom among mental health practitioners that it has become accepted as established fact in many quarters. Perhaps this is due, in part, to the absence of a clearly articulated treatment alternative.

Just recently, for instance, we recommended adjunct couples therapy to a woman who had been in individual therapy at TRIP for about a year. When the couples counselor found out that the treatment this woman had been receiving at TRIP did not involve extensive attention to her actual abuse experiences, she told her that she was "wasting time" and would "never get anywhere" without directly addressing the trauma. This pronouncement was made despite the fact that the therapist had no expertise in trauma or abuse. The counselor's presumption that trauma-focused treatment is the only avenue to progress for child abuse survivors was so entrenched that it apparently never even occurred to her to inquire about what, if anything, the client had accomplished after almost a year of therapy. This client had successfully broken a long-standing pattern of obsessive-compulsive cleaning and organizing. She left a physically abusive relationship and established an independent residence. Most significantly, she was able to affect a major shift in the quality of her relationships, which in the past had been marked by tremendous difficulty being assertive and by extensive lying in order to avoid conflict. Instead, she learned to set limits, refuse requests she considered unreasonable, and directly ask others for what she wanted.

☐ The Shift Away From A Primarily Trauma-Focused Perspective

An exclusively trauma-centered viewpoint seems to be adhered to less frequently by therapists who specialize in treating the long-term effects of child abuse. This impression is consistent with the recent writings of some experts in the field who acknowledge that a focus on traumatic material early in treatment is destructive and ill-advised. However, these authors generally attribute this adverse outcome to a failure to help the client develop sufficient safety and containment skills before proceeding to address the specifics of the abuse (see, e.g., Herman, 1992a; Phillips & Frederick, 1995).

This is a position that I myself advocated not long ago (Gold, 1998b). The contextual model of prioritized treatment goals originated, in a sense, as an attempt to more fully articulate the safety and containment skills that PCA survivors needed to develop before they could be expected to effectively confront, process, and come to terms with traumatic material. The more progress that was made as we continued to explore the implications of this approach, however, the less evidence there seemed to be that explicitly confronting traumatic material in a detailed manner was a sensible and productive facet of treatment for most PCA survivors.

At TRIP and in my own clinical work with PCA survivors, I found that when we entrusted our clients to direct the course of therapy and to educate us about their needs and concerns, specific instances of abuse became an increasingly peripheral focus of attention. Instead, the scope of treatment, while it subsumed overt incidents of maltreatment, became much broader. The picture that began to develop was one in which explicitly abusive events were landmarks in a much more expansive terrain of emotional rejection, isolation, and deprivation. Observations such as these are what led to the development of a conceptual framework centered around features of the family-of-origin environment and of the larger social context in which PCA survivors grew up. These conditions overlapped with and contributed to the occurrence and persistence of overt abuse, but also unquestionably extended beyond it. As this interpersonal context model of PCA evolved, we began to perceive that much of what we had initially thought of as the establishment of safety and containment preparatory to the direct confrontation of abuse trauma in fact constituted the remediation of daily-living skills. Our clients' reports strongly suggested that in most cases these were not capacities that had been mastered and later disrupted by abusive experiences, but rather abilities in which proficiency had never been attained because the opportunity to learn them had not been present. (The transcript of Rick's therapy session in Chapter 3 is a particularly vivid illustration of this scenario.)

The further in this direction our clinical investigations took us, and the more we saw how much substantive progress PCA survivors made when we employed a contextual approach to treatment, the less rationale we saw for viewing confrontation of traumatic experiences as an indispensable component of therapy. At first, our assumption was that their mastery of daily-living skills would place PCA survivors on similar ground with single event trauma survivors who had no appreciable adjustment problems before the trauma occurred. Once this level of functioning was attained, we reasoned, we could then implement exposure-based interventions to resolve the residual impact of abuse trauma.

What we repeatedly discovered, however, was that by the time sufficient gains had been made to warrant the introduction of trauma-centered methods, they often no longer seemed needed. In most instances, by this point in treatment freedom from distress (including the absence of intrusion and other symptoms of posttraumatic stress disorder, and increased effectiveness of daily functioning) and general quality of life had reached such proportions that no further intervention of any sort seemed necessary. In essence, once our clients were functioning well enough to process traumatic material productively, usually neither they nor we saw any substantive need to address it. There was no longer appreciable reason to believe that exposure would be destabilizing, but neither was there evidence of the presence of sufficient residual symptoms to indicate a need for these methods.

☐ Addressing Trauma: Keeping the Client in Charge

This does not mean, however, that addressing abuse and its impact had been avoided or ignored with these clients. While the content of the abusive incidents themselves was not the primary focus, their influence on the formation or intensification of distorted beliefs about self and others was an integral part of the treatment enterprise. This was a naturally occurring component of the process of identifying and challenging erroneous cognitions. Much of this aspect of addressing trauma, therefore, was subsumed under the cognitive work associated with learning to exercise critical thinking. Tracing many of the PCA survivor's erroneous beliefs to their source led clients and practitioners to family-of-origin deficits, abuse experiences, or, most commonly, a combination of both factors. These two elements often interacted to engender and mutually reinforce core distorted convictions that adversely impacted daily functioning, and helped maintain repetitive maladaptive patterns of behavior.

We also found, in working on disrupting compulsive cycles of behavior by closely examining particular instances of their occurrence, that a connection to abusive experiences would frequently arise. One of the most common and conspicuous examples of this phenomenon was the link that often came to light between sexually compulsive behaviors and experiences of childhood sexual abuse. One male survivor, for instance, in addition to suffering ongoing sexual abuse by his father, had also as a teenager been violently anally raped by one man while being forcibly held down by another. Without being aware of the connection, he had for years been periodically recruiting men to participate with him in threesomes in which he was the recipient of sadistic sexual practices. When he suddenly recognized that he was recreating and replaying the scenario of his own rape as an adolescent, his urge to participate in this type of activity immediately ceased.

Clinical experiences such as these led specialists in the field to the general conclusion that collaborating with PCA survivors in order to understand their current erroneous beliefs, disturbed feelings, or dysfunctional cycles of behavior would lead us back to a connection to traumatic experiences where one existed and needed to be resolved, without needing to expressly encourage extensive exploration of the abusive incidents themselves. Acknowledging and exploring this link was almost invariably constructive, particularly when we were careful to explicitly place the timing, pace and depth of examination of the traumatic material under the control of the client. Under these conditions, what we generally found was that with some monitoring and guidance by the therapist, the client could be trusted to effectively judge when and in exactly how much detail it was necessary to process the traumatic experience in order to benefit without becoming overwhelmed or destabilized. The most common exception to this general rule was those clients who had been convinced by clinicians in previous treatment, or through reading or popular media presentations, that exhaustive recollection and confrontation of their abusive experiences was essential to attaining therapeutic improvement. It rarely took more than one or two instances of experiencing the debilitating and counterproductive consequences of excessive self-exposure to this material, however, for them to revise their beliefs about the wisdom of this approach.

Nevertheless, we have generally seen that when PCA survivors have the power to control the investigative process, and are not operating under preconceptions obtained from professionals or other outside sources,

they are unlikely to lead themselves into territory that they are not prepared to manage. As a rule, accounts of traumatic experiences will be
volunteered by clients when they are ready to face them without being
destabilized by symptoms of intrusion and arousal, and not before. For
the most part it has been only when clients were coaxed by others into
addressing traumatic material that we have seen them rush prematurely
into exposing themselves to this type of content.

Pressuring PCA survivors into exploring recollections of abuse is detrimental not only because it carries the risk of exacerbating symptoms, but
because of the additional, more subtle but extremely detrimental consequences it can have. Persuading these clients to confront traumatic
material, even when they are hesitant or fearful about doing so, is regret-
tably all too easy. Extensive experiences of abuse, neglect, and rejection
have commonly instilled a willingness to please others, even at the expense of their own safety and comfort, that can render them extremely
vulnerable to ignoring their own judgment and feelings to passively comply
with external demands and expectations. In the most disturbing instances,
both parties in the therapeutic situation end up blaming the client when
exposure to traumatic material leads to deterioration rather than progress,
and conclude that with greater diligence and continued confrontation
improvement will occur. When this happens, especially if it involves revisiting abusive experiences, it is especially likely that the interaction will be
experienced by the client as recapitulating the coercive interpersonal situation experienced with the original abuse perpetrator, and thereby reinforce
her or his negative beliefs about self and others (Gold & Brown, 1997).

In order to guard against outcomes of this sort, it is imperative that we
as practitioners recognize that PCA survivors are the ultimate experts about
their own experiences. This is most powerfully communicated by encouraging them to take the lead exploring the factors that led to and maintain
current difficulties, unrestricted by the theoretical preconceptions to which
a clinician might subscribe. When intervention proceeds in this way, the
interchange conveys an inherent respect for the client's perceptions and
judgment that is an important corrective to the destructive repercussions
of previous abusive, coercive, neglectful, rejecting, and invalidating interpersonal experiences.

The general principle that we have found useful in dealing with traumatic content, therefore, is that it is productive for PCA survivors to address this material if this is where investigation of present-day difficulties
leads. Recognizing that current beliefs, reactions, feelings, and behaviors
are not manifestations of the client's own inherent defects but rather responses to past trauma proved helpful in making them more comprehensible and less of a source of shame and self-denigration for the client.
Understanding that these responses are not primarily due to the influ-

ence of current circumstances provided clients with enough distance and leverage to loosen the lingering impact of abusive experiences. The establishment of this type of perspective facilitated the development of new, more effective ways of thinking and acting, unencumbered by the reverberations of abuse trauma.

One way to succinctly summarize the difference in the approaches we favor in most instances for PCA as opposed to single event trauma survivors is in the sequence and direction of therapeutic focus. Once sufficient trust, safety, and security are established, survivors of circumscribed trauma can productively confront and thereby decondition the trauma, and as a consequence, reduce and eliminate the attendant symptoms. Among PCA survivors, in contrast, the process of directly addressing and resolving current problems and symptoms may bring up associated traumatic content in a titrated, manageable form that can then be assimilated without being overwhelming.

One of the implications of making distress reduction and enhanced functioning, rather than the specifics of the abusive incidents, the centerpiece of therapy for PCA survivors is that it drastically reduces the complications that the issue of delayed recall of trauma can introduce to their treatment. Since exploring the content of the trauma in detail is not a major intervention strategy, we have found that many of the survivors we work with remember little more about the specifics of the abuse upon terminating therapy than they did when they entered treatment. Nevertheless, they understand and perceive the significance of what they did know about the abuse in a radically different way than they had before, and live in a way that is no longer appreciably damaged by it.

☐ When Exposure to Traumatic Material Is Appropriate

While exposure methods rarely seem to be indicated as the favored initial strategy in the treatment of PCA survivors, this does not mean that this type of intervention is to be scrupulously avoided with this population at all times and under any circumstance. When precautions are taken to limit extensively addressing traumatic material to certain circumscribed conditions, this can be a productive procedure for some PCA survivors. We would advocate, however, that these types of methods are only employed in instances where:

- It is the client who comes to the conclusion that processing a particular abusive incident would be helpful because it remains especially disturbing to her or him, without urging or pressure from the practitioner.

- Exposure is only initiated once both therapist and client are in agreement that the capacities to modulate distress and dissociation, to engage in constructive reasoning and exercise critical judgment, and to resist retreating back to compulsive behaviors and to mobilize adaptive resources have been firmly established.
- Confrontation of traumatic material is planned and discussed in advance, and executed through a systematized intervention protocol.

Once these conditions are met, any of a number of approaches for confronting and resolving trauma, such as prolonged exposure (PE; Foa & Rothbaum, 1998), stress innoculation training (SIT; Foa & Meadows, 1997), or eye movement desensitization and reprocessing (EMDR; Shapiro, 1995) may ensue. However, in keeping with the recognition of the value of a client-directed approach to addressing abuse trauma, in those instances in which the extensive processing of traumatic material appears warranted, we favor using a procedure known as Traumatic Incident Reduction (TIR; French & Harris, 1999; Moore, 1993; Valentine, 1995). TIR is similar to exposure therapy in that it consists of having the client recount a traumatic incident repeatedly. It is reminiscent of Meichenbaum's narrative constructivist approach (Hoyt, 1996; Meichenbaum & Fong, 1993) in its emphasis on allowing the client to tell her or his own story in her or his own terms. It differs from these and other trauma-focused procedures, however, in several critical respects:

- It is the client, without influence by the practitioner, who selects the event to be reviewed.
- Retelling and processing of the incident by the client proceed without interpretation, reframing, interruption, or other forms of interference by the therapist.
- Once processing of a particular incident is intiated, it continues, without a predetermined session time limit, until resolution is achieved.

There are a number of reasons why we consider TIR preferrable to other techniques with similar aims in working with PCA survivors. There is some empirical evidence that TIR may be more effective than more conventional exposure methods for individuals who have been subjected to repeated similar traumas (Bisbey, 1995). In addition, the client is clearly in charge of directing the exploratory and explanatory process. This feature helps her or him to avoid experiencing the procedure as recapitulating the coercive interpersonal qualities that characterized the original abusive event. It also permits the client to arrive at her or his own revised understanding of the incident, fostering a sense of competency and circumventing the possibility of attributing credit for her or his new perspective and resolution of the trauma to the practitioner. Consequently, TIR bolsters the client's sense of empowerment and promotes the capacities for self-sufficiency that are integral to the contextual approach to treating PCA survivors.

Regardless of the particular type of intervention used to address traumatic material with PCA survivors, the outcome is much more likely to be positive when it is conducted within a larger framework that is not exclusively trauma-centered. Many authors have noted the importance of helping a traumatized individual to firmly establish safety and security before embarking on exploration of the trauma itself (Courtois, 1988; Dolan, 1991; Herman & Schatzow, 1987; Simonds, 1994; Watkins, 1992). Contextual therapy takes an even more cautious approach by making remediation of adaptive living skills rather than resolution of traumatic experiences the primary goal of treatment. This is not to suggest that there is no legitimate place for trauma-focused interventions in contextual treatment. It does mean, however, that these approaches play a decidedly secondary role in the course of therapy as a whole. When abuse trauma is not the major focus of treatment, it is considerably less probable that being an abuse survivor will become an integral, defining characteristic of the client's identity, thereby avoiding reinforcing the implications of hopelessness and helplessness that such a self-image can carry. Moreover, when distress is reduced and functioning is strengthened by the acquisition of adaptive coping skills, the debilitating effects of trauma are often adequately resolved so as to render direct confrontation of these episodes unnecessary.

Transformation: The Miracle of Living Well

It is exceedingly difficult to adequately convey through the written word the intricacies of conducting psychotherapy with individuals whose formative years were riddled with instances of maltreatment and whose social environments inadequately prepared them for competent daily living. In order to be effective, treatment for survivors of prolonged child abuse (PCA) must be grounded in a well thought-out, systematized plan of action. At the same time, therapy will not only fail to be productive, but runs the risk of causing considerable harm when preconceptions and a predetermined program of intervention are adhered to in a way that ignores the need to be mindful of and accommodate individual differences.

☐ The Challenge of Maintaining Flexibility

Throughout the preceding chapters, I have purposefully employed qualifiers such as "some," "often," and "may," not as a superfluous stylistic convention, but to acknowledge that any particular generalization about survivors cannot be assumed to hold true for every individual. I hope that the use of terms such as these have helped to alert the reader that the trends I have discussed are not likely to be manifested by *all* PCA survivors. In some instances they may only be prominent in the most extreme cases. My intention has been to alert clinicians to be prepared for these more severe or unusual features without creating the expectation that they will invariably be present. It is imperative that therapists understand this. Losing sight of the significance of individual variations among PCA survivors and therefore failing to be responsive to these differences can have every bit as disastrous an influence on treatment outcome as attempting to conduct therapy with this population without the benefit of thorough case conceptualization and carefully organized treatment planning. Lockstep conformity to a standardized treatment plan may be effective for more circumscribed target problems, but it will not do justice to the complexities that are often created by an upbringing characterized by chaos and unpredictability.

It is enormously important to emphasize, therefore, that inherent in the concept of therapy structured around prioritized goals is a certain degree of flexibility that is indispensable to working effectively with this population. It is expected and built into the model. In other words, its appropriate and effective implementation will require the practitioner to utilize her or his own judgement in order to be responsive to the unique situation of each particular client. These types of adjustments can be more clearly illustrated now that each of the component prioritized goals of contextual treatment for survivors has been fully delineated.

Intervention for dissociation, for instance, does not receive the relatively high priority it does because it can be presumed to be an essential aspect of therapy for *every* PCA survivor. For some clients it may be the most extensive facet of intervention, but for others, dissociative symptomatology will be minimal or even nonexistent. In these instances, consequently, it may not enter into the treatment plan at all. Dissociation is accorded a high priority because when it is present, until the client develops some ability to moderate it and thereby stabilize the capacity for focused and continuous awareness, little progress is likely made toward achieving those goals assigned lesser priorities in the treatment model.

The presence, absence, or pervasiveness of a difficulty, however, is not the only criterion for determining whether, when, or how extensively it will be a target of treatment. As some of the cases mentioned in the previous chapter illustrate, certain clients with very extensive histories of abuse will successfully complete their entire course of therapy without ever having engaged in direct confrontation of traumatic material. For other clients, regardless of the pervasiveness of the abuse they have experienced, trauma-focused intervention will play a more prominent role in their treatments. The significance of basing treatment for PCA survivors on a framework of prioritized goals is that a particular target goal is addressed only once adequate progress has been made toward the attainment of those goals with a higher priority that make the skills necessary to productively work toward the target available. In the case of exposure to traumatic material, for example, this means that the client has developed enough proficiency in managing distress, modulating dissociation, exercising critical judgment, and responding to stress with adaptive coping skills instead of compulsive habits to provide a reasonable degree of assurance that addressing traumatic content will lead to resolution rather than exacerbation of the difficulties associated with it.

It is not expected that goals with lower priorities will be attended to only once the objectives comprising a higher priority goal are fully achieved. With rare exceptions, work on several prioritized goals will be occurring at any given point in treatment. In most instances, aspects of more than one prioritized goal will be covered in each session. However, at each phase of treatment, the goals that are focused on are likely to fall within a circumscribed range. Early in therapy, for example, session time usually will be devoted primarily to distress reduction, and more peripherally to modulating dissociation and bolstering constructive reasoning. In later phases, it is not uncommon for there to be periods of time when intervention will focus almost completely on breaking compulsive patterns or on processing traumatic material, to the relative exclusion of other goals.

One of the consequences of conducting therapy that takes into consideration individual needs, rather than adhering to a fixed, preset schedule, is that the course, pace, and most notably the length of treatment will vary enormously from one case to another. I have seen some PCA survivors make tremendous progress and appropriately terminate therapy in less than a year (although most of those in this category had received at least some treatment previously). More commonly, the duration of a full course of treatment will extend anywhere from 2 to 7 years.

Particularly in an era when the restrictions of managed care create pressure to complete a course of therapy within a handful of sessions, these may seem to be inordinately protracted time frames. However, when one grasps the extraordinary quality and magnitude of therapeutic change that it is possible to achieve with an approach such as this, it is difficult to argue that the investment of time and effort is not justified. Treatment of this type certainly can lead to the resolution of circumscribed difficulties. Anxiety abates. Depression subsides. Flashbacks cease. Chronic insomnia dissipates. Self-mutilation is discontinued. Compulsive habits are broken.

As important as accomplishments such as these can be, however, they only represent a limited segment of the kinds of alterations that PCA survivors routinely experience when a more ambitious mode of intervention is undertaken and pursued to completion. When therapy is directed toward helping survivors attain more fundamental and sweeping changes than symptomatic relief, the results can be no less than transforming. The entire quality of life changes in a way that the client could not have begun to anticipate or imagine. The following case study illustrates the complications that trauma-focused treatment can create for PCA survivors, depicts the ways in which the pacing and application of the model of prioritized skills-based treatment goals were tailored to meet the needs of a particular client, and demonstrates the types of fundamental changes in quality of life that this approach can facilitate.

☐ Case Example: Resolving the Impact of Multiple Forms of Abuse and Disturbed Family Context

Brad entered therapy in his early thirties after 2 years of abstinence from alcohol and drug abuse and regular active participation in both Alcoholics Anonymous and Narcotics Anonymous. Despite his success in maintaining sobriety from alcohol and drugs during the 2 previous years, in many respects his life continued to be permeated by disorganization and anguish. He was working at a job that offered little security and failed to provide consistent income. Although he had taken on a second job in an effort to make ends meet, his car was repossessed because he was unable to keep current on the payments. Circumstances such as these were not foreign to Brad. Throughout his adult life he had never been able to achieve financial stability.

The nature of his relationship with his lover, Mark, was consistent with those of the intimate partnerships he had formed throughout his late teens and twenties while he was still actively drinking and abusing drugs. Long periods of mutual guardedness, emotional distance, and uncommunicativeness were punctuated by outbreaks of intense anger and conflict that periodically erupted into physical violence. In some of his past relationships these altercations had been so severe that Brad had to seek medical treatment in hospital emergency rooms on several occasions.

One of the precipitants of these fights was Brad's compulsive pattern of seeking out and engaging in anonymous sexual encounters in public places and pursuing brief affairs with other men. Mark had become aware of these activities, and reacted with jealousy, insecurity, and anger that exacerbated an already contentious relationship. Brad revealed that both with Mark and in his anonymous sexual contacts he was rarely able to achieve and maintain an erection. He disclosed that in those rare instances where he was able to have a satisfactory erection, it was accomplished by concentrating on fantasies of having pain inflicted upon him. Although he yearned for affection, neither his primary relationships nor his most fleeting outside affairs had ever been characterized by warmth or emotional intimacy.

Brad acknowledged a wide range of psychological difficulties. He experienced depressed mood, a pessimistic outlook, fatigue, and a deep sense of inadequacy. His self-image was extremely negative and his level of self-confidence was exceptionally low. He suffered from constant tension and anxiety which manifested in the form of tremors, dizziness, nightmares, and physical symptoms such as headaches and stomach upsets. Interpersonally, he described himself as unassertive, insecure, shy, and lonely.

At the outset of treatment Brad's primary focus was on his history of childhood sexual abuse (CSA). His parents had divorced when he was 7 years old, after a marriage permeated by arguments and physical altercations. Brad recounted that subsequently, during visitations, his father would sexually molest him. Although he had always known about these incidents, his recollection of them was extremely fragmentary. He indicated that he remembered some of the events immediately preceding and following the actual assaults, but did not recall the molestation itself in extensive or continuous detail. He did have sufficient memory to know that his father would masturbate in front of him and fondle Brad's genitals. Beyond this, his recollection of the abuse consisted of disorganized, discrete flashes of images and sensory impressions.

However, his memory of the circumstances surrounding the cessation of the abuse was much clearer. One day after his father had gone to work Brad snuck out to a nearby store, told one of the people who worked there about his father's sexual assaults on him, and asked that his grandmother be contacted. His grandmother came for him and packed up his things. She took him to stay at her house, and his visitations with his father permanently ended.

Brad first entered therapy at a time when childhood sexual abuse was receiving a great deal of attention in the popular media and in the twelve-step recovery movement, and before the controversy regarding the validity of delayed recall of traumatic memories arose. He strongly believed that remembering the specifics of his incestuous experiences was pivotal to overcoming his numerous difficulties in functioning. His therapist, although he had misgivings about the wisdom of this approach, agreed to this general strategy of intervention. However, he impressed upon Brad the importance of becoming adept at stress reduction methods and the necessity of establishing a reliable network of social supports before initiating processing of his memories of abuse. The two of them agreed, in effect, that significant progress would need to be made toward learning to reduce and modulate distress before confrontation of traumatic material could be productively initiated.

Brad had completed a Dissociative Experiences Scale (DES; Bernstein & Putnam, 1986) during his first therapy session. He endorsed items indicating the presence of dissociative absorption (e.g., becoming so absorbed in a movie that he was unaware of events happening around him), flashbacks (e.g., recalling past events with such vividness that he felt as if they were reoccuring), and dissociative amnesia (e.g., finding evidence of having done things he did not remember doing), but not items indicating the presence of depersonalization, derealization, or identity fragmentation. With the attainment of substantive gains in reducing his level of anxiety and tension, his experience of flashbacks, memory gaps, and losing touch with his surroundings appreciably diminished.

After 3 months of training in anxiety reduction procedures and developing other strategies for safety, containment, and self-soothing, Brad and his clinician felt that he was adequately prepared to begin addressing his CSA experiences. To his surprise, however, in the first session allocated to this task, the moment he initiated the relaxation procedure he had learned and before he had even begun to approach the content of the abusive incidents, Brad became acutely fearful and began crying. Consequently, once he regained his composure, instead of resuming attempts to retrieve and process traumatic material, the remainder of the session was devoted to an examination of Brad's unexpected reaction. This debriefing led to the identification of his general tendency to impulsively throw himself into situations without adequately recognizing or attending to his thoughts and feelings about them. In the session immediately following, therefore, a new intervention plan was negotiated. Brad agreed that it would be best to concentrate more directly on improving and stabilizing his immediate life circumstances before resuming direct exploration of his CSA experiences.

From the outset of treatment, despite his earlier conviction that addressing his CSA history was the key to therapeutic progress, Brad had also expressed a great deal of disturbance about many other aspects of his past and current relationships with his family. He reported that his mother, father, and step-father were all alcoholic. For a period of several years during his childhood, for reasons that were never explained to him, he and his siblings were reared by their grandparents. Brad also indicated that in addition to having been molested by his father and having witnessed ongoing violence between his parents, he had often received beatings from his father, and later from his brother, throughout his childhood and adolescence. He alleged, moreover, that from the time his family found out that he was gay during his mid-teens, his mother and siblings blatantly expressed intolerance of his sexual preference. He explained that they did not speak to him at all or respond to any requests he made of them for the first 4 months after he came out, and that they had continued to make their disapproval clear since that time. He also expressed considerable hurt and confusion that, unlike his siblings, from the age of 12 onward he was expected to earn the money he needed to purchase his own clothes, toiletries, and other personal items. He had no idea why he was treated differently in this respect.

This tendency to act without sufficient forethought and without adequately taking his feelings and preferences into account that had characterized his initial insistence on addressing his CSA memories became a pivotal theme in Brad's treatment. In various areas of his life, both in terms of long-term goals and day-to-day living, he started to make a purposeful effort to approach situations in a more deliberate, planned manner. He enrolled in a program to obtain training in a new trade in the hope that this would provide him with a more reliable income. He also dedicated himself to investing more time and energy into creating a more stable and fulfilling partnership with Mark. Both in an attempt to improve their relationship and to save money so he could put his finances in order, Brad moved in with Mark.

As the focus of treatment shifted away from processing CSA incidents toward bettering his present-day situation, Brad became increasingly aware of how much his decisions, choices and actions repeated, or were continuations, of patterns established in his family of origin. He felt manipulated and belittled by Mark in a way that reminded him of previous interactions, not only with other romantic partners, but with both of his parents as well. His continuous efforts to please Mark elicited rejection and condemnation rather than approval, confirming Brad's feelings of being unlovable, reprehensible, and doomed to remain isolated and alone. Once he began to resist the compulsion to engage in anonymous sexual encounters, he came to recognize that this urge was often triggered by anger. More specifically, the temptation to act out sexually appeared to arise in response to resentment he experienced when he perceived he was being criticized, controlled, pushed away, or otherwise mistreated.

Soon after he started to arrest and explore his patterns of sexually compulsive behavior and realized the degree to which these activities were driven by spiteful feelings, Brad indicated that he was beginning to communicate more openly and directly with Mark. He also said that he found himself focusing less exclusively on the sexual aspects of their relationship and becoming more concerned with seeking affection and developing emotional intimacy. His ability to achieve an erection was still erratic but now more frequent than it had been previously. He became aware that he consistently lost erections when his partner would touch his genital area, and realized that this was because this stimulus triggered flashbacks of his father fondling his penis.

However, as he continued to venture toward exploring greater emotional closeness and disclosure with Mark, Brad was confronted with fundamental problems in their relationship. He noticed that Mark seemed to expect emotional support from him but did not reciprocate. Mark also continued to rationalize being irritable with and cruel toward him even after Brad stopped his sexual acting out and infidelity. He was unsure how to address this with Mark, because he found that when he confronted him directly, he received little or no response.

In the midst of grappling with these relationship difficulties, Brad was making significant progress in other aspects of his life. As he began to identify and successfully challenge the negative self-attributions he had developed in his family of origin—that he was incompetent, lazy, and irresponsible—his behavior started to change accordingly. He successfully completed the trade school program in which he had enrolled, was working full time and making a more regular income, and had been able to manage his money well enough that his past debts were paid off. He began to devote himself to strengthening his network of friendships and social supports outside of his relationship with Mark.

The more closely he examined the nature of his interactions with Mark, the more obvious its continuity with his past relationships with lovers and family members became to him. A cycle of consistently catering to others to gain their approval without expecting or requesting reciprocity, eventually leading him to feel taken advantage of and resentful, became apparent. As Brad saw with increasing clarity the fallacy behind this way of conducting his relationships, he was moved to decisively change this pattern. He resolved to leave Mark and establish his own residence so that he could learn to be more self-sufficient and break his habit of becoming immersed in pleasing other people to the exclusion of taking responsibility for his own needs.

It was almost a full year before Brad was able to follow through on his commitment to move out on his own and another year before he completely severed his relationship with Mark. As he gradually moved through this transition, however, he grew increasingly self-confident and reported greater assertiveness, initially at work and eventually in his personal life as well. A grave setback created by a serious physical injury that forced him into several months of unemployment, threatened his financial security, and disrupted his career plans did precipitate a major depressive episode, but did not prevent him from continuing to press forward. Brad started on a regimen of antidepressant medication, and actively continued in his eff s to assume greater responsibility for himself. As he grappled with   issue, he found himself confronting deep feelings of bitterness that   had been deprived of much of his childhood. He had been forced to end for himself financially, instrumentally, and emotionally from a very early age. It occurred to him that the premature self-sufficiency imposed on him without adequate preparation or assistance and the consequent resentment he experienced had strongly contributed to his difficultly assuming responsibility for himself as an adult.

Although he had moved into his own apartment and begun to meet and become involved with men who treated him with more kindness and respect than those he had previously dated, he periodically found himself being drawn back into volatile and short-lived encounters with Mark. In the process, he realized how unlovable and unattractive he had always felt. He was desperate for acceptance and affection, but convinced that he did not deserve to be treated well and that he was doomed to be rejected if he let anyone get close enough to really know him well. In a strange way, Mark's poor treatment of him was comforting in its familiarity. It was reminiscent, on some level, of the criticism and rejection he had experienced from his family as a child.

The influence Mark had exerted over him, however, was waning. Therapy increasingly focused on building upon Brad's changing view of himself to help him envision and establish the type of lifestyle and life structure to which he aspired. Extensive coaching was provided in dealing with practical daily matters at home, at work, and his social life in an organized, goal-directed manner. Brad's self-esteem was strongly bolstered as he found that he was able to effectively manage maintaining his own household. After recovering from his physical injuries, he successfully resumed steady employment, paid off the medical bills he had incurred, and reestablished financial stability. As he moved back and forth between being treated contemptuously by Mark and being dealt with more considerately by others, the contrast grew more and more incongruous. He could not help but notice that he experienced erectile difficulties with the greatest regularity when he was with Mark. He came to understand this as a concrete indication of how unsafe and detached he felt with him. With distance, Brad became more cognizant of the extent of the verbal, emotional and physical abuse Mark had inflicted upon him. Months elapsed between contacts with Mark, and the belligerence that characterized each of their encounters only served to loosen the grip of Brad's old patterns of relating and reinforce his conviction that he did not deserve to be mistreated. He vividly realized how intensely Mark's disdainful manner of interacting with him had elicited old feelings of worthlessness associated with the rejection and maltreatment experienced throughout his childhood. He soon found that rather than being drawn to Mark, he was increasingly afraid of him and his rage, and he stopped communication with him all together.

Brad's management of his practical affairs was by then markedly more effective and stable than it had ever been. He was relieved and gratified to find that he could maintain his own residence efficiently and with much less effort than he had anticipated. He was exhibiting an exemplary degree of dedication and reliability at work that was rewarded by a series of promotions to increasing levels of responsibility and monetary compensation. For the first time in his life he was not only out of debt, but also able to manage his finances so that he accrued a cushion of savings rather than struggling to make it from one paycheck to the next.

Another major series of gains was catalyzed when Brad met and became involved with a man, Dwayne, with whom he felt a deep sense of safety and connection that he had not experienced previously. He found, at this point, that he was able to draw upon the interpersonal skills he had acquired to develop a relationship with Dwayne that was characterized by open and direct communication, mutuality, and respect. By processing conflicts that occurred early in the relationship with his therapist, he was able to see how much misunderstanding was generated when he fell back on his old habits of shutting down or communicating his feelings in indirect and confusing ways. He was able to quickly overcome this tendency as he found out how much more effective direct and assertive forms of self-expression were in fostering emotional intimacy, rapid resolution of conflicts, and a relationship based on mutually gratifying reciprocity. Within a few weeks of becoming sexually active with Dwayne, Brad found that he no longer had erectile difficulties. In addition, he was astonished to discover a depth and intensity of sexual feelings and responsiveness that were entirely new to him. It was only with the emergence of these sensations that Brad realized how much numbness and detachment had characterized his former sexual interactions. He was also developing capacities for affection, closeness, emotional intimacy, interpersonal security, and a sense of self-worth and personal attractiveness, that he had never experienced before.

At follow-up over a year after the termination of therapy, Brad remained free of major psychological symptomatology and was continuing to construct an increasingly stable and satisfying life structure. He was still working for the same company and had continued to advance in responsibility and income. He and Dwayne had a strong and committed relationship and had been living together for several months. In contrast to the anxiety and depression that he had manifested at the outset of treatment, Brad's demeanor was now conspicuously upbeat, calm, and contented.

☐ Theoretical, Clinical, and Empirical Implications

Brad's therapy extended over a period of just under 3 years. Due to a number of both planned and unanticipated breaks in treatment, the number of sessions totaled 55. At the time Brad underwent therapy, the prioritized goal approach to treatment was not as fully articulated as it currently is. In fact, it was cases such as his that led to the conclusions that:

- A focus on traumatic material is not required for PCA survivors to make substantial progress in therapy, and in many cases it may disrupt rather than enhance adaptive functioning.
- Chaos, conflict, and limited opportunities to learn adaptive living skills are common characteristics of the early family life of PCA survivors, and can have as much or more to do with their psychological difficulties as the overtly abusive events they have experienced.
- Treatment for PCA survivors based upon the remediation of inadequately mastered daily living skills can be extremely effective in both the amelioration of specific symptoms and enrichment in basic areas of adaptation.
- There is an optimal sequence in which to address the major goals comprising a skills-based course of therapy for PCA survivors.

It is possible that gains might have been attained more rapidly if the somewhat greater structure provided by subsequently developed refinements of the model had been employed. However, due to the tenuous sense of trust and control experienced by many PCA survivors, there is a limit to how rapidly substantive and enduring gains can be made.

One of the strengths of the model is that it has evolved on the basis of the clinical observations and experience of dozens of practitioners working with hundreds of PCA survivors over an extended period of time. Anecdotal evidence for the effectiveness of the treatment program, such as that presented in the case of Brad, is strong. However, it must be acknowledged that controlled empirical assessment of this model's efficacy has yet to be conducted. While no appreciable outcome research on any form of treatment for PCA survivors has been generated to date, this does not relieve us of the responsibility to evaluate the contextual model of treatment in this way. Ultimately, this form of therapy must be submitted to more systematic evaluation. Until substantial progress has been made toward that goal, contextual treatment for survivors of prolonged child abuse can at best be considered a promising, but as yet not empirically validated, approach to treating this population.

Another factor that must be acknowledged is that while the results can be extremely impressive when it works, this form of treatment is far from universally effective. There are still too many clients we see at TRIP for whom our methods do not produce substantial changes such as those exhibited by Brad. In this respect, contextual therapy for PCA survivors is still very much in need of further development and refinement. The greatest obstacle to reaching and engaging the clients we see at TRIP, on top of the constraints posed by the distrust, pessimism, and other consequences of growing up in an ineffective family context and being subjected to abuse and maltreatment, is their current life circumstances. Our clientele comprise, on the whole, a relatively indigent and disadvantaged group. Many, 44%, are unemployed, and only 36% are employed full time. The vast majority of them, 73%, have household incomes under $20,000. Few have extensive social supports, and a substantial minority are faced with debilitating physical illnesses and disabilities yet lack access to adequate medical coverage or facilities. These factors often create circumstances, such as limited availability of transportation or child care and frequently facing emergent situations that require immediate attention, which hamper their ability to regularly attend and benefit from psychotherapy.

Complications such as these, however, can not be allowed to constitute an apologia for our or any other treatment model. They must, rather, be addressed. Many of the hardships that interfere with PCA survivors' abilities to benefit from treatment are directly or indirectly related to the very same conditions—childhood abuse and inadequate family background—that engendered the difficulties for which these individuals are seeking therapy in the first place (Herman et al., 1997; McCauley et al., 1997). They need treatment because of the deprivation and maltreatment they have already experienced. To allow them to continue to be penalized by conditions that restrict their access to or ability to benefit from intervention that would help remediate the damage they have suffered is inexcusable. Although the model of treatment provided must take these factors into account, in all likelihood, amelioration of these practical issues is a task that no form of psychotherapy can be expected to achieve in and of itself. To a large degree the response to these concrete problems needs to be social and political. As a society, we have failed to protect these individuals during their formative years and to provide them with the assistance they require to be adequately equipped for effective functioning as adults. We owe it to them and to ourselves to develop and supply them with the resources they require to remediate the deficits that prevent them from leading productive and fulfilling lives. We need to do this not only for moral reasons, but for practical ones as well: it is not only these individuals who suffer the consequences of and are diminished by what they have endured, but all of us as a community.

☐ The Miracle: It's Not a Big Deal At All

While the duration of treatment varies considerably, the gains Brad made are typical of those we have observed among PCA survivors who successfully complete a course of contextual therapy. Not only are circumscribed problems such as depression, anxiety, low self-esteem, nightmares, flashbacks, physical symptoms, and compulsions resolved, but, even more importantly, major spheres of daily adult living—participating in an intimate relationship, maintaining stable employment, nurturing a network of social support, overseeing the responsibilities of sustaining a household, and effectively managing finances—are mastered. These types of accomplishments provide clients with a quality of life dramatically different from and discontinuous with what they had known previously.

In those instances where we have had opportunities to follow up after termination, we have found that therapeutic gains are not merely maintained, but serve as the foundation for substantial continued achievement and further growth. Detailed documentation of these types of effects in one such case treated at TRIP, in the form of scores on standardized tests administered at admission, termination, and follow-up, can be found in Gold & Elhai (1999). During a taped follow-up interview with her therapist, Jon Elhai (E), and myself (G) 8 months after termination, the client (C) in that case described the changes she had experienced in response to treatment. She is, undeniably, exceptionally articulate. Her expression of the magnitude of the changes she had experienced and their impact on her life, however, very closely approximates sentiments voiced by other PCA clients who have completed treatment with this model.

C: The work I've done with Jon has been very existential. And very, very good for me. In fact, that brings me to where I am today, because I feel today like, yes there's still a lot of crap in my past that I could go through, one way or another, and I'm sure, you know, maybe there's more out there for me. Maybe I don't have to lose time at all, maybe eventually in some sort of metamorphosis I can go through. But I am so happy right now, and I feel that it's been such a big change for me. I mean big changes like sleeping 5 or 6 hours at a stretch, and not waking up in a panic, but just, you know, noticing that I'm awake and being able to have that physical rest. As opposed to sleeping for 20 or 30 minutes, waking up always with the knowledge that some dread has happened. . . . And I'm kind of free of all that now . . . On some level we talked about what the kinds of things that happened to me when I was little. But we really didn't get into that too extensively, and actually I'm glad.

G: Well it sounds like you're saying that, "Well, and maybe some day that might be worthwhile and maybe there's more I can achieve at some point if I do that. But in the meantime I just want to enjoy the gains that I'm experiencing now and stop pushing, and pushing, and pushing . . . "

C: Yeah. This is the first time in ten years that I've been, like, 'shrinkless.' And I kept saying to myself, "Am I okay?" You know? Because I've been suicidal in my life, I've had so many episodes of cutting myself and burning myself and, one way or another saying to myself, "Hey, you know, you really need to be in treatment." You know, "You're behavior concerns me." And, and now I feel so amazed that I actually have this oasis in time where my behavior is not harmful to me, and I have so much more of myself. You know, in terms of, of good energy. So that's why I'm just like, "Let's just stop right here and see how this goes for a while."

G: So what is day-to-day life like—work, home, social life. What is it like now?

C: It's a lot better. Um, I have a lot less of my energy dealing with fear. So many firsts are happening for me now. Two weekends ago my husband went, um, for the weekend. And he was gone for three days. I was alone in my house for three days. This has never happened in my adult life that I was aware of, that I was alone by choice for three days. I slept upstairs in my bed. I was not fearful. I really slept. I ate. I watched TV. I never forced any of my [adult] children to come and stay with me. You know, I would do that in the past by paying them off. You know, "Come, mommy will take you shopping. Come, I'll do this for you, I'll do that." I didn't do any of those things. And I just am amazed at how relaxing that was. To be in my house. You know, by myself. I wasn't, I, I'm not checking the doors and the windows all the time. I'm not terrified if I hear a sound. So for me it's so much noticing the things that don't scare me, it's kind of like Disneyland for me in that way. . . .

After discussing her work, at which she had been extremely successfully after many years of unemployment, and her plans to return to school for an advanced degree, the interviewer raises the topic of her personal life.

G: Any changes in your relationship with your husband?

C: Tremendously. First of all he is my husband. Douglas and I are legally married.

G: Congratulations.

C: Thank you. And um, yeah, well, being, being able to trust him, you know, that far. And being lovers with him is a huge difference in my life. And a wonderful difference in my life. And on some level I think if I've been mad about any one thing it's, um, the huge, physical price that I've paid, um, for all the abuse that I suffered as a child. And one of the, one big thing was that I could not enjoy sex. In fact the other side of it was that I had to hate it. Because if I didn't hate it then I was the whore that, you know my mother swore I was. So I, I'm past that, you know. And I think that both for Douglas and I, we have discovered something, and he said to me, "There are very few men who end up with a 45 year old virgin." This is like, you know, a whole fun thing for him too. And so that whole thing has opened up for us.

G: So am I right in understanding that is not something that you and Jon worked on, but something that you pretty much achieved on your own?

C: Yes, and I think that that kind of evolved out of the work that we were doing. And also all of the many bizillion questions that I answered brought up questions in my mind that, um, that—The many, many research questions that I answered allowed me to think about things that I had never allowed myself to think about that opened up sexuality to me. [The client is referring here to a measure of sexual experiences that was part of the packet of instruments administered to clients in TRIP who were willing to be research participants.]

C: . . . So in reading the research packet, the questions... it was clear to me that these questions were not constructed for me. These were constructed for a large group of people. So these are the concerns of many people. And that was the beginning of being more relaxed with the questions. . . . I have been many, many times told that I need medication or I'm going to need hospitalization and, um, that I will deteriorate over time. And, um, many, many pronouncements that in fear, um, became blown up bigger than life. But I was able to see beyond those pronouncements and decide that no, that's not necessarily the case with me.

G: So even though they scared you, those pronouncements, you were able all, pretty much all along, to say, "No, I'm sorry, I'm not going for that."

C: Right! Right. And eventually to actually trust that. And, uh, as it turns out, voila, here I am. No psychotropic meds, no dependency on any kind of, uh, milieu like that. I can pop out what I need, my, my psychological tool, if you will, and protect myself. And what I have left is so much greater an ability to function than I had in the past that, you know, I have to believe that the future is better than I even imagined it could be. Because really what I was hoping for, first of all, to, you know, to never be cut or burned again [through self-mutilation]. Or allow people, I mean, prior to that I had people in my life who cut me and burned me and kicked me and hurt me. And that was just what life was gonna be. So when I, as I came through the various developmental stages, actually to believe in living my life, not only without being physically abused in any way, but perceiving any kind of, um, any kind of stimulus or input from other people or things or events, and being able to back off and have the, the emotional or intellectual tool that will put it back in focus for me. And exactly, the way I see things now, I was looking at life through a badly fractured lens. And I now have clearer lenses. I don't imagine that it's window pane at this point in time. But it's certainly a lot closer to that than I ever imagined it could be. And I'm also aware that other people have failings and frailties that I was unaware of because I was so busy thinking how screwed up I was, I was unable to see that other people are just regular people too. And they can be screwed up and screw up something. Like if a boss would say a report was missing. Oh my God I would be maniacal to reproduce my original notes, the date of the notes, when did I make the note that I would formally do the report. I had everything back to the first, you know dot on the "i" that I would do the report. And now, I'm like, "Oh, all right, I'll send you another copy." It's not that big a deal. You know, it's really become manageable to me. . . .

E: Seems like the hypervigilence we talked about has really gone down a lot.

C: Right, which was my life. I couldn't sit, like, for instance, if I had to sit where you are, then I would be continuously worrying about where the door is, and whether or not I could get out the door. That was like, like, an absolute given in my life. I could be in the biggest business meeting, it could be many things going on, but I had to be able to get out. You know? And now I think I, if I really felt like getting out I could say to you, "Listen, I'm gonna to leave." And—or maybe just not say anything, just be rude and walk out. And, and continue to live my life, and know you the next time I see you. Which is the miracle. Now it's not lost information. Or if it's lost information within a few minutes the information I need will just kind of kick off in my head. And I am able to go back to people and say, "You know what? When I spoke to you an hour ago, I don't know my, my, I had tabula rosa going on here. I remember now, now let's, you know, re-go over it with the information I have." And it works. People don't say, "Oh my God! You have memory loss! Do you have a dissociative disorder?" You know, they're like, "Oh great, okay, right, right, right." You know, and then it just, it just moves along without any big glaring, you know, thing about me. It's not a big deal at all.

CONCLUSION

Chapter 1 opened with an overview of the origins of the concepts of trauma and posttraumatic stress disorder in the social and political movements of the 1970s. The final chapter of Part I returned to the issue of social context by considering how the perpetuation of ongoing child abuse and deficient family environment are in the final analysis, attributable to conditions at the level of society as a whole. The concluding section of this volume leads us back yet again to our starting point, the broad perspective of social context.

Epilogue:
The Inextricable Tie

You decide what's good.
You decide alone.
But no one is alone.
"No One Is Alone," Stephen Sondheim, 1988

One of the most intriguing aspects of the contextual approach to the treatment of survivors of prolonged child abuse (PCA) is the patterning of the changes it promotes. Although substantive progress is unquestionably made during therapy, application of the skills acquired in the course of treatment may lead to even greater client gains subsequent to termination (see Gold & Elhai, 1999 for documented evidence of this effect). In a very real sense, therefore, cessation of the formal psychotherapeutic process marks the inauguration of a series of further transformations, rather than the attainment of a stagnant plateau. Neither practitioner nor client can fully anticipate where this trajectory will lead.

In analogous fashion, the contextual model of psychotherapy for PCA survivors presented here, although an outgrowth of many years of clinical observation, supervisory experience, and empirical investigation, is in many respects still very much in the nascent stages of its development. While the initial outcomes engendered by the approach described here are encouraging, there is still much to be done in the way of further articulating the conceptual model, refining intervention strategies, and researching the assessment of clinical effectiveness. The specific therapeutic methods comprising the current version of the treatment model and their generalizability need to be empirically tested. The model will undoubtedly unfold and transform in unanticipated directions.

The impetus for the creation of the contextual model was the observation that in response to trauma-centered treatment, adult survivors of prolonged child abuse manifested conspicuous elevations in distress and reductions in adaptive functioning, without indications of productive therapeutic gains. The accounts of their life histories imparted by survivor clients suggested that many of the fundamental daily-living skills most of us take for granted were never conveyed to them. Concentrating on helping them to remediate these apparent gaps in their learning history in order to fortify their capacities to withstand distress and to function more productively led to radically better clinical results than treatment grounded in the uncovering and processing of traumatic material. While the particulars of the treatment methodology are bound to evolve, this conception has been and is likely to continue to form the cornerstone of the contextual treatment model. The trauma model provided practitioners with the awareness that many of the difficulties experienced by survivors of protracted maltreatment are not a reflection on them, but on what happened to them. The contextual model alerts clinicians that many of the deficits and problems exhibited by survivors are similarly not an indictment of these individuals, but of a society that disturbingly often fails to adequately prepare its young for the considerable demands of adult living.

In spite of my reservations about doing so, throughout this book I have used the terms "survivor" and "PCA survivor" to refer to the individuals for whom contextual therapy was designed. On one hand, it is in a practical sense unavoidable to use some type of terminology to refer a group of people who share certain features. On the other hand, while the term "survivor" is as good as or better than any other to serve this purpose, the convention of employing such a designation is one that arouses qualms in me. It is all too easy to reify nomenclature by forgetting that the one thing that invariably distinguishes survivors of prolonged child abuse from anyone else is not their personal character, but what they have lived through. It is imperative that we remember this. It is imperative that we are mindful that the only thing that differentiates PCA survivors from anyone else is that they had the misfortune of having to endure the extraordinary experience of a childhood characterized by ongoing maltreatment. In doing so, we can guard against allowing "survivorship" to come to be considered a stigma, and recognize that it should be more accurately considered grounds for compassion and humility among those who have not had the liability of being burdened with growing up under similar conditions.

Personally, I have found it to be a tremendously humbling experience to work with individuals striving to overcome the impediments created by a history of prolonged childhood abuse. My own impression of those clients who have successfully completed contextual therapy is that they are not just functioning adequately, but in many respects are navigating through life in a manner that is exceptional. The level of intimacy in their relationships, depth of purpose in their work, intensity of their sexual and sensual responsiveness, generosity of spirit, and general appreciation of daily living seems to considerably exceed that displayed and experienced by most people who have been blessed with more fortunate life histories.

How can one explain how some people who have endured inconceivable hardships and experienced extensive impairment as a result can not only overcome the damage they have sustained, but can achieve a quality of life that appreciably exceeds the norm? For those of them who grew up in the most dire circumstances, it was only through a sheer act of will that they survived. At some point, or in some instances repeatedly at various junctures in their lives, they literally found themselves faced with the decision of whether to persevere or to surrender, and determined, often not without considerable hesitancy, to go on. For certain individuals confronting a choice that dreadful not only takes a debilitating toll, but also imbues them with an aura of sobriety, genuineness, honesty, wisdom and depth of character that can be awe-inspiring. If they are to persevere, mere existence will not suffice. Just getting by is not enough for them. Life must have purpose. What they have suffered through must have meaning. Invariably, that purpose and meaning entails breaking through their sense of aloneness and in some way passing on what they have gained to others.

Another factor which I believe contributes to their superior capacity for living is a keen awareness of what many of us take for granted. Commonplace daily occurrences, such as going to work, being with loved ones, maintaining financial solvency, developing friendships, and experiencing the immediacy of emotions, are hard-won accomplishments for them. They experience an intense joy and sense of appreciation for what is usually considered mundane and therefore overlooked.

These qualities, admittedly, are far from universal among survivors, and where they do exist, they are often obscured by the difficulties and limitations in functioning that they manifest. That is why these characteristics are most conspicuous in those fortunate and determined individuals who have successfully overcome the impediments that the injurious aspects of their background have created. If therapists can look closely enough to recognize and to honor the reserves of depth and sincerity that these individuals bring with them to treatment, they will be infinitely better equipped to be helpful to them.

We need to understand, therefore, that while the hardships that survivors of prolonged child abuse have suffered are vastly more damaging than those encountered by most of us, at least in some instances this misfortune has fostered qualities that endow them with the potential to function at a level that is, and make contributions to others that are, exceptional. Conversely, when society forsakes them, we relegate survivors to fates—alcoholism and drug abuse (Wilsnack et al., 1997), criminal activity and victimization of others (Widom, 1998), unemployment, poverty, and homelessness (Herman et al., 1997)—for which all of us pay incalculably. Above all, what distinguishes survivors of prolonged child abuse from others is not the trauma they have suffered, but their pervasive sense from their earliest memories onward of being profoundly *alone*— intangibly but palpably segregated from the larger human community. Unlike survivors of more circumscribed trauma occuring in adulthood, they have not lost their connection with others, but in many instances never felt supported by or affiliated with others to begin with. Their best hope, and consequently that of the rest of us, is to recognize that although they have been abandoned and feel alienated and alone, their destiny, and that of society as a whole, are in actuality inextricably intertwined.

REFERENCES

Alexander, P. C. (1992). Application of attachment theory to the study of sexual abuse. *Journal of Consulting and Clinical Psychology, 60,* 185–195.

Alexander, P. C. (1993). The differential effects of abuse characteristics and attachment in the prediction of long-term effects of sexual abuse. *Journal of Interpersonal Violence, 8,* 346–362.

Alexander, P. C., & Lupfer, S. L. (1987). Family characteristics and long-term consequences associated with sexual abuse. *Archives of Sexual Behavior, 16,* 235–245.

Alexander, P. C., & Schaeffer, C. M. (1994). A typology of incestuous families based on cluster analysis. *Journal of Family Psychology, 8,* 458–470.

Alpert, J. L., Brown, L. S., & Courtois, C. A. (1996). Symptomatic clients and memories of childhood abuse: What the trauma and child sexual abuse literature tells us. In J. Alpert, L. S. Brown, S. J. Ceci, C. A. Courtois, E. F. Loftus, & P. A. Ornstein (Eds.), *Final report of the working group on the investigation of memories of childhood abuse* (pp. 15–105). Washington, DC: American Psychological Association.

Alter, M. G. (1997). Parents: Psychotherapy's scapegoats. *Pastoral Psychology, 45,* 343–351.

American Psychiatric Association. (1980). *Diagnostic and statistical manual of mental disorders* (3rd ed.). Washington, DC: Author.

American Psychiatric Association. (1987). *Diagnostic and statistical manual of mental disorders* (3rd ed., revised). Washington, DC: Author.

American Psychiatric Association. (1994). *Diagnostic and statistical manual of mental disorders* (4th ed.). Washington, DC: Author.

Anderson, C. L., & Alexander, P. C. (1996). The relationship between attachment and dissociation in adult survivors of incest. *Psychiatry: Interpersonal & Biological Processes, 59,* 240–254.

Anderson, G., Yasenik, L., & Ross, C. A. (1993). Dissociative experiences and disorders among women who identify themselves as sexual abuse survivors. *Child Abuse & Neglect, 17,* 677–686.

Anderson, N., & Coleman, E. (1991). Childhood abuse and family sexual attitudes in sexually compulsive males: A comparison of three clinical groups. *American Journal of Preventive Psychiatry and Neurology, 3,* 8–15.

Barach, P. M. M. (1991). Multiple personality disorder as an attachment disorder. *Dissociation, 4,* 117–123.

Bartholomew, K., & Horowitz, L. M. (1991). Attachment styles among young adults: A test of a four-category model. *Journal of Personality and Social Psychology, 61,* 226–244.

Bass, E., & Davis, L. (1988). *The courage to heal: A guide for women survivors of child sexual abuse.* New York: Harper & Row.

Beck, A. T. (1979). *Cognitve therapy of depression.* New York: Guilford Press.

Beck, A. T., & Steer, R. A. (1987). *Beck depression inventory manual.* San Antonio, TX: The Psychological Corporation, Harcourt Brace Javanovich, Inc.

245

Beitchman, J. H., Zucker, K. J., Hood, J. E., DaCosta, G. A., Akman, D., & Cassavia, E. (1992). A review of long-term effects of child sexual abuse. *Child Abuse & Neglect, 16,* 101–118.

Bellack, A. S., & Hersen, M. (Eds.). (1988). *Behavioral assessment: A practical handbook* (3rd ed.). New York: Permagon Press.

Bennett, E. M., & Kemper, K. J. (1994). Is abuse during childhood a risk factor for developing substance abuse problems as an adult? *Journal of Developmental & Behavioral Pediatrics, 15,* 426–429.

Bernstein, E. M., & Putnam, F. W. (1986). Development, reliability, and validity of a dissociation scale. *Journal of Nervous & Mental Disease, 174,* 727–735.

Billings, A. G., & Moos, R. H. (1982). Family environment and adaptation: A clinically applicable typology. *American Journal of Family Therapy, 10,* 26–38.

Bisbey, L. B. (1995). No longer a victim: A treatment outcome study for crime victims with post-traumatic stress disorder (Doctoral dissertation, California School of Professional Psychology, 1995). *Dissertation Abstracts International, 5,* 1692.

Blake-White, J. & Kline, C. M. (1985). Treating the dissociative process in adult victims of childhood incest. *Social Casework, 66,* 394–402.

Bleich, A., Koslowsky, M., Dolev, A., & Lerer, B. (1997). Post-traumatic stress disorder and depression. *British Journal of Psychiatry, 170,* 479–482.

Bloch, J. P. (1991). *Assessment and treatment of multiple personality and dissociative disorders.* Sarasota, FL: Professional Resource Press.

Bloom, B. L. (1985). A factor analysis of self-report measures of family functioning. *Family Process, 24,* 225–239.

Blume, E. S. (1990). *Secret survivors: Uncovering incest and its aftereffects in women.* New York: John Wiley and Sons.

Bourne, P. G. (1978). Foreword. In C. R. Figley (Ed.), *Stress disorders among Vietnam veterans: Theory, research, and treatment* (pp. vii–ix). Philadelphia: Brunner/Mazel.

Briere, J. (1989). *Therapy for adults molested as children: Beyond survival.* New York: Springer Publishing Company.

Briere, J. N. (1996). *Therapy for adults molested as children: Beyond survival.* (2nd ed., Rev.). New York: Springer Publishing Company.

Briere, J., & Conte, J. (1993). Self-reported amnesia for abuse in adults molested as children. *Journal of Traumatic Stress, 6,* 21–31.

Briere, J., & Elliott, D. M. (1993). Sexual abuse, family environment, and psychological symptoms: On the validity of statistical control. *Journal of Consulting and Clinical Psychology, 61,* 284–288.

Briere, J., & Elliott, D. M. (1997). Psychological assessments of interpersonal victimization effects in adults and children. *Psychotherapy, 34,* 353–364.

Briere, J., & Runtz, M. (1986). Suicidal thoughts and behaviors in former sexual abuse victims. *Canadian Journal of Behavioural Science, 18,* 413–423.

Briere, J., & Runtz, M. (1988a). Multivariate correlates of childhood psychological and physical maltreatment among university women. *Child Abuse & Neglect, 12,* 331–341.

Briere, J., & Runtz, M. (1988b). Symptomatology associated with child sexual victimization in a nonclinical adult sample. *Child Abuse & Neglect, 12,* 51–59.

Briere, J., & Runtz, M. (1989). The trauma sypmtom checklist (TSC-33): Early data on a new scale. *Journal of Interpersonal Violence, 4,* 151–163.

Briere, J., & Runtz, M. (1990). Differential adult symptomatology associated with three types of child abuse histories. *Child Abuse & Neglect, 14,* 357–364.

Brown, D. P., & Fromm, E. (1986). *Hypnotherapy and hypnoanalysis.* Hillsdale, NJ: Erlbaum.

Brown, L. S. (1996). Politics of memory, politics of incest: Doing therapy and politics that really matter. *A Feminist Heritage of Speaking About Incest, 19,* 5–18.

Browne, A., & Finkelhor, D. (1986). Impact of sexual abuse: A review of the research. *Psychological Bulletin, 99,* 66–77.

Brownmiller, S. (1975). *Against our will: Men, women, and rape.* New York: Bantam.

Breuer, J., & Freud, S. (1955). Studies on hysteria. *The standard edition of the complete psychological works of Sigmund Freud* (Vol. II). London: Hogarth Press. (Original work published 1895)

Bryant, D., Kessler, J., & Shirar, L. (1992). *The family inside: Working with the multiple.* New York: W. W. Norton.

Bryer, J. B., Nelson, B. A., Miller, J. B., & Krol, P. A. (1987). Childhood sexual and physical abuse as factors in adult psychiatric illness. *American Journal of Psychiatry, 144,* 1426–1430.

Burgess, A. W., & Holstrom, L. (1974). Rape trauma syndrome. *American Journal of Psychiatry, 131,* 981–986.

Cardeña, E. (1994).The domain of dissociation. In S. J. Lynn & J. W. Rhue (Eds.), *Dissociation: Clinical and theoretical perspectives* (pp. 15–31). New York: Guilford.

Carnes, P. (1991). *Don't call it love: Recovery from sexual addiction.* New York: Bantam Books.

Cattell, R. B., & Scheier, I. H. (1976). *The IPAT anxiety scale.* Champaign, IL: Institute for Personality and Ability Testing.

Chancer, L. S.(1991). New Bedford, Massachusetts, March 6, 1983–March 22, 1984: The "before and after" of a group rape. In J. Lorber & S. A. Farrell (Eds.), *The social construction of gender* (pp. 288–307). Newbury Park, CA: Sage Publications.

Cherry, E. L., & Gold, S. N. (1989). The therapeutic frame revisited: A contemporary perspective. *Psychotherapy, 26,* 162–168.

Chesler, P. (1998, Winter). No safe place. *On the Issues: The Progressive Women's Quarterly,* 7(1), 12–17.

Chu, J. A. (1998). *Rebuilding shattered lives: The responsible treatment of complex posttraumatic stress and dissociative disorders.* New York: John Wiley & Sons.

Chu, J. A., & Dill, D. L. (1990). Dissociative symptoms in relation to childhood physical and sexual abuse. *American Journal of Psychiatry, 147,* 887–892.

Chu, J. A., Frey, L. M., Ganzel, B. L., & Matthews, J. A. (1999). Memories of childhood abuse: Dissociation, amnesia, and corroboration. *American Journal of Psychiatry, 156,* 749–755.

Collins, N. L., & Read. S. J. (1990). Adult attachment, working models and relationship quality in dating couples. *Journal of Personality and Social Psychology, 59,* 644–663.

Conte, J. R., & Schuerman, J. R. (1987). Factors associated with an increased impact of child sexual abuse. *Child Abuse & Neglect, 11,* 201–211.

Conte, J., Wolfe, S., & Smith, T. (1989). What sexual offenders tell us about prevention strategies. *Child Abuse and Neglect, 13,* 293–301.

Coopersmith, S. (1981). *Manual of the adult self-esteem scale.* Palo Alto, CA: Consulting Psychologists Press.

Courtois, C. A. (1988). *Healing the incest wound: Adult survivors in therapy.* New York: W. W. Norton.

Courtois, C. A. (1991). Theory, sequencing, and strategy in treating adult survivors. *Directions for Mental Health Services, 51,* 47–60.

Davis, M., Eshelman, E R., & McKay, M. (1995). *The relaxation & stress reduction workbook.* (4th ed.). Oakland, CA: New Harbinger Publications.

Deering, C. G., Glover, S. G., Ready, D., Eddleman, H. C., & Alarcon, R. D. (1996). Unique patterns of comorbidity in posttraumatic stress disorder from different sources of trauma. *Comprehensive Psychiatry, 37,* 336–346.

de Groot, J., & Rodin, G. M. (1999). The relationship between eating disorders and childhood trauma. *Psychiatric Annals, 29,* 225–229.

Derogatis, L. R. (1983). *SCL-R-90: Administration, scoring, and procedures manual-II.* Towson, MD: Clinical Psychiatric Research.

Derogatis, L. R., Lipman, R. S., & Covi, L. (1973). The SCL-90. An outpatient psychiatric rating scale—Preliminary report. *Psychopharmacology Bulletin, 9,* 13–28.

Dolan, Y. M. (1991). *Resolving sexual abuse: Solution-focused therapy and Ericksonian hypnosis for survivors.* New York: W. W. Norton.

Egendorf, A. (1978). Psychotherapy with Vietnam veterans: Observations and suggestions. In C. R. Figley (Ed.), *Stress disorders among Vietnam veterans: Theory, research, and treatment implications* (pp. 231–253). Philadelphia: Brunner/Mazel.

Elliott, D. (1997). Traumatic events: Prevalence and delayed recall in the general population. *Journal of Consulting and Clinical Psychology, 65,* 811–820.

Elliott, D. M. & Briere, J. (1992, August). Child sexual abuse and family environment: Combined impacts and the effects of statistical control. Paper presented at the 100th Annual Convention of the American Psychological Association, Washington, DC.

Elliott, D. M., & Briere, J. (1995). Posttraumatic stress associated with delayed recall of sexual abuse: A general population study. *Journal of Traumatic Stress, 8,* 629–647.

Erickson, M. H., & Rossi, E. L. (1980). The indirect forms of suggestion. In E. L. Rossi (Ed.), *The collected papers of Milton H. Erickson on hypnosis. Vol. 1: The nature of hypnosis and suggestion* (pp. 452–477). NewYork: Irvington Publishers.

Fallon, P., & Wonderlich, S. A. (1997). Sexual abuse and other forms of trauma. In D. M. Garner & P. E. Garfinkel (Eds.), *Handbook of treatment for eating disorders* (pp. 394–414). New York: Guilford Press.

Felitti, V. J., Anda, R. F., Nordenberg, D., Williamson, D. F., Spitz, A. M., Edwards, V., Koss, M. P., & Marks, J. S. (1998). Relationship of childhood abuse and household dysfunction to many of the leading causes of death in adults. *American Journal of Preventative Medicine, 14,* 245–258.

Figley, C. R. (1978a). *Stress disorders among Vietnam veterans: Theory, research, and treatment implications.* Philadelphia: Brunner/Mazel.

Figley, C. R. (1978b). Introduction. In C. R. Figley (Ed.), *Stress disorders among Vietnam veterans: Theory, research, and treatment implications* (pp. xiii–xxvi). Philadephia: Brunner/Mazel.

Finkelhor, D. (1980). Risk factors in the sexual victimization of children. *Child Abuse and Neglect, 4,* 265–273.

Finkelhor, D. (1990). Early and long-term effects of child sexual abuse: An update. *Professional Psychology, 21,* 325–330.

Finkelhor, D., & Browne, A. (1985). The traumatic impact of child sexual abuse: A conceptualization. *Journal of Orthopsychiatry, 55,* 530–541.

Finkelhor, D., Hotaling, G., Lewis, I. A., & Smith, C. (1990). Sexual abuse in a national survey of adult men and women: Prevalence, characteristics, and risk factors. *Child Abuse & Neglect, 14,* 19–28.

Fischman, Y. (1996). Sexual torture as an instrument of war. *American Journal of Orthopsychiatry, 66,* 161–162.

Foa, E. B., & Meadows, E. A. (1997). Psychosocial treatments for posttraumatic stress disorder: A critical review. In J. Spence, J. M. Darley, & D. J. Foss (Eds.), *Annual review of psychology* (Vol. 48, pp. 449–480). Palo Alto, CA: Annual Reviews.

Foa, E. B., & Rothbaum, B. O. (1998). *Treating the trauma of rape: Cognitive-behavioral therapy for PTSD.* New York: Guilford Press.

Foa, E. B., Rothbaum, B. O., Riggs, D., & Murdock, T. (1991). Treatment of posttraumatic stress disorder in rape victims: A comparison between cognitive-behavioral procedures and counseling. *Journal of Consulting and Clinical Psychology, 59,* 715–723.

French, G. D., & Harris, C. J. (1999). *Traumatic incident reduction (TIR).* Boca Raton, FL: CRC Press.

Freud, S. (1959). On the psychical mechanisms of hysterical phenomena (J. Riviere, Trans.). In E. Jones (Ed.), *Sigmund Freud: Collected papers. Vol. 1* (pp. 24–41). New York: Basic Books. (Original work published 1893)

Freud, S. (1959). The aetiology of hysteria (J. Riviere, Trans.). In E. Jones (Ed.), *Sigmund Freud: Collected papers. Vol. 1* (pp. 183–219). New York: Basic Books. (Original work published 1896)

Freyd, J. J. (1996). *Betrayal trauma: The logic of forgetting child abuse.* Cambridge, MA: Harvard University Press.

Fromuth, M. E. (1986). The relationship of childhood sexual abuse with later psychological and sexual adjustment in a sample of college women. *Child Abuse & Neglect, 10,* 5–15.

Gasquoine, P. G. (1998). Historical perspectives on postconcussion symptoms. *The Clinical Neuropsychologist, 12,* 315–324.

Gaudin, J. M., & Polansky, N. A. (1986). Social distancing of the neglectful family: Sex, race, and social class influences. *Children & Youth Services Review, 8,* 1–12.

Gauthier, L., Stollack, G., Messé, L., & Aronoff, J. (1996). Recall of childhood neglect and physical abuse as differential predictors of current psychological functioning. *Child Abuse & Neglect, 20,* 549–559.

Gelinas, D. J. (1983). The persisting negative effects of incest. *Psychiatry, 46,* 312–332.

Gelles, R. J. (1987). The family and its role in the abuse of children. *Psychiatric Annals, 17,* 229–232.

Gill, E. (1988). *Treatment of adult survivors of childhood abuse.* Walnut Creek, CA: Launch Press.

Gleberzon, W. (1983–1984). Academic freedom and Holocaust denial literature: Dealing with infamy. *Interchange, 14*(4)–15(1), 62–69.

Gold, S. N. (1998a). Dealing with defensiveness. In M. Hersen & V. B. van Hasselt (Eds.), *Basic interviewing: A practical guide for counselors and clinicians* (pp. 151–168). Mahwah, NJ: Lawrence Erlbaum Associates.

Gold, S. N. (1998b). Training professional psychologists to treat survivors of childhood sexual abuse. *Psychotherapy, 34,* 365–374.

Gold, S. N., & Brown, L. S. (1997). Therapeutic responses to delayed recall: Beyond recovered memory. *Psychotherapy, 34,* 182–191.

Gold, S. N., & Brown, L. S. (1999). Adult survivors of sexual abuse. In R. T. Ammerman and M. Hersen (Eds.), *Assessment of family violence: A clinical and legal sourcebook (2nd ed.).* (pp. 390–412). New York: John Wiley & Sons.

Gold, S. N., & Cherry, E. L. (1997). The therapeutic frame: On the need for flexibility. *Journal of Contemporary Psychotherapy, 27,* 147–155.

Gold, S. N., & Elhai, J. D. (1999, November). Skills-based treatment of dissociation: Case presentation, outcome, and follow-up. Paper presented at the 16th Annual Conference of the International Society for the Study of Dissociation, Miami, Florida.

Gold, S. N., & Heffner, C. L. (1998). Sexual addiction: Many conceptions, minimal data. *Clinical Psychology Review, 18,* 367–381.

Gold, S. N., Hughes, D. M., & Swingle, J. M. (1996). Characteristics of childhood sexual abuse among female survivors in therapy. *Child Abuse & Neglect, 20,* 323–335.

Gold, S. N., Russo, S. A., Lucenko, B. A., & Vermont, P. (1998, November). *Sexual abuse survivors' family environments: Intra- and extra- group comparisons.* Poster session presentated at the International Society of Traumatic Stress Studies Annual Meeting, Washington, DC.

Green, B. L., Lindy, J. D., Grace, M. C., & Leonard, A. C. (1992). Chronic posttraumatic stress disorder and diagnostic comorbidity in a disaster sample. *The Journal of Nervous and Mental Disease, 180,* 760–766.

Haley, S. A. (1978). Treatment implications for postcombat stress response syndromes for mental health professionals. In C. R. Figley (Ed.), *Stress disorders among Vietnam veter-*

ans: *Theory, research, and treatment implications* (pp. 254–267). Philadelphia: Brunner/ Mazel.

Hamilton, V. L. (1986). Chains of command: Responsibility attribution in hierarchies. *Journal of Applied Social Psychology, 16,* 118–138.

Hammond, D. C. (Ed.), (1990). *Handbook of hypnotic suggestions and metaphors.* New York: W. W. Norton.

Harter, S., Alexander, P. C., & Neimeyer, R. A. (1988). Long-term effects of incestuous abuse in college women: Social adjustment, social cognition, and family characteristics. *Journal of Consulting and Clinical Psychology, 56,* 5–8.

Hathaway, S. R., & McKinley, J. C. (1983). *The Minnesota multiphasic personality inventory manual.* New York: Psychological Corporation.

Herman, D. B., Susser, E. S., Struening, E. L., & Link, B. L. (1997). Adverse childhood experiences: Are they risk factors for homelessness? *Journal of Public Health, 87,* 249–255.

Herman, J. L. (1981). *Father-daughter incest.* Cambridge, MA: Harvard University Press.

Herman, J. L. (1992a). *Trauma and recovery: The aftermath of violence—from domestic abuse to political terror.* New York: Basic Books.

Herman, J. L. (1992b). Complex PTSD: A syndrome in survivors of prolonged and repeated trauma. *Journal of Traumatic Stress, 5,* 377–391.

Herman, J. L., Perry, J. C., & van der Kolk, B. A. (1989). Childhood trauma in borderline personality disorder. *American Journal of Psychiatry, 146,* 490–495.

Herman, J., Russell, D., & Trocki, K. (1986). Long-term effects of incestuous abuse in children. *American Journal of Psychiatry, 143,* 1293–1296.

Herman, J. L., & Schatzow, E. (1987). Recovery and verification of memories of childhood sexual trauma. *Psychoanalytic Psychology, 4,* 1–14.

Horowitz, M. J. (1969). Psychic trauma: Return of images after a stress film. *Archives of General Psychiatry, 20,* 552–559.

Horowitz, M. J. (1970). *Image formation and cognition.* New York: Appleton-Century-Crofts.

Horowitz, M. J. (1986). *Stress response syndromes* (2nd ed.). Northvale, N J: Jason Aronson.

Horowitz, M. J., & Solomon, G. F. (1978). Delayed stress response in syndromes in Vietnam veterans. In C. R. Figley (Ed.), *Stress disorders among Vietnam veterans: Theory, research, and treatment implications* (pp. 268–280). Philadelphia: Brunner/Mazel.

Hoyt, M. F. (1996). Cognitive-behavioral treatment of posttraumatic stress disorder from a narrative constructivist perspective: A conversation with Donald Meichenbaum. In M. F. Hoyt (Ed.), *Constructive therapies: Vol. 2.* (pp. 124–147). New York: Guilford Press.

International Society for the Study of Dissociation. (1997). *Guidelines for treating dissociative identity disorder (multiple personality disorder) in adults.* Retrieved February 23, 2000 from the World Wide Web: http://www.issd.org/iskguide.htm. Northbrook, IL: International Society for the Study of Dissociation.

Jacobson, E. (1938). *Progressive relaxation.* Chicago: University of Chicago Press.

Janet, P. (1973). *L'automatisme psychologique: Essai de psychologie experimentale sure les formes inferieures de l'activite humaine* [Psychological automatisms: Experimental psychology essay on the lower forms of human activity]. Paris: Societe Pierre Janet/Payot. (Original work published 1889).

Janoff-Bulman, R. (1992). *Shattered assumptions: Towards a new psychology of trauma.* New York: Free Press.

Kanfer, F. H., & Phillips, J. S. (1970). *Learning foundations of behavior therapy.* New York: John Wiley & Sons.

Kelly, G.A. (1955). *The psychology of personal constructs.* New York: W. W. Norton.

Kelman, H. C., & Hamilton, V. L. (1989). *Crimes of obedience: Toward a social psychology of authority and responsibility.* New Haven, CT: Yale University Press.

Kempe, R. S., & Kempe, C. H. (1978). *Child abuse.* Cambridge, MA: Harvard University Press.

Kendall-Tackett, K. A., Williams, L. M., & Finkelhor, D. (1993). Impact of sexual abuse on children: A review and synthesis of recent empirical studies. *Psychological Bulletin, 113,* 164–180.

Kirby, J. S., Chu, J. A., & Dill, D. L. (1993). Correlates of dissociative symptomatology in patients with physical and sexual abuse histories. *Comprehensive Psychiatry, 34,* 258–263.

Kluft, R. P. (1982). Varieties of hypnotic intervention in the treatment of multiple personality. *American Journal of Clinical Hypnosis, 26,* 73–83.

Kluft, R. P. (Ed.). (1990).*Incest-related syndromes of adult psychopathology.* Washington, DC: American Psychiatric Press.

Kluft, R. P. (1996). Multiple personality disorder: A legacy of trauma. In C. R. Pfeffer (Ed.), *Severe stress and mental disturbance in children* (pp. 411–448). Washington, DC: American Psychiatric Press, Inc.

Koch, K., & Jarvis, C. (1987). Symbiotic mother-daughter relationships in incest families. *Social Casework, 68,* 94–101.

Kuchinsky, B. L. (1996). *Childhood sexual abuse and adult revictimization: Repeating the traumatic relationship.* Unpublished doctoral dissertation, Nova Southeastern University.

Lang, R. A., & Frenzel, R. R. (1988). How sex offenders lure children. *Annals of Sex Research, 1,* 303–317.

Lankton, S. R., & Lankton, C. H. (1983). *The answer within: A clinical framework of Ericksonian hypnotherapy.* Philadelphia: Brunner/Mazel.

Leavitt, F. (1997). False attributions of suggestibility to explain recovered memory of childhood sexual abuse following extended amnesia. *Child Abuse & Neglect, 21,* 265–277.

Lehrer, P. & Carr, R. (1997). Progressive relaxation. In W. T. Roth & I. D. Yalom (Eds.). *Treating anxiety disorders* (pp. 83–116). San Francisco: Jossey-Bass.

Levinson, D. J., & Huffman, P. E. (1955). Traditional family ideology and its relation to personality. *Journal of Personality, 23,* 251–273.

Linden, W. (1990). *Autogenic training: A clinical guide.* New York: Guilford Press.

Linehan, M. M. (1993). *Cognitive-behavioral treatment of borderline personality disorder.* New York: Guildford Press.

Lipschitz, D. S., Winegar, R. K., Nicolaou, A. L., Hartnick, E., Wolfson, M., & Southwick, S. M. (1999). Perceived abuse and neglect as risk factors for suicidal behavior in adolescent inpatients. *Journal of Nervous & Mental Disease, 187,* 32–39.

Loevinger, J. (1976). *Ego development: Conceptions and theories.* San Francisco: Jossey-Bass.

Loftus, E. F. (1993). The reality of repressed memories. *American Psychologist, 48,* 518–537.

Loftus, E. F., Polonsky, S., & Fullilove, M. T. (1994). Memories of childhood sexual abuse: Remembering and repressing. *Psychology of Women Quarterly, 18,* 67–84.

Long, P. J., & Jackson, J. L. (1991). Children sexually abused by multiple perpetrators: Familial risk factors and abuse characteristics. *Journal of Interpersonal Violence, 6,* 147–159.

Long, P. J., & Jackson, J. L. (1994). Childhood sexual abuse: An examination of family functioning. *Journal of Interpersonal Violence, 9,* 270–277.

Loos, M. E., & Alexander, P. C. (1997). Differential effects associated with self-reported histories of abuse and neglect in a college sample. *Journal of Interpersonal Violence, 12,* 340–360.

Lucenko, B. A., Gold, S. N., Elhai, J. D., Russo, S. A., & Swingle, J. M. (2000). Relations between coercive strategies and MMPI-2 scale elevations among women survivors of childhood sexual abuse. *Journal of Traumatic Stress, 13,* 169–177.

Mancini, C., van Ameringen, M., & MacMillan, H. (1995). Relationship of childhood sexual and physical abuse to anxiety disorders. *Journal of Nervous and Mental Diseases, 183,* 309–314.

Masson, J. M. (1984). *The assault on truth: Freud's suppression of the seduction theory.* New York: Farrar, Straus and Giroux.

McCann, L., & Pearlman, L. A. (1990). *Psychological trauma and the adult survivor: Theory, treatment, and transformation.* Philadelphia: Brunner/Mazel.

McCauley, J., Kern, D. E., Koladner, K., Dill, L., Schroeder, A. E., DeChant, H. K., Ryden, J., Derogatis, L. R., & Bass, E. B. (1997). Clinical characteristics of women with a history of childhood abuse: Unhealed wounds. *Journal of the American Medical Association, 277,* 1362–1368.

Meadows, E.A. & Foa, E.B. (1999). Cognitive behavioral treatment of traumatized adults. In P.A. Saigh & J. D. Bremner (Eds.), *Posttrataumatic stress disorder: A comprehensive text* (pp. 376–390). New York: Allyn & Bacon.

Meichenbaum, D. (1995). Disasters, stress, and cognition. In S. E. Hobfoll & M. W. de Vries (Eds.), *Extreme stress and communities: Impact and intervention* (pp. 33–61). Boston: Kluwer Academic Publishers.

Meichenbaum, D., & Fitzpatrick, D. (1993). A constructivist narrative perspective on stress and coping: Stress inoculation applications. In L. Goldberger & S. Breznitz (Eds.), *Handbook of stress: Theoretical and clinical aspects* (2nd ed., pp. 706–723). New York: Free Press.

Meichenbaum, D., & Fong, G. T. (1993). How individuals control their own minds: A constructive narrative perspective. In D. M. Wegner & J. M. Pennebaker (Eds.), *Handbook of mental control* (pp. 473–490). Englewood Cliffs, NJ: Prentice-Hall.

Messman, T. L., & Long, P. J. (1996). Child sexual abuse and its relationship to revictimization in adult women: A review. *Clinical Psychology Review, 16,* 397–420.

Miller, A. (1984). *Thou shalt not be aware: Society's betrayal of the child.* New York: Meridian.

Millon, T. (1987). *Manual for the MCMI-II.* Minneapolis, MN: National Computer Systems.

Moeller, T. P., Bachmann, G. A., & Moeller, J. R. (1993). The combined effects of physical, sexual, and emotional abuse during childhood: Long-term health consequences for women. *Child Abuse & Neglect, 17,* 623–640.

Moore, R. H. (1993). Traumatic incident reduction: A cognitive-emotive treatment of post-traumatic stress disorder. In W. Dryden & L. K. Hill (Eds.), *Innovations in rational-emotive therapy* (pp. 116–159). Newbury Park, CA: Sage Publications.

Moos, R. H., & Moos, B. S. (1986). *Family environment scale manual* (2nd ed.). Palo Alto, CA: Consulting Psychologists Press.

Mullen, P. E. (1993). Child sexual abuse and adult mental health: The development of disorder [Special Issue: Research on treatment of adults sexually abused in childhood]. *Journal of Interpersonal Violence, 8,* 429–432.

Mullen, P. E., Martin, J. L., Anderson, J. C., Romans, S. E., & Herbison, G. P. (1996). The long-term impact of the physical, emotional, and sexual abuse of children: A community study. *Child Abuse & Neglect, 20,* 7–21.

Nash, M. R., Hulsey, T. L., Sexton, M. C., Harralson, T. L., & Lambert, W. (1993a). Long-term sequelae of childhood sexual abuse: Perceived family environment, psychopathology, and dissociation. *Journal of Consulting and Clinical Psychology, 61,* 276–283.

Nash, M. R., Hulsey, T. L., Sexton, M. C., Harralson, T. L., & Lambert, W. (1993b). Reply to comment by Briere and Elliott. *Journal of Consulting and Clinical Psychology, 61,* 289-290.

Nash, M. R., Zivney, O. A., & Hulsey, T. (1993). Characteristics of sexual abuse associated with greater psychological impairment among children. *Child Abuse & Neglect, 17,* 401–408.

Nelson, R. O., & Hayes, S. C. (1986). *Conceptual foundations of behavioral assessment.* New York: Guilford Press.

Neumann, D. A., Houskamp, B. M., Pollack, V. E., & Briere, J. (1986). The long-term sequelae of childhood sexual abuse in women: A meta-analytic review. *Child Maltreatment, 1,* 6–16.

Nichols, C. (1982). The military installation: How the company town deals with rape, spouse abuse and child abuse. *Victimology, 7,* 242–251.

Nijman, H. L. I., Dautzenberg, M., Merkelbach, H. L. G. J., Jung, P., Wessel, I., & a Campo, J. (1999). Self-mutilating behaviour of psychiatric inpatients. *European Psychiatry, 14,* 4–10.

Ofshe, R., & Watters, E. (1994). *Making monsters: False memories, psychotherapy, and hysteria.* New York: Charles Scribner's Sons.

Olson, D. H., Russell, C. S., & Sprenkle, D. H. (1983). Circumplex model of marital and family systems: VI. Theoretical update. *Family Process, 22,* 69–83.

Pearlman, L. A., & Saakvitne, K. (1995). *Trauma and the therapist.* New York: W. W. Norton.

Perry, J. C., Herman, J. L., van der Kolk, B. A., & Hoke, L. A. (1990). Psychotherapy and psychological trauma in borderline personality disorder. *Psychiatric Annals, 20,* 33–43.

Phillips, M., & Frederick, C. (1995). *Healing the divided self: Clinical and Ericksonian hypnotherapy for post-traumatic and dissociative conditions.* New York: W. W. Norton.

Pope, K. S., & Brown, L. S. (1996). *Recovered memories of abuse: Assessment, therapy, forensics.* Washington, DC: American Psychological Association.

Price, V., Tewksbury, D., & Huang, L. (1998). Third-person effects on publication of a holocaust-denial advertisement. *Journal of Communication, 48,* 3–26.

Putnam, F. W. (1989). *Diagnosis & treatment of multiple personality disorder.* New York: Guilford Press.

Ray, K. C., Jackson, J. L., & Townsley, R. M. (1991). Family environments of victims of intrafamilial and extrafamilial child sexual abuse. *Journal of Family Violence, 6,* 365–374.

Resick, P. A., Jordan, C. G., Girelli, S. A., Hutter, C. K., & Marhoefer-Dvorak, S. (1988). A comparative victim study of behavioral group therapy for sexual assault victims. *Behavior Therapy, 19,* 385–401.

Rivera, M. (1996). *More alike than different: Treating severely dissociative trauma survivors.* Toronto: University of Toronto Press.

Robinson, L. H. (1990). In defense of parents. In S. C. Feinstein, A. H. Esman, J. G. Looney, G. H. Orrin, J. L. Schimel, A. Z. Schwartzberg, A. D. Sorosky, & M. Sugar (Eds.), *Adolescent psychiatry: Developmental and clinical studies. Vol. 17* (pp. 36–50). Chicago, IL: University of Chicago Press.

Rodriguez, N., Ryan, S. W., Rowan, A. B., & Foy, D. W. (1996). Posttraumatic stress disorder in a clinical sample of adults survivors of childhood sexual abuse. *Child Abuse & Neglect, 20,* 943–952.

Roesler, T. A., & McKenzie, N. (1994). Effects of childhood trauma on psychological functioning in adults sexually abused as children. *The Journal of Nervous and Mental Diseases, 182,* 145–150.

Roscoe, B., & Peterson, K. L. (1983). Parents of battered and neglected children: What child care providers should know. *Journal of Child Care, 1,* 21–29.

Rosen, L. N., & Martin, L. (1996). Impact of childhood abuse history on psychological symptoms among male and female soldiers in the U. S. army. *Child Abuse & Neglect, 12,* 1149–1160.

Ross, C. A. (1997). *Dissociative identity disorder: Diagnosis, clinical features, and treatment of multiple personality* (2nd ed.). New York: John Wiley & Sons.

Ross, C. A., Ellason, J. W., & Anderson, G. (1995). A factor analysis of the Dissociative Experiences Scale (DES) in dissociative identity disorder. *Dissociation, 8,* 229–235.

Ross, C. A., Joshi, S., & Currie, R. (1991). Dissociative experiences in the general population: A factor analysis. *Hospital & Community Psychiatry, 42,* 297–301.

Roth, S., Newman, E., Pelcovitz, D., van der Kolk, B., & Mandel, F. S. (1997). Complex PTSD in victims exposed to sexual and physical abuse: Results from the DSM-IV field trial for posttraumatic stress disorder. *Journal of Traumatic Stress, 10,* 539–555.

Rowan, A. B., & Foy, D. W. (1993). Posttraumatic stress disorder in child sexual abuse survivors: A literature review. *Journal of Traumatic Stress, 6,* 3–20.

Russell, D. E. (1986). *The secret trauma: Incest in the lives of girls and women.* New York: Basic Books.

Ryan, W. (1971). *Blaming the victim.* New York: Pantheon Books.

Sanders, B., & Green, J. A. (1994). The factor structure of the Dissociative Experiences Scale in college students. *Dissociation, 7,* 23–27.

Scheflin, A. W., & Brown, D. (1996). Repressed memory or dissociative amnesia: What the science says. *Journal of Psychiatry and Law, 24,* 143-188.

Shapiro, F. (1995). *Eye movement desensitization and reprocessing.* New York: Guilford Press.

Shultz, J. H., & Luthe, W. (Eds.). (1969). *Autogenic therapy: Volume 1.* New York: Grune & Stratton.

Simonds, S. L. (1994). *Bridging the silence: Nonverbal modalities in the treatment of adult survivors of childhood sexual abuse.* New York: W. W. Norton.

Spak, L., Spak, F., & Allebeck, P. (1997). Factors in childhood and youth predicting alcohol dependence and abuse in Swedish women: Findings from a general population study. *Alcohol & Alcoholism, 32,* 267–274.

Stacey, J. (1996). *In the name of the family: Rethinking family values in a postmodern age.* Boston: Beacon Press.

Suyemoto, K. L. (1998). The functions of self-mutilation. *Clinical Psychology Review, 18,* 531–554.

Tedesco, A., & Bola, J. R. (1997). A pilot study of the relationship between childhood sexual abuse and compulsive sexual behaviors in adults. *Sexual Addiction and Compulsivity, 4,* 147–157.

Timms, R. J., & Conners, P. (1992). Adult promiscuity following child abuse: An introduction. *Psychotherapy Patient, 8,* 19–27.

Treirweiler, S. J., & Stricker, G. (1992). Research and evaluation competency: Training the local clinical scientist. In R. L. Peterson, J. D. McHolland, R. J Bent, E. Davis-Russell, G. E. Edwall, K. Polite, D. L. Singer, & G. Stricker (Eds.), *The core curriculum in professioanl psychology.* Washington, DC: American Psychological Association.

Tsai, M., Feldman-Summers, S., & Edgar, M. (1979). Childhood molestation: Variables related to differential impacts on psychosexual functioning in adult women. *Journal of Abnormal Psychology, 88,* 407–417.

Uzzell, B. P. (1999). Mild head injury: Much ado about something. In N. R.Varney & R. J. Roberts (Eds.), *The evaluation and treatment of mild traumatic brain injury* (pp. 1–13). Mahwah, NJ: Lawrence Erhlbaum Associates.

Valentine, P. (1995). Traumatic incident reduction: A review of a new intervention. *Journal of Family Psychotherapy, 6*(2), 79–85.

van der Hart, O., Steele, K., Boon, S., Brown, P. (1993). The treatment of traumatic memories: Synthesis, realization, and integration.*Dissociation, 6,* 162–180.

van der Kolk, B. A. (1996). The body keeps score. In B. A. van der Kolk, A. C. McFarlane, & L. Weisaeth (Eds.), *Traumatic stress: The effects of overwhelming experience on mind, body, and society* (pp. 214–241). New York: Guilford Press.

van der Kolk, B. A., & Fisler, R. E. (1994). Childhood abuse and neglect and loss of self-regulation. *Bulletin of the Menninger Clinic, 58,* 145–168.

van der Kolk, B. A., & McFarlane, A. C. (1996). The black hole of trauma. In B. A. van der Kolk, A. C. McFarlane, & L. Weisaeth (Eds.), *Traumatic stress: The effects of overwhelming experience on mind, body, and society* (pp. 3–23). New York: Guilford Press.

van der Kolk, B. A., Weisaeth, L., & van der Hart, O. (1996). History of trauma in psychiatry. In B. A. van der Kolk, A. C. McFarlane, & L. Weisaeth (Eds.), *Traumatic stress: The effects of overwhelming experience on mind, body, and society* (pp. 47–74). New York: Guilford Press.

Waites, E. A. (1993). *Trauma and survival: Posttraumatic and dissociative disorders in women.* New York: W. W. Norton.

Wakefield, H., & Underwager, R. (1992). Recovered memories of alleged sexual abuse: Lawsuits against parents. *Behavioral Sciences and the Law, 10,* 483–507.

Walker, L. (1979). *The battered woman.* New York: Harper & Row.

Watkins, J. G. (1992). *Clinical hypnosis. Vol 1: Hypnoanalytic techniques.* New York: Irvington.

Watkins, J. G., & Watkins, H. H. (1997). *Ego states: Theory and therapy.* New York: W. W. Norton.

Weiler, B. L., & Widom, C. S. (1996). Psychopathy and violent behavior in abused and neglected young adults. *Criminal Behavior & Mental Health, 6,* 253–271.

Widom, C. S. (1998). Child victims: Searching for opportunities to break the cycle of violence. *Applied & Preventive Psychology, 7,* 225–234.

Widom, C. S. (1999). Posttraumatic stress disorder in abused and neglected children grown up. *American Journal of Psychiatry, 156,* 1223–1229.

Widom, C. S., Ireland, T., & Glynn, P. J. (1995). Alcohol abuse in abused and neglected children followed-up: Are they at increased risk? *Journal of Studies on Alcohol, 56,* 207–217.

Widom, C. S., & Kuhns, J. B. (1996). Childhood victimization and subsequent risk for promiscuity, prostitution, and teenage pregnancy: A prospective study. *American Journal of Public Health, 86,* 1607–1612.

Williams, L. M. (1994). Recall of childhood trauma: A prospective study of women's memories of child sexual abuse. *Journal of Consulting and Clinical Psychology, 62,* 1167–1176.

Williamson, J. M., Borduin, C. M., & Howe, B. A. (1991). The ecology of adolescent maltreatment: A multilevel examination of adolescent physical abuse, sexual abuse, and neglect. *Journal of Consulting and Clinical Psychology, 59,* 449–457.

Wilsnack, S. C., Vogeltanz, N. D., Klassen, A. D., & Harris, T. R. (1997). Childhood sexual abuse and women's substance abuse: National survey findings. *Journal of Studies on Alcohol, 58,* 264-271.

Wind, T. W., & Silvern, L. (1992). Type and extent of child abuse as predictors of adult functioning. *Journal of Family Violence, 7,* 261–281.

Wiser, S., & Telch, C. F. (1999). Dialectical behavior therapy for binge-eating disorder. *Journal of Clinical Psychology, 55,* 755–768.

Wolpe, J. (1969). *The practice of behavior therapy.* New York: Pergamon Press.

Wyatt, G. E., Guthrie, D., & Notgrass, C. M. (1992). Differential effects of women's child sexual abuse and subsequent sexual revictimization. *Journal of Consulting and Clinical Psychology, 60,* 167–173.

Yaeger-von Birgelen, C. (1996). *Off the hook: Stop blaming your parents and shaming yourself.* New York: Insight Books/Plenum Press.

Yama, M. F., Tovey, S. L., & Fogas, B. S. (1993). Childhood family environment and sexual abuse as predictors of anxiety and depression in adult women. *American Journal of Orthopsychiatry, 63,* 136–141.

Yama, M. F., Tovey, S. L., Fogas, B. S., & Teegarden, L. A. (1992). Joint consequences of parental alcoholism and childhood sexual abuse, and their partial mediation by family environment. *Violence & Victims, 7,* 313–325.

Yapko, M. D. (1994). *Suggestions of abuse: True and false memories of childhood sexual trauma.* New York: Simon & Schuster.

Yelland, L. M., & Stone, W. F. (1996). Belief in the Holocaust: Effects of personality and propaganda. *Political Psychology, 17,* 551–562.

Zlotnick, C., Shea, M.T., Pearlstein, T., Begin, A., Simpson, E., & Costello, E. (1996). Differences in dissociative experiences between survivors of childhood incest and survivors of assault in adulthood. *Journal of Nervous & Mental Diseases, 184,* 52–54.

SUBJECT INDEX

AUTHOR INDEX